Energy Security Logics in Europe

This book analyzes energy security dynamics in Europe through the prism of security logics.

Drawing on the literature on securitization, security logics and security contexts, it scrutinizes energy security debates and policy developments in Germany, Poland and Ukraine, focusing on the pipeline politics, nuclear energy and renewables sector. The contextualized analysis accounts for the wider historical, socio-economic and cultural background from which energy policies emerge and gives a voice to the different stakeholders—from policymakers to the local NGO sector. The book sheds light on the root causes of different energy policy decisions and illustrates that European energy security is currently driven by four security logics—war, subsistence, risk and emancipation. The logic of emancipation is a newly emergent phenomenon embraced by many bottom–up citizens' initiatives and manifested in their drive to self-reliance, the rhetoric of liberation and local practices of energy production. The conceptualization and analysis of the emancipatory logic vis-à-vis other energy security logics help to explain European energy context most effectively—with its background conditions, emerging trends and often controversial national policy approaches.

This book will be of much interest to students of critical security studies, energy policy and European politics in general.

Izabela Surwillo is a postdoctoral researcher at the Metropolitan University Prague. She earned her PhD from the Central European University in Budapest and her master's degree from the University of St. Andrews, UK. Her research interests include international relations theory, security studies and energy security.

Routledge New Security Studies
Series Editor: J. Peter Burgess
École Normale Superieur (ENS), Paris

The aim of this book series is to gather state-of-the-art theoretical reflection and empirical research into a core set of volumes that respond vigorously and dynamically to new challenges to security studies scholarship. This is a continuation of the PRIO New Security Studies series.

The Securitisation of Climate Change
Actors, processes and consequences
Thomas Diez, Franziskus von Lucke and Zehra Wellmann

Surveillance, Privacy and Security
Citizens' perspectives
Edited by Michael Friedewald, J. Peter Burgess, Johann Čas, Rocco Bellanova and Walter Peissl

Socially Responsible Innovation in Security
Critical reflections
Edited by J. Peter Burgess, Genserik Reniers, Koen Ponnet, Wim Hardyns and Wim Smit

Visual Security Studies
Sights and spectacles of insecurity and war
Edited by Juha A. Vuori and Rune Saugmann Andersen

Privacy and Identity in a Networked Society
Refining privacy impact assessment
Stefan Strauß

Energy Security Logics in Europe
Threat, risk or emancipation?
Izabela Surwillo

For more information about this series, please visit: www.routledge.com/Routledge-New-Security-Studies/book-series/RNSS

Energy Security Logics in Europe

Threat, Risk or Emancipation?

Izabela Surwillo

Routledge
Taylor & Francis Group
LONDON AND NEW YORK

First published 2019
by Routledge
2 Park Square, Milton Park, Abingdon, Oxon OX14 4RN

and by Routledge
605 Third Avenue, New York, NY 10017

First issued in paperback 2020

Routledge is an imprint of the Taylor & Francis Group, an informa business

British Library Cataloguing-in-Publication Data
A catalogue record for this book is available from the British Library

Library of Congress Cataloging-in-Publication Data
A catalog record has been requested for this book

ISBN 13: 978-0-367-72969-1 (pbk)
ISBN 13: 978-1-138-38768-3 (hbk)

Typeset in Times New Roman
by Wearset Ltd, Boldon, Tyne and Wear

To my parents

Contents

Illustrations

Figures

Tables

Abbreviations

BDEW	Federal Association of the Energy and Water Industry
BDI	Federation of German Industry
BEB	Citizens Energy Cooperative Berlin
BEE	German Renewable Energy Federation
BMUB	Federal Ministry for the Environment, Nature Conservation and Nuclear Safety
CDU	Christian Democratic Union of Germany
CEE	Central and Eastern Europe
CS	Copenhagen School
CSU	Christian Social Union in Bavaria
DGAP	German Council on Foreign Relations
EC	Energy Community
FDP	Free Democratic Party (Germany)
GIZ	German Society for International Cooperation
HBF	Heinrich Böll Foundation
IEA	International Energy Agency
INES	International Nuclear Event Scale
LNG	liquefied natural gas
MP	Member of Parliament
NATO	North Atlantic Treaty Organization
NECU	National Ecological Centre of Ukraine
NEURC	National Energy and Utility Regulatory Commission
NGO	non-governmental organization
NPP	nuclear power plant
NYER	National Agency for Effective Use of Energy Resources
PGE	Polish Energy Group
SGGW	Warsaw University of Life Sciences
SPD	Social Democratic Party of Germany
SWP	German Institute for International and Security Affairs

Introduction

As the combined challenge of climate change and diminishing fossil fuels further complicates the questions of economic growth, sustainability or political and social stability, the concept of energy security emerges on the European policy agenda as one of its top priorities for decades to come. Establishing ambitious climate and energy policy frameworks does not come easy in the union of states, which frequently opt for diverse policy solutions and at times openly contradict the common goals of greenhouse gas emissions or increasing the share of renewables in their national energy mixes. Simultaneously, building a strong Energy Union and maintaining good cooperation with strategic partners within the Energy Community proves challenging in the face of projects, which, as in the case of Nordstream, are established by the selected few and seem to go against European energy independence or solidarity. Despite its high policy standing, the challenges to European energy security are mounting, largely owing to the discrepancies in national policy approaches. Germany, Poland and Ukraine are key players here, which often face similar energy policy challenges yet represent a puzzling mix of vastly different policy responses that have a crucial impact on the energy security of the continent.

Germany, with its ambitious project of energy transition coupled with the denuclearization of its energy portfolio, could be the single most important European energy context to study. It is therefore the more perplexing that its policies on renewables, nuclear energy and pipeline politics are all contradicted by the energy policies of the CEE states, such as Poland and Ukraine. Whereas "Energiewende" aims to achieve a goal of 80 percent of electricity from renewable energy sources by 2050 and cut its overall energy consumption in half by that date,[1] the policy approaches in the same issue areas in Poland and Ukraine appear stagnant in comparison. Especially Poland, with its domestic coal sector and unfavorable regulations for the development of alternative energy scenarios, is often hesitant to adhere to the common climate protection goals. Moreover, while Germany committed to a full phase-out of its nuclear energy, the plans for building first nuclear power plants are currently under way in Poland, while Ukraine aims to expand its share of nuclear energy despite its legacy of the Chernobyl catastrophe. This picture is complicated further by the divergent policies in the area of pipeline politics. The German–Russian cooperation on the development of the Nordstream project in particular has been perceived in the CEE region as undermining European solidarity and contradicting the ambitious goals of the Energy Union, which aims at diversification of energy supply and liberalization of the internal gas market, among other things. Strengthening Russian influence in the European energy sector by promoting pipeline projects with the omission of the CEE transit states has been seen as a sign of ignoring their interests and a particularly insensitive policy move towards Ukraine, which remains in a state of war with Russia.

These contradictory energy policy approaches hinder prospects for effective regional collaboration and cause frustration and lack of understanding at the policymaking level. It might then be difficult for the German side to fully grasp why its eastern neighbors support nuclear energy instead of making more profound investments in renewables. On the other hand, the continuation of the German pipeline policy course following the outbreak of the Ukrainian–Russian conflict in 2014 raises deeper concerns not only regarding Europe's energy solidarity, but also its shared values. Understanding and overcoming such challenges seems to be a daunting, yet pressing task. Gaining an in-depth understanding of the background conditions and security rationales that shape starkly different national approaches to energy security is crucial for addressing them effectively. Establishing efficient energy policy at the EU level, mitigating the effects of climate change or cooperating in the area of regional gas projects will continue to be key goals of the broader European energy and security agenda. However, if one would like to uncover deeper factors shaping national energy security dynamics in Europe, it quickly turns out that the analytical and conceptual tools for doing so are rather limited.

A number of disciplines deal with the issue of energy security—energy studies, public policy, traditional political science focused on state-level policy analysis or different strands of political economy. However, they all have a tendency to either largely simplify their respective theoretical and analytical frameworks or to increase the number of predominantly economic indicators incorporated into the definitions of energy security at the most.[2] Moreover, the mainstream research is primarily conducted from a limited methodological perspective that often relies on economic modeling, but rarely includes qualitative data that would give more consideration to the multiplicity of local actors, agendas and perspectives.[3] Unfortunately, energy security continuously slips away from such simplifications[4] and—similarly to the concept of *security*—proves to be rather ambiguous.[5] Although the literature on the subject provides over 45 different definitions of energy security,[6] various political and societal actors are continuously involved in the everyday usage and practical redefinition of the concept.

Energy security escapes any established categorizations and its constant reconceptualization happens according to diverse rationales and security logics in practice.[7] As Chester noted, energy security means different things in different places, and its multidimensional character makes it "inherently slippery because it is polysemic in nature, capable of holding multiple dimensions and taking on different specificities depending on the country (or continent), timeframe or energy source to which it is applied."[8] What it means, however, goes much deeper than the scope of potential indicators that can be either omitted or added to its multiple definitions. Combining such multidimensional notions as "energy" and "security" results in a variety of rationales that drive multiple actors towards different types of energy sources and diverse policy solutions for ensuring energy access. This process also reflects the deeply rooted understandings of the energy security phenomenon itself—as different actors define, categorize and hierarchize its multiple dimensions and practices differently—with all its normative and policy implications. This process is clearly visible in the example of the variety of energy security understandings and conceptualizations in Europe. Such understandings range from the militarized competition over energy resources, through the fulfillment of diverse functional needs or risk scenarios to holistic approaches, which highlight the broad character of energy security that cuts through multiple sectors of human activity—environmental and societal included. Energy security constitutes the field in which both individual and collective security practices are continuously produced and contested, and where calls for establishing "energy NATO" or risk analyses of future supply trends mesh with common concerns about "keeping the lights on" or individual desire to produce one's energy.[9] As energy security is continuously redefined, its priorities and understandings happen in everyday practice and are strongly informed by the multiple background conditions; analysis of mainstream policy trends tend to only scratch the surface of this complexity. Official statements, documents or policy briefs can point to the economic and political rationale behind key decisions, but they do not provide a deeper insight into the root causes of energy policies or to the reasoning about energy security goals and priorities more broadly. And the latter are likely to be heavily entrenched in national contexts and influenced not only by economic, but also political, societal, historical and cultural factors. Therefore, understanding the dynamics and far-reaching implications of diverse energy security understandings requires going beyond neat conceptual clarifications or mainstream definitions.

Given this state of the art, this book utilizes the analytical toolbox derived from critical security studies and, by engaging with the literature on securitization, security contexts and security logics, it establishes an analytical approach to the contextual analysis of energy security in Europe. Since the way in which the notion of energy security is perceived, approached and exercised will continue to have wide political, economic, environmental and societal consequences, the book makes a significant empirical contribution by unpacking multiple rationales driving domestic energy security agendas in Germany, Poland and Ukraine. These three cases serve as an analytical background against which the slippery notion of energy security and the multiple logics that govern its dynamics are investigated. In the process, the book seeks to address a number of questions: What security logics are at play across different energy contexts in Europe and what are the mechanisms of their diffusion and interaction? How do competing security rationales influence domestic energy policy agenda in

Germany, Poland and Ukraine in relation to gas politics, nuclear energy and renewables? What do energy security logics in Europe and their contextual dynamics tell us about the nature of contemporary security more broadly?

Whereas securitization theory prominently focused on how the logic of exception leads to emergency measures that curtail "normal" democratic politics,[10] the debate has since shifted towards the exploration of what other security logic(s) might be at play.[11] The analysis of energy security conducted in this book—similarly to the analyses of environmental security[12]—defies the logic of exception as the dominant and universal logic of security and instead shows a multiplicity of energy security logics that drive the debates, policy developments and reasoning about energy security in Europe. In doing so it follows the calls for contextualization of security analysis[13] and agrees with the statement that "we learn to know the meaning of security through the practices which embody a particular interpretation of it."[14] The claim that actors "speak security"[15] is taken seriously, and consequently the debates over the meaning of energy security in the three analyzed cases are seen as a site of contestation where multiple visions and rationales interact and compete—to different outcomes. While acknowledging that vastly different energy policy solutions and agendas derive as much from material constraints as from deeply rooted understandings of actors on the ground, the analysis pays special attention to the latter. The analytical lens is widened to embrace not only the agenda of the main policymakers, but similar attention is given to how the energy security label is framed and utilized by a variety of other relevant actors in each national context studied—including energy experts, businesses, NGOs and environmentalists. The situated actors contribute their own definitions, understandings and conceptualizations of energy security and elaborate on their energy security rationale, which is influenced by the diverse background conditions specific to the three analyzed countries. As this book demonstrates, giving voice to the diversity of local actors provides a wide range of conceptualizations of energy security in Europe that often go far beyond a set of "dry" economic indicators and differ in all dimensions: Starting from what constitutes energy security, how to prioritize its various aspects, in what way to fulfill them, with the involvement of which actors, through which channels and on what levels. Simultaneously, the contextualized methodological approach alleviates the risk that such a broadly defined analysis will stretch the concept of energy security endlessly and make it insignificant. The book operationalizes context within the triangle of *distal factors* (widely defined socioeconomic, historical and cultural backgrounds), the *embeddedness of security mechanisms* (how easily are different understandings of energy security articulated and acted upon) and a *constellation of actors* (variety of stakeholders in the domestic energy security setting). As such, all the meanings, understandings and practices of energy security analyzed are bound to and limited by local contexts from which they emerge. The study of German, Polish and Ukrainian contexts focuses then on how diverse meanings and practices of energy security operate in between these three dimensions according to different logics. Informed by the existing typologies of security logics/grammars in the literature,[16] the three case study chapters take the reader through the manifestations of multiple energy security logics that have different normative implications and are linked differently to their respective policy and practice across a number of domestic energy sectors—fossil fuels, nuclear energy and renewables. Special attention is given here to the manifestation and interaction of the logics: levels in which they intertwine or compete; aspects of energy security that they prioritize or reject; congruence of factors that brings certain energy security logics to the dominant public agenda while hindering the development of others; constellations of actors that uphold the status quo or shift in relation to different energy sources and security rationales. Such an approach allows us to sketch a broader picture of the fluid energy security dynamics in Europe and sheds light not only on the roots of the mainstream debates and policy developments, but also on the alternative voices and approaches that might be currently of lesser scope and influence. As such, the analysis not only explains the current "state of energy affairs," but also points to the potential future energy security scenarios in Europe—together with the trajectories of their discursive and policy development.

The contextual analysis of energy security in Germany, Poland and Ukraine reveals both the anticipated logics that have been previously depicted in the literature and that revolve around the imperative of survival, sustenance or prevention, and an emerging one—which calls for social emancipation in the energy sphere and for the gradual change of energy security status quo from within. In other words, it is not only the logic of risk, war and subsistence that shapes local energy security agendas, but this book shows that the rising logic of emancipation that drives the bottom–up democratic movements in the energy sector increasingly plays a role in different European contexts.

The very term "energy democracy" was initially developed by some NGOs, civil society groups and think tanks to either refer to the dual challenge of decarbonization and energy transformation or to describe the ongoing bottom–up initiatives focused on the development of citizens' energy.[17] Although one of its main prerequisites is energy production in a liberalized energy market by energy prosumers,[18] the idea of energy democracy additionally implies ambitious goals of social, economic and workplace justice[19] that would result from the democratization of the means of production and changing attitudes towards energy consumption.[20] Therefore the concept of energy democracy often combines resistance towards fossil fuel exploitation with progressive solutions in the energy sector[21] and its definitions emphasize justice, fairness, access to energy, redistribution of energy production and consumption, and environmental sustainability.[22] The idea of energy democracy has been increasingly advocated in recent years not only by NGOs and think tanks,[23] but also by renewable energy businesses and local communities, which often stress the importance of renewables and energy-efficiency measures as the means of increasing local energy ownership. It has also been the subject of some recent studies on the grassroots movements for the democratization of energy and their relative impact on energy policymaking in the big Western economies such as Germany and the US.[24] As the concept grows in popularity, its analyses scrutinize it from different angles, including its historical roots, the role of bottom–up initiatives with their activist strategies and practices, as well as the impact of democratization of energy for the economic, environmental and societal sectors.[25] This book, which similarly includes the case study of Germany, additionally argues that technological energy transition coupled with a strengthening of democracy and social participation marks yet another mutation of the meaning and practice of energy security. Driven by an imperative of self-reliance in energy affairs, the emerging emancipatory logic—through societal participation and regaining control over energy production and consumption by individual users/local communities—not only leads to the gradual democratization of energy systems, but also to the transformation of the notion of energy security into a positive and inclusive one. Therefore, although the book departs from the analytical blueprint based on security logics identified in the literature,[26] depicting the emancipatory logic across cases adds even greater complexity to the analysis of the diverse energy security logics in Europe.

The book unpacks the contextual mutations of the emancipatory logic across the cases vis-à-vis other energy security logics. The emancipatory logic manifests strongly in the German context, as driven by the strong imperative of self-reliance—different local communities manifest it both in their rhetoric of social empowerment/liberation and through the practices of various local citizens' energy initiatives. The German case illustrates not only the multi-layered dynamics of the emancipatory agenda in the energy sector, but also its cosmopolitan character—as the transnational network of actors and NGOs in the CEE region builds upon the German experience and seeks to promote the emancipatory agenda locally. A combination of historical (Soviet legacy) and socioeconomic factors determines that the emancipatory logic starts to be visible in the rhetoric in Poland and Ukraine, but there is a lack of sufficient imperative to act upon the rationale of self-reliance on a larger scale. Nevertheless, the first bottom–up energy initiatives are slowly emerging and, because of the specifics of the CEE region, some local NGOs express hope that the decentralization of energy production can both remodel domestic energy systems and empower citizens to implement further democratic changes beyond the energy sector. More specifically, in the CEE states, with traditionally centralized political authority and the Soviet legacy of separating societal actors from the management of resources, the democratization of energy is often seen as a mechanism for the profound transformation of the entire political and socioeconomic models into ones where people "have a say."[27] Thanks to their scalability and distributed character, renewables not only enable individuals, cooperatives and local communities to invest and benefit from their development,[28] but through shifting the responsibility for energy production to citizens, they empower them to bring about widely defined sociopolitical change as societal actors realize the power of their political agency. Therefore, a number of interviewees expressed hope that the emancipatory agenda could have transformative power in the Polish context. Although the ideas of the democratization of energy and social empowerment in the energy sector slowly emerge also in Ukraine, they are of a more marginal yet growing presence there. If Ukrainian society used to be largely disengaged from the issues of energy policy, the outbreak of the conflict with Russia shook up the status quo in the domestic energy sector with its traditional focus on fossil fuels underpinned by the oligarchic interests. As such, it not only shifted Ukrainian energy policy closer to the EU agenda and accelerated a number of domestic reforms, but also led to an increased mobilization that translates into higher societal involvement in the energy sector. Despite a number of obstacles that hinder the development of the emancipatory logic in the Ukrainian energy context, the rationale of self-reliance and small energy-autonomous communities becomes increasingly appealing in the state that is at war with Russia and that seeks greater energy independence from it at all costs.

From the empirical point of view, the emerging emancipatory agenda in the energy sector adds greater nuance to and further complicates the analysis of energy security contexts as highlighted by the case studies of Germany, Poland and Ukraine. It makes more explicit the variety of the contextual factors that make the progressive energy policies (e.g., small-scale renewables and energy efficiency measures) more or less likely. Together with the analysis of the energy security logics of war, subsistence and risk, the book sheds light on the rationale behind key energy policies across a number of energy sectors and sources that are otherwise hard to grasp for the outsider. It is then highlighted how the contextual analysis of energy security through the prism of its logics allows us to understand regional discrepancies in approach to energy security in Europe more effectively. The high subsistence and risk logics explain the German attitude to pipeline politics and the nuclear phase-out respectively, whereas the contestation of the sustenance rationale that accompanies "Energiewende" lays the groundwork for the emergence of the emancipatory logic in the German energy context. Further east, the deeply entrenched geopolitical and historical factors give rise to the logic of war in the Polish and Ukrainian energy policy approach. In Poland, the war logic constitutes the only challenge to the sustenance imperative that revolves around economic calculations and that otherwise dominates Polish energy affairs. In Ukraine, where the energy security lies at the very core of the national struggle for independence in the military conflict with Russia, the war logic increasingly permeates and influences the entire policy agenda—from the national to the local level. Although the analysis of the dominant subsistence and war logics, and a puzzling lack of the logic of risk in CEE shed light on a number of national and regional energy policy developments, the logic of emancipation similarly emerges here, inspired by the German example of energy transition. The book not only uncovers the main economic and political calculations behind key policy decisions and approaches, but also how seemingly remote historical factors, legacies of previous political systems, deeply rooted societal attitudes, media debates or cultural backgrounds can all give rise to or hinder different logics and influence national policy agendas. Tracing and understanding these linkages is key to understanding current and future energy policy trends in Europe, including how given logics:

uphold centralized energy systems or lead to diffused participatory models; facilitate international cooperation or trigger confrontation; and aid in prioritizing local economic and political interests or the global environmental agenda. As such, the book makes an important empirical contribution to the studies on European energy security and policy.

Simultaneously, the complexity of the energy security phenomenon, which makes it difficult to grasp empirically, conceptually and theoretically, opens up the analysis to new insights—in all of these dimensions. Therefore, its contextual analysis not only enriches the undertheorized and economic-centered energy studies literature, but also contributes to a number of debates in wider security studies. First, the analytical engagement with the literature on securitization that aids in establishing contextual approach based on energy security logics and its empirical application highlights once again the pitfalls of the Copenhagen School theory and point to the "liminal" policy/theory sphere as an analytical ground where the emergence, operation and legitimization of different security logics can be traced. As such the study contributes to the discipline's key debates regarding the theorization of security.

Second, since the research conducted relates to the critical security studies debate on the nature of security and its logics—the analysis not only shows how a multiplicity of security logics depicted in the literature play out in the energy realm, but it additionally identifies the energy security logic of emancipation to be operative in different empirical contexts. This finding runs counter to the intuitive analytical guesses: Given its usual "hard security" standing it would seem that energy security does not lend itself as easily as some other "soft security" issues (e.g., environment) to the alternative understandings and interpretations of security. The emergence of emancipatory logic in the energy sector is therefore puzzling. It provides new insights into the conventional energy studies which largely reject such an option as well as adds a new quality to critical security studies which tend to deal with emancipatory issues within the "soft security" or "societal sector."

Third and consequently, the analysis makes a two-fold conceptual contribution. On the one hand, it uncovers a wide variety of conceptualizations of energy security in CEE—as depicted in local rhetoric and as framed in semi-structured interviews by the situated actors. On the other hand, the emancipatory agenda uncovered in the energy sector leads to an alternative conceptualization of the logic of emancipation. Although marked by individuals as the referent objects of security, the rhetoric of social inclusion/liberation and reflexive security practice, the energy security logic of emancipation cannot be easily confined to any of the existing definitions of emancipation. As opposed to Booth's depiction of "security" as means and "emancipation" as ends,[29] the energy sphere indicates a reversed dynamic—as it is through emancipatory practices (removal of intermediaries, co-ownership of energy infrastructure and production of one's energy) that individuals achieve energy security. The fact that the emancipatory logic in the energy sector has a tangible element to it—energy output—also means that as opposed to the wider discussion of the security–emancipation nexus, this energy security logic revolves around the primary imperative of self-reliance. In other words, it is through regaining control over energy production/consumption that individuals and communities become more "secure." Although the energy security logic of emancipation is certainly bound to social empowerment, it also diverges from some of the most prominent calls for "empowering security" in the literature and their respective normative agendas.[30] If some scholars propagated the use of immanent critique as an emancipatory tool for freeing up space for dialogue and inclusion of marginalized voices to "speak security,"[31] the sphere of energy constitutes a case of "emancipation without emancipator." Namely, its analysis indicates that the emancipatory processes happen organically and are very context-dependent. Although the emancipatory agenda can be promoted by the transnational/"green" actors, it is ultimately the interplay of the constellation of domestic actors and background conditions that are decisive in determining which security articulations and practices manifest. As such, emancipatory rhetoric and practice can be either already at play in different energy contexts or they struggle to fully manifest because of local conditions, but they do not depend on the discursive empowerment or the figure of emancipator to be brought about. Therefore, the emancipatory logic of energy security is primarily characterized not so much by its "empowering," but rather by its "transformative" nature. First, the democratization of the energy sector shifts the agency back to the individual users and further transforms the practice and meaning of energy security; second and consequently, the social empowerment in the energy sphere has a potential to transform the entire socioeconomic models. Moreover, the analysis shows that democratization of energy does not equal desecuritization of the issue either. If some scholars would link "emancipation" with "democratic politics" and put it at the opposite end of the securitization spectrum,[32] the sphere of energy indicates that it is precisely through "energy democracy" that energy security can be achieved—albeit within a different kind of a paradigm. In other words, democratizing energy does not lead in this case to the "unmaking" of security,[33] but on the contrary—energy security conceptualized in reflexive and positive terms appears to be "made" in the process.

In reaching these empirical, theoretical and conceptual contributions, the book undertakes an interdisciplinary approach, as it merges the analysis of energy security in CEE with theoretical insights derived from the critical security studies and interpretivist methodology. The first chapter grounds the theoretical argument of the book within the wider debate on security logics.[34] Similarly to numerous voices in this debate, the argument starts by reviewing the insights and pitfalls of the theoretical framework that sought to account for the contextual construction of security issues—the Copenhagen School securitization theory.[35] The book scrutinizes different critical re-engagement with the framework to tease out some of its inherent tensions—most prominently its reliance on a single security logic and problems with the contextualization of analysis. In particular, the calls for the consideration of *"embeddedness" of security mechanisms,*[36] *distal context*[37] and *"setting" of a securitization*[38] are utilized for the operationalization of the book's contextualized methodological approach. Such approach allows accounting for the interplay between distal factors (historical, political and socioeconomic), shifting constellation of actors and the degree to which certain security mechanisms/channels are likely to be utilized in a given setting. The chapter moves, then, to some existing typologies of security logics/ grammars[39] in its search for an adequate analytical starting point for the contextual analysis of energy security. Notably, Ciută's classification of the energy security logics[40] and Corry's typology of security grammars[41] are discussed and utilized for the establishment of an analytical blueprint that aids in discerning energy security logics in the empirical case studies. This blueprint consists of the energy security logics of war, subsistence and risk and is confronted with the contextual conceptualizations of energy security in the three analyzed states.

The three empirical chapters that follow take the reader through an in-depth case-by-case analysis of the German, Polish and Ukrainian energy contexts. The analysis is conducted with the view to uncover security logics operating in the European energy sphere and to account for the channels of their diffusion and interaction as well as policy relevance in the given domestic settings. In doing so, the research combines discourse analysis (of media coverage, parliamentary debates, national energy policy strategies and domestic literature on energy security) with semi-structured interviews (with energy experts, politicians, ministerial representatives, NGO workers and environmental activists) as primary research methods. Employing the contextualized methodology that hinges on the logic of subsistence—marked by the multiplicity of actors and meanings of energy security[42]—as the de facto main site of contestation, each empirical chapter starts with the analysis of the competing definitions and understandings of energy security in a given context. The security logics behind those understandings are then unpacked further as manifested by the rhetoric and practice related to a number of "trigger events" in the European energy sector in the last decade. The latter include the Ukrainian gas crises, the development of the Nordstream project, the nuclear accident in Fukushima and the European debate on the Energy and Climate package. With attention being paid not only to the mainstream discourse, but also to the debates taking place at the sub-state level among a variety of societal actors, the analysis maneuvers between meanings and understandings of energy security embraced in the theory, policy and practice to uncover a number of security logics in the energy sphere of the CEE region.

The analysis depicts the energy security logics of subsistence, war and risk as well as the emerging logic of emancipation in the three countries analyzed and scrutinizes the logics' occurrence and interaction patterns. Whereas the logic of war (in Poland and Ukraine) and the logic of risk (in Germany) tend to periodically rise and fall while exerting immediate policy responses, the logic of subsistence and emancipation are intertwined and come to the fore of the public policy agenda through incremental processes of contestation. On the one hand, prioritization of the fulfillment of societal needs and continuous economic growth within given definitions, understandings and practices of energy security—often at the expense of the environmental agenda—points to a strong economic orientation that characterizes the subsistence logic. On the other hand, once this hierarchy reverses and environmental concerns start to shape the frame of the energy security debate, other dimensions not only go down in the hierarchy, but become transformed in the process: The imperative of sustenance is replaced by the idea of sustainable development while the emphasis on economic growth is minimized. Once that happens, a favorable frame for the further diffusion of the centralized energy system is established. This shift—driven by the imperative of self-reliance and upheld by the rhetoric of social empowerment and dismantling of energy monopolies—favors the emergence of the emancipatory logic in the energy sector.

The final chapter constitutes an in-depth summary of the theoretical and empirical findings of the book. The analytical blueprint of energy security logics from the first chapter is extended by the energy security logic of emancipation that was identified in the three analyzed cases. Since, because of the specificity of the energy security phenomenon, the emancipatory logic manifests uniquely in the energy sphere, it is conceptualized against the background literature on emancipation. All energy security logics uncovered in the empirical chapters are then juxtaposed to illustrate their key characteristics and interdependencies. Together with a comparison of the logics' empirical manifestation across the cases, the analysis points to the existing patterns and their respective normative and policy implications. It also highlights how the dominance of the respective energy security logics across the German, Polish and Ukrainian distal contexts explains a number of recent policy decisions and energy sector developments in recent years. The chapter concludes by providing some final remarks regarding the book's theoretical contribution to the broader security studies. First, it is emphasized that security is indeed a contextual phenomenon and that one-fits-all frameworks or approaches will inherently miss the nuances that can be discovered only in the process of contextualized analysis. Second, the conducted research illustrates that the realist logic of security appears to be merely one of the security logics at play and there is nothing certain about its dominant position or endurance. As the analyses of the energy sector show, it might be challenged by other logics that emerge from the areas of contestation or rise triggered by external events—and that come to the fore of public discourse and policy agenda. Third, positive conceptualizations of energy security and reflexive individual practices of energy production coupled with the rhetoric of social liberation indicate the emergence of the energy security logic of emancipation. This finding challenges both theoretical frameworks geared on a single security logic (such as the Copenhagen School theory) as well as some of the existing typologies of security logics/grammars. From the empirical side, it problematizes contemporary mainstream analysis of energy security and adds new conceptual clarity and analytical quality to the interdisciplinary research on energy security, which will increasingly have to account for the multifaceted and cross-sectoral nature of this "new" security area.

Notes

1 Berst, "German Shift to Wind Power."
2 Valentine, "The Fuzzy Nature of Energy Security."
3 Sovacool, "Diversity."
4 Ciută, "Conceptual Notes on Energy Security."
5 *International Energy Security: Common Concept for Energy Producing, Consuming and Transit Countries*, 10.
6 Sovacool, *Routledge Handbook of Energy Security*, 3.
7 Ciută, "Conceptual Notes on Energy Security."
8 Chester, "Conceptualising Energy Security and Making Explicit Its Polysemic Nature."
9 Sovacool, *Routledge Handbook of Energy Security*; Victor and Yueh, "The New Energy Order"; Hildyard, Lohmann, and Sexton, "Energy Security for Whom? For What?"
10 Buzan, Wæver, and De Wilde, *Security*.
11 Ciută, "Conceptual Notes on Energy Security"; Trombetta, "Environmental Security and Climate Change"; Balzacq, *Contesting Security*; Doty, "Immigration and the Politics of Security."
12 Trombetta, "Environmental Security and Climate Change."
13 Ciută, "Security and the Problem of Context."
14 McSweeney, *Security, Identity and Interests*, 21
15 Wæver, "Securitization and Desecuritization," 55.
16 E.g., Ciută, "Conceptual Notes on Energy Security"; Corry, "Securitisation and 'Riskification'."
17 Kunze and Becker, *Energy Democracy in Europe*; Szwed and Maciejewska, *Demokracja Energetyczna*, 19.
18 Simultaneous producers and consumers of energy.
19 Angel, *Strategies of Energy Democracy*.
20 Büro für eine demokratische Energiewende 2012 http://energie-demokratie.de/what-is-energy-democracy.
21 Kunze and Becker, *Energy Democracy in Europe*.
22 Szulecki, Ancygier, and Szwed, "Energy Democratization?" 9.
23 E.g., Green Institute Foundation, Rosa Luxemburg Foundation.
24 Morris and Jungjohann, *Energy Democracy*; Fairchild and Weinrub, "Energy Democracy."
25 Ibid.
26 E.g., Ciută, "Conceptual Notes on Energy Security"; Corry, "Securitisation and 'Riskification'."
27 Dariusz Szwed, Interview; Chancellery of the Sejm, Interview; SGGW, Interview; demosEUROPA, Interview; Greencubator, Interview.
28 Szulecki, Ancygier, and Szwed, "Energy Democratization?"
29 Booth, *Theory of World Security*, 115.
30 E.g., McDonald, *Security, the Environment and Emancipation*.
31 McDonald, *Security, the Environment and Emancipation*, 41; McDonald, "Emancipation and Critical Terrorism Studies."
32 Aradau, "Security and the Democratic Scene."
33 Balzacq, Depauw, and Leonard, "The Political Limits of Desecuritization."
34 Ciută, "Conceptual Notes on Energy Security"; Trombetta, "Environmental Security and Climate Change"; Balzacq, *Contesting Security*; Doty, "Immigration and the Politics of Security."
35 Buzan, Wæver, and De Wilde, *Security*.
36 Stritzel, "Towards a Theory of Securitization."
37 Balzacq, *Securitization Theory*, 17.

38 Salter, "Securitization and Desecuritization."
39 Corry, "Securitisation and 'Riskification'"; Ciută, "Conceptual Notes on Energy Security."
40 Ibid.
41 Corry, "Securitisation and 'Riskification'."
42 Ciută, "Security and the Problem of Context."

References

Angel, James. *Strategies of Energy Democracy.* Brussels: Rosa-Luxemburg-Stiftung. www.rosalux.de/publication/42125/strategien-der-energiedemokratie.html.

Aradau, Claudia. "Security and the Democratic Scene: Desecuritization and Emancipation." *Journal of International Relations and Development* 7, no. 4 (2004): 388–413.

Balzacq, Thierry. *Contesting Security: Strategies and Logics*. London: Routledge, 2014.

Balzacq, Thierry. *Securitization Theory: How Security Problems Emerge and Dissolve.* London: Routledge, 2010.

Balzacq, Thierry, Sara Depauw, and Sarah Leonard. "The Political Limits of Desecuritization: Security, Arms Trade, and the EU's Economic Targets." In *Contesting Security: Strategies and Logics*, 104–21. London: Routledge, 2015.

Berst, Jan. "German Shift to Wind Power Slams Neighboring Grids." *Smartgridnews.com* [blog], 2012. www.smartgridnews.com/artman/publish/Technologies_DG_Renewables/German-shift-to-wind-power-slams-neighboring-grids-4373.html#.UPRPO-SZnao.

Booth, Ken. *Theory of World Security*. Cambridge: Cambridge University Press, 2007.

Buzan, Barry, Ole Wæver, and Jaap De Wilde. *Security: A New Framework for Analysis.* Boulder, CO: Lynne Rienner Publishers, 1998.

Chancellery of the Sejm. Interview, June 7, 2013.

Chester, Lynne. "Conceptualising Energy Security and Making Explicit Its Polysemic Nature." *Energy Policy* 38, no. 2 (2010): 887–95.

Ciută, Felix. "Conceptual Notes on Energy Security: Total or Banal Security?" *Security Dialogue* 41, no. 2 (2010): 123–44.

Ciută, Felix. "Security and the Problem of Context: A Hermeneutical Critique of Securitization Theory." *Review of International Studies* 35, no. 2 (2009): 301–26.

Corry, Olaf. "Securitisation and 'Riskification': Second-Order Security and the Politics of Climate Change." *Millennium-Journal of International Studies* 40, no. 2 (2012): 235–58.

demosEUROPA. Interview, Warsaw, May 24, 2013.

Doty, Roxanne Lynn. "Immigration and the Politics of Security." *Security Studies* 8, no. 2–3 (1998): 71–93.

Fairchild, Denise and Al Weinrub, "Energy Democracy." In *The Community Resilience Reader.* Washington, DC: Island Press, 2017.

Greencubator. Interview, Kiev, October 30, 2013.

Hildyard, Nicholas, Larry Lohmann, and Sarah Sexton. "Energy Security for Whom? For What?" *The Corner House*, February 16, 2012.

International Energy Security: Common Concept for Energy Producing, Consuming and Transit Countries. Energy Charter Secretariat, 2015. www.energycharter.org/fileadmin/DocumentsMedia/Thematic/International_Energy_Security_2015_en.pdf.

Kunze, Conrad, and Sören Becker. *Energy Democracy in Europe: A Survey and Outlook.* Brussels: Rosa Luxemburg Stiftung, 2014.

McDonald, Matt. "Emancipation and Critical Terrorism Studies." *European Political Science* 6, no. 3 (2007): 252–9.
McDonald, Matt. *Security, the Environment and Emancipation: Contestation over Environmental Change*. London: Routledge, 2011.
McSweeney, Bill. *Security, Identity and Interests: A Sociology of International Relations*. Cambridge: Cambridge University Press, 1999.
Morris, Craig and Arne Jungjohann. *Energy Democracy*. Basingstoke: Palgrave Macmillan, 2016.
Salter, Mark B. "Securitization and Desecuritization: A Dramaturgical Analysis of the Canadian Air Transport Security Authority." *Journal of International Relations and Development* 11, no. 4 (2008): 321–49.
SGGW. (Warsaw University of Life Sciences) Interview, Warsaw, June 12, 2013.
Sovacool, Benjamin K. "Diversity: Energy Studies Need Social Science." *Nature* 511, no. 7511 (July 30, 2014): 529–30.
Sovacool, Benjamin K. *Routledge Handbook of Energy Security*. London: Routledge, 2010.
Stritzel, Holger. "Towards a Theory of Securitization: Copenhagen and Beyond." *European Journal of International Relations* 13, no. 3 (2007): 357–83.
Szulecki, Kacper, Andrzej Ancygier, and Dariusz Szwed. "Energy Democratization? Societal Aspects of de-Carbonization in the German and Polish Energy Sectors." *Environmental Studies and Policy Research Institute: Wroclaw*, March 9, 2015.
Szwed, Dariusz, and Beata Maciejewska. *Demokracja Energetyczna*. Warsaw: Zielony Instytut, 2014.
Szwed, Dariusz. Interview, Warsaw, May 27, 2013.
Trombetta, Maria Julia. "Environmental Security and Climate Change: Analysing the Discourse." *Cambridge Review of International Affairs* 21, no. 4 (2008): 585–602.
Valentine, Scott Victor. "The Fuzzy Nature of Energy Security." In *Routledge Handbook of Energy Security*, 56–73. London: Routledge, 2011.
Victor, David G., and Linda Yueh. "The New Energy Order." *Foreign Affairs* 89, no. 1 (2010): 61–73.
Wæver, Ole. "Securitization and Desecuritization." In *On Security*. New York: Columbia University Press, 1995.

1 Energy security and its logics

Towards contextual analysis

Introduction

This chapter departs from briefly sketching conceptual challenges of energy security analysis and demonstrates how theoretically-oriented security studies provide a useful analytical lens for in-depth research on the practice-oriented energy security field. The Copenhagen School (CS) securitization theory[1] is taken as a starting point for establishing an analytical framework of the book. Since the CS theory constituted a genuine advancement in the discipline, as it sought to account for the mechanism of security issues' construction, the chapter reviews some critical re-engagement with the framework—in particular those tackling its problematic adherence to the Schmittian logic of security (based on exception and existential threats) and the consequential obstacles with the contextualization of analysis.[2] The insights derived from these critiques are used to establish a theoretical and analytical approach that is grounded within a wider critical security studies debate on security logics.[3] Felix Ciută's typology of the energy security logics[4] and Olaf Corry's classification of the security grammars[5] in particular are utilized for developing an analytical blueprint for the study of German, Polish and Ukrainian energy security dynamics. Additionally, the chapter operationalizes a broader analytical approach to the study of energy contexts by building on the critiques of the CS framework that call for the inclusion of the *"embeddedness" of security mechanisms*,[6] *distal context*[7] and *"setting" of a securitization*[8] in the analysis. The discussion concludes with outlining the adopted interpretivist methodology and research practice grounded in hermeneutics. It is illustrated how this particular approach allows scrutinizing the multiple actors, meanings, understandings and background conditions that influence the diverse and context-bound conceptualizations of energy security in Europe most effectively.

The challenge of energy security analysis

An overwhelming number of the contemporary energy security definitions might raise doubts whether different actors that invoke the "energy security" label—including the politicians, energy experts, business representatives or NGOs—do not end up talking past each other most of the time. This has not always been the case. The initial conceptualizations of energy security derived largely from the energy studies literature,[9] and the "security" aspect of energy was often linked to the global market forces determining energy supply trends within the geopolitical context and its mechanisms.[10] Therefore, in line with the realist logic of security that perceives security/insecurity as the outcome of states' power struggles within the international system, traditional energy security studies saw energy security/insecurity as an outcome of the inescapable market forces.[11] Such conceptualizations of energy security linked to the geopolitical power plays were largely appropriated by a narrow circle of analysts working from the limited theoretical perspective.[12]

With time these definitions began to be questioned and the emerging reconceptualizations of energy security aimed at more inclusive definitions that would incorporate new energy sources, more economic indicators and various "qualitative" aspects. First, energy security started to focus on energy sources other than oil, such as biofuels, nuclear energy or renewables; second, not only a wider range of economic indicators was taken into consideration, but many definitions were broadened to encompass various "qualitative" dimensions of energy security (e.g., sustainability) or went beyond purely economic rationale; third, the multiplicity of actors—and consequently meanings—of energy security was gradually acknowledged, which led to the development of more complex analytical frameworks.[13, 14] As a consequence, the concept of energy security became rather elusive and started to function as an "umbrella term" for heterogeneous scales, frames and policies.[15] However, whereas the literature on the subject provides over 45 different definitions of energy security,[16] neither the various working definitions and indicators of energy security provided for the broader understanding of this phenomenon, nor the major pieces of legislation[17] answered the conceptual dilemma of *"what does energy security mean?"*[18] As Valentine put it:

> Some analysts have attempted to address the fuzzy nature of energy security by creating aggregate indices that conflate a number of different energy security criteria. Unfortunately, approaching energy security analysis through the application of multiple indicators does not lead to the "broader understanding" that some colleagues purport; rather, adding more indicators to an energy security assessment simply serves to enhance intellectual discord by introducing contentious debate over the weighting of multiple indicators and inveigling academic tantrums over criteria that was unfairly omitted or thoughtlessly added to the assessment. Comprehensive indices or methodologies for measuring energy security merely represent more complex mobilization of ideological bias.[19]

These conceptual challenges largely owe to the fact that despite energy security's high policy standing, its definitions are appropriated by multiple different actors, who exhibit strong discrepancy in basic beliefs and attitudes towards it. Such differences between energy consumers and energy experts, as well as between energy "thinkers" (e.g., university experts and civil society stakeholders) and energy "doers" (e.g., businesspersons and government officials), have been highlighted by a number of studies.[20] Simultaneously, neither the expert community has a monopoly on defining energy security vis-à-vis other societal actors nor are the current energy systems solely in the hands of nation states or energy companies. On the contrary, attaching the tangible aspect of "energy" (resources, supply and use) to "security" (dimensions and practices) means that both the broadening moves (incorporation of various "new" dimensions to energy security definitions) and the deepening moves (from states and large energy companies to energy cooperatives and individual consumers) lead to the continuous reformulations of the energy security concept in the "liminal" sphere between its theory, policy and practice.[21] Consequently, as Ciută argued, energy security dynamics is "marked by such a diversity of uses and understandings that it poses a difficulty of establishing any categorical or political boundaries to delineate it."[22] Therefore, energy studies incorporate diverse dimensions of energy security that already function within the mainstream policy approaches to their definitions, while the policymakers focus on establishing viable working frameworks for the purpose of domestic energy policies. Both strategies are sound given the respective orientations of the two fields. However, neither the application of the existing conceptualizations of energy security in the literature nor the analysis of the mainstream policy agendas can explain the nuanced energy security dynamics in different European states. There is no one-fits-all framework to be successfully applied to the empirical study of energy security, and adopting the mainstream methodological perspective that rarely includes qualitative data that would give more consideration to the multiplicity of local actors, agendas and perspectives is equally ill-suited for this task.[23] In this sense, Valentine' s critique regarding the ongoing disputes over the adequacy of the indicators to be included in the energy security definitions highlights the fact that the latter cannot be accurate unless they are sufficiently contextualized. And paying sufficient attention to contexts in which energy policies are shaped is a challenging task indeed. Combining such multifaceted notions as "energy" and "security" by multiple stakeholders in relation to different energy sources (fossil fuels, renewables or nuclear) is likely to result in a matrix of competing policy approaches and security rationales. Such approaches are heavily influenced not only by the economic concerns about the security of energy supply at affordable prices, but also by the more or less obvious political, societal, historical and cultural factors. Since energy security is a "total" field as it influences and permeates all sectors of human activity,[24] the reasoning behind it is also highly contextual and reflects wider security considerations of different stakeholders—together with their preferred solutions for attaining energy security in a given setting. Yet, if analyzing such root factors of energy security conceptualizations is understandably not in line with the traditional energy studies or mainstream policy analysis, this book proposes to do precisely that. It utilizes analytical tools derived from its critical engagement with the literature on securitization, security contexts and security logics and applies it to the in-depth study of German, Polish and Ukrainian energy security.

Turning into critical security studies for the analysis of a "hard" security issue such as energy might seem counterintuitive at first. Yet, the theoretical insights developed in the discipline's own search for the broader approach to security analysis prove useful here. If the concept of security was for the most part of the twentieth century locked up in the realist-informed understanding,[25] equated with an absence of threat[26] and bound to the military rationale that saw the international scene as a system of competing, self-reliant state units,[27] the end of the Cold War led to the "broadening," "widening," "sectorization" and constructivist critique of the traditional security studies agenda. On the one hand, security studies started to incorporate a number of "new" security issues, such as environmental degradation, economic well-being, migration and population.[28] On the other hand, attempts at disentangling the analysis of security from its empirical and normative dimensions started to be questioned as a number of critical security scholars[29] chose to focus on the "background assumptions and discourses belonging to a culture from which threats are defined."[30] This allowed for new ways of reasoning and a better contextualization of analysis. Following the rationale that "we learn to know the meaning of security through the practices which embody a particular interpretation of it,"[31] the critical research agenda began to challenge the state-centric traditional definitions of security by focusing on its context-dependent discourse and practice.

As such, critical security studies can aid the energy security analysis by providing means for untangling its complex conceptualizations that are strongly bound to national contexts. Their theoretical lens not only allows to adopt more inclusive analytical frameworks that scrutinize background factors of energy security reasoning, but also problematize the very "security" aspect of energy—regarding its logics, practices and mechanisms of operation. Simultaneously, the highly practice and policy-oriented energy security field is a fascinating terrain for security analysis in its own right. Since, as opposed to security studies, the practical reformulation of the energy security concept is continuously taking place in its practice, it not only challenges the often assumed primacy of the theoretical constructs over the practical meanings,[32] but also opens up security analysis to new insights. The question of "how certain ideas about security develop, enter the realm of public policy, and become dominant and legitimated in public discourses," whereas others do not,[33] is one of security studies' most important, yet least understood ones to date. The multidimensional character of energy security on the one hand poses a challenge to security studies' drives aimed at establishing an "essence" of security.[34] On the other hand, it can serve as an analytical testing ground for tracing the variety of mechanisms of conceptual formation, legitimation and proliferation of security issues more broadly.

The remainder of this chapter engages with the chosen debates in security studies in order to establish an analytical approach to the contextual analysis of energy security based on its logics. It starts with reviewing a couple of critiques of the Copenhagen School securitization theory, which sparked the debate on the mechanisms of security issues' construction. Although the CS securitization framework has been extensively criticized on the conceptual, theoretical and normative grounds[35]—with the debate moving onto an exploration of other approaches to the contextual analysis of security and other security logics[36]—teasing out some of its inherent theoretical tensions provides much analytical insight. The chapter specifically focuses on two interconnected criticisms of the theory that aid in the establishment of an analytical framework to energy security analysis—one related to the framework's ability to account for context,[37] and the other to its single security logic approach.[38]

Copenhagen School securitization theory: the problem of context and a single logic approach

If looking for an approach that would seek to account for the emergence of the "new" security issues in an innovative manner, the Copenhagen School securitization theory is the first point of reference. The Copenhagen School framework had often been referred to as a shorthand for the construction of security.[39] If some voices within critical security studies suggested focusing on how "security is *used* ... [and] examine it as a field of practices, including how it typically works,"[40] the CS attempted to account for the process of security issues' construction. It focused on the mechanisms through which security, which is typically about survival and an existential threat to a particular valued referent object, enters the national policy agenda through the "speech act" mechanism.[41] If this discursive move proves successful and its audience acknowledges the issue as a security one, we enter the realm of emergency politics, which legitimizes extraordinary measures to deal with that issue. As such, the securitization theory sought to tease out a major tension between traditional and critical approaches to security, by accommodating the realist-informed understanding of security focused on "existential threats" with the critical claim of social constructedness of security issues within a single theoretical framework.[42] Linking these two elements both lies at the core of the framework's relative success and causes a number of analytical problems. Although, in addition to answering the "who, what, where and how" of security, the CS theory allows for potentially new interpretations of what security actually *means*,[43] and sees it as an outcome of a specific kind of social process, susceptible to criticism and change,[44] relying on the realist logic of security limits its ability to account for contexts in which security issues come about. These two problems are inextricably linked and understanding their limitations helps to steer the security analysis in a different direction.

To start with, the "contextual" problem category among the criticisms of the Copenhagen School is particularly important to consider here, as Ciută noticed, it embraces the normative, epistemological and conceptual dilemmas of the framework "at the moment when securitization theory delivers its answer to the primordial question ... *what is security?*"[45] Securitization theory contextualizes at two levels: process-specific and region-specific. The former relates to the analysis of the speech act and its accompanying facilitating conditions that determine which issues are securitized and how different actors act and interact with their audience. The latter combines the cross-sectoral dynamics of security with a regional level of analysis—a result of which is the regional security complex theory.[46] However, this two-level contextualization does not solve the problem of context within the framework, which is a more profound one and has been depicted by a number of scholars from different angles. McDonald, for example, distinguished three characteristics of the framework's theoretical design that have problematic implications for context. First, the *form* of the act of constructing security was defined narrowly, with the focus on the speech of dominant actors. Second, the *context* of the act was defined narrowly, with the focus only on the moment of intervention. And third, the *nature* of the act was defined solely in terms of the designation of threats.[47] The respective limitations of these shortcomings imply that non-discursive representations and voices of less empowered actors are entirely excluded from the analysis, whereas "the potential for security to be constructed over time through a range of incremental processes and representations is not addressed" at all.[48] Therefore, as Wilkinson argued:

> Not only is the securitization framework likely to produce a version of events that has been 'edited' to ensure chronological order and a linear and step-wise progression (from actor to speech-act to audience to outcome), but the final analysis is likely to erase the local knowledge that can be generated by fieldwork even if empirical details are included.[49]

Moreover, the preoccupation with existential threats "ignores the central importance of the way in which security—as a normative goal or expression of core values—is understood in particular contexts."[50] In this light, a mere consideration of the "facilitating conditions" present at the moment of the "speech act" is insufficient to contextualize the analysis.[51] The latter point, which seems to lie at the core of the CS's problem with context, was elaborated further by Ciută in his "hermeneutical critique" of the framework.[52] The critique highlighted that the default definition of "security" within the CS theory is dual and contradictory: First, "discursive" (security as a speech act), and second equated with "survival in the face of existential threats."[53] Moreover, these two definitions are put in the hierarchy that favors the second understanding of security and, as a result, eliminates contextualization from the CS framework.[54] From the more practical side, such hierarchical relation "locks-in the *meaning* of security and insulates it from conceptual variation or practical reformulation."[55]

The roots of this dilemma seem to go back to the Copenhagen School's initial argument that security studies should adopt an understanding of the "duality" of security—a combination of state security concerned with *sovereignty* and societal security concerned with *identity*.[56] This dual approach proves problematic once its elements become uneven, as downplaying the "societal" aspect of security ultimately means that in the CS security acquires meaning only as long as it is fixed in a Schmittian *logic* based on exclusion and exception.[57] Consequently, securitization theory seems to be torn between its aim to establish the "essence" of security, and its claim that security is "what actors make of it."[58] The impossibility of eliminating this contradiction results in both the logic of security and its definition remaining relatively "fixed" and politically conservative in the Copenhagen School's approach.[59] Moreover, this "fixedness" seems to translate into an indirect assumption that security has an unchanging essence, which in turn largely explains why CS attempts to unproblematically apply its framework to various contexts, without exploring *how* and *why* the instances of securitization could have taken place in these contexts in the first place. In Wæver's view, the application of the same logic to different areas meant that, while remaining true to the classical meaning of security, we could "show how these old elements operate in new ways and new places."[60] This kind of inquiry runs contrary to a broader understanding of the intersubjective processes through which security is constructed in different contexts. Moreover, as Doty noticed, such approach implies that the logic of securitization is the same in all realms of security, and that this is the only logic worth considering—an assumption that would eliminate from analysis "other important logics which do not fit within the classical security logic but might be operative."[61]

Some studies devoted to specific security areas confirm Doty's point. For example, Trombetta in her analysis of securitization of the environment showed that the process of securitization in the environmental realm does not follow a single logic, as the environmental sector transforms existing security practices and this process is a part of a "a broader re-articulation of the spaces in which a *logic of security* based on *emergency and contingency* is legitimated and those in which a *logic of prevention and management* prevails."[62] Therefore, as she argues:

> the transformation of an issue into a security issue can follow different modalities and different logics, which eschew the confrontational logic of the national security model suggested by the [Copenhagen] School. Through the appeal to security, other logics, which characterize different contexts, can be brought into existence and new actors can gain relevance in security policies.[63]

This dynamic playing out in relation to some "new" security areas is crucial, as it implies that simple re-appropriations of the CS securitization framework do not address its main intrinsic shortcomings.

For instance, Balzacq proposed a "sociological" reformulation of the securitization theory that approached it as a more complex intersubjective process that could be "discursive and non-discursive, intentional and non-intentional, performative, but not an *act in itself*."[64] However, if the "sociological" approach resigned completely from the innovative parts of the CS framework (role of the speech act and the structured mechanism of security construction), it, similarly to the CS, defined security mainly in the realist notion of threats. As such the understanding of security within the "sociological" approach is defined a priori to analysis and then sought among policies, discourses and practices of the situated actors. Another take on the securitization theory was proposed by Guzzini, who saw it as just one of the mechanisms of security issues' construction—a state-centric one that is geared on threats and confrontation.[65] Drawing on Elster's definition of security mechanisms,[66] Guzzini also suggested that the causality of the security mechanisms should be considered here in a non-positivist manner, as such mechanisms could be "contingent in their prompting or indeterminate in their effect" and highly dependent upon history and "circles of recognition" for the collective identities of a country.[67] Guzzini's latter point highlights yet again the importance of context, as it states that it is the congruence of contextual factors that are decisive for the securitizations to occur.[68] However, both theoretical re-appropriations of the framework raise the question of: Why not propose a looser approach geared on the contextual construction of security instead? Similarly to the environmental security, the highly practice-oriented field of energy security slips away from simple categorizations, as its understandings, meanings and practices are continuously appropriated by multiple actors and tend to be highly contextual. Therefore, the CS framework that relies on the realist logic of security could indeed uncover one of the mechanisms of the energy security issues' construction—one linked to the competition and confrontation as often reflected in the geopolitics of energy supply. However, unpacking the nuances of contemporary energy security requires a more critical analytical lens that would account for its different voices and manifestations—and for its potentially different logics.

Security and its logics

As Balzacq noted, the debate on whether *security* has a *logic*, or none, or multiple ones that depend on context traces back to a choice between the critical and traditional approaches to security, between "security as a given" and "security as a construct," and between security that is immutable and security that is variable.[69] Hence, as Hansen noted, the debate over the logic of security cannot be solved, "as it rests upon deeper philosophical and political commitments that are themselves 'unsolvable'."[70] On the one hand, subscribing to the threat–defense modality is still very common even among the more "critically" oriented security scholars, e.g., with Aradau writing about "the exclusionary logic of security" that upholds and legitimizes "forms of domination,"[71] or Van Munster describing "the logic of security" as one based on "political organization on the exclusionary basis of fear."[72] On the other hand, the research on security logics that challenges and transforms the realist notion of security across various issue areas aims to enhance our understanding of the changing nature of the security phenomenon and can shed more light on current and future policy developments. Energy security that cannot be confined to the threat–defense modality is a case in point as far as the latter approach is concerned. However, before attempting to account for security logics in the energy field and their wider normative and practical implications for the European energy security, a key question that has to be answered is: What is a "security logic"?

Despite a common assumption that there exists a shared understanding of the concept of security logic, the latter remains in fact largely under-theorized.[73] Balzacq argued that what is referred to as "the logic of security" is frequently an attempt to ascribe a logic to an abstract concept.[74] However, if scrutinizing the existing debate in the literature, it rather turns out that the authors either point to the security logics' possible manifestations and mechanisms of operation or describe the necessary conditions that have to be in place for the security logics to play out. Huysmans, for instance, considers the logic of security as "an ensemble of rules that is immanent to security practice and that defines the practice in its specificity."[75] This reasoning of security logics being "parasitic upon security practices" is further undertaken by Balzacq, for whom "the logic of security is always already the logic of a concept as expressed by, or engraved in various practices."[76] He further distinguishes between its two constitutive features—the "rule or grammar of the practice" and the "conditions which make the practice both possible and vulnerable."[77] For instance, the realist-informed understanding of the security logic would indicate that "military rules inform the characteristic grammar of security practices and the concept of 'existential threats' provides the background condition, which enables the different components of security practices to operate in a distinctive way."[78] The focus on security practices could also be spotted in the analysis of the logic that underpins the widely defined securitization process. For instance, Bourbeau argues that the current literature on securitization relies mainly on two logics: the logic of exception and the logic of routine.[79] Whereas the former sees security as a process that aims to combat existential threats via exceptional measures, the latter views securitization "as a collection of routinized and patterned practices, typically carried out by bureaucrats and security professionals, in which technology comes to hold a prominent place."[80] Although very different, both logics, according to Bourbeau, rely on security performance, as securitization is first and foremost about a performance—a process of doing something.[81]

The variety of the above definitions touch upon security logics' possible characteristics and ways of operation. For instance, Huysmans' definition of the logic of security as "an ensemble of rules that is immanent to security practice and that defines the practice in its specificity"[82] focuses on how the security logic "comes about" via an ensemble of given rules that guide its dynamic. In a way, his definition resembles the definition of the logic in the IT field, as "a system or set of principles underlying the arrangements of elements in a computer or electronic device so as to perform a specified task"[83] When it comes to security theory, the very attainment of security constitutes such task that is "performed" by security practices. The rules here determine the characteristics of a specific course of action or a performative effect. As such, an assembly of rules—even if immanent to security practice—defines rather the logic of operation of security practices, not the security logic itself. However, what defines and determines the rules? This question is especially pressing if subscribing to the view that security logics might indeed mutate and multiply, which would indicate that there are different possible assemblies of rules guiding their dynamic. In other words, what lies at the core of the security logic? And how do we discern security logics and account for their emergence and possible mutations? The above definitions of security logic in the literature hint at the existence of such core (e.g., Balzacq's approach) and at the potential multiplication of the logics themselves, but their primary focus on the logics' operation mechanisms makes accounting for these two questions rather difficult.

A certain exception in the ongoing debate is Olaf Corry's article on security grammars. Corry suggested a pluralistic view of security logics and, while departing from the Copenhagen School framework, attempted to identify the distinct logic of speech acts that turn issues into questions of risk politics.[84] Overall, he distinguished among three "grammars of security": securitization, riskification and politicization.[85] Whereas securitization would be marked by the construction of scenario of direct harm (an existential threat) to a valued referent object, riskification would mean construction of conditions of possibility of harm (risk) to a governance-object, and politicization the construction of object as governable.[86] The political imperative that would inform the respective "plan of action" would then include defense against the threat in the case of securitization, increased governance in the case of riskification and maximization of utility in trade-offs with other goods in the case of politicization.[87] Consequently, the "performative effects" that follow would imply the legitimation of exceptional measures aiming for survival, legitimation of precautionary measures and legitimation of trade-offs in relation to other goods respectively.[88] Corry theorized security logics as ideal types for rules of action to be found *across* contexts. As such his typology, similarly to the securitization framework, avoids analytical contextualism that would scrutinize wider background conditions impacting upon security issues construction. Nevertheless, the distinction between different grammars, political imperatives and performative effects is a useful tool for distinguishing between different security logics—at least in their discursive manifestations. It can also aid in defining the very security logic itself.

Arguably, political imperative is key to consider here. Different plans of action that arise in response to the construction of security scenarios point to an internal drive of various actors that causes them to recognize what "counts" as a security issue and to employ adequate means for addressing it. In essence this recognition points to what lies at the core of the particular security logic in any given circumstances. The security logic could then be defined as an *intrinsic guiding imperative for attaining security*. Intrinsic, because security logics are always more or less internalized by actors who employ them. They can be learned over time or quickly adopted in the face of specific developments. Guiding, because more than one option might be available to actors, who can choose to employ different security logics in similar circumstances (e.g., security or risk)—or none at all. And this is likely to be very context-dependent. Imperative, because security logic requires a significant drive to be set in motion and manifest. Imperatives are internalized rationales that might be acted upon. Whereas the underlying security rationale of each logic can point to what that imperative is (e.g., survival within the realist logic of security), it is not until this rationale is sufficiently internalized in the favorable contextual conditions by the actors who bring it about via corresponding rhetoric and practices. Crucially, different imperatives transform the very understanding of security within each logic, as they are ultimately determining what contextually counts as "security." Depicting the rhetoric and practices that are in line with a given imperative is therefore key for the analysis, as the way in which energy security is conceptualized and practiced contextually points to the security logics' multiplication and mutation and helps to distinguish between them across different empirical settings. In this approach, security logics are indeed parasitic upon security practices and security rhetoric, but they don't equal either. Even if given rhetoric is invoked or certain practice manifests in line with a distinct security rationale (e.g., survival), but the latter is not sufficiently internalized/does not fall on fertile ground in a given context, the security logic might either fail to emerge or play out only very marginally. Therefore, this approach to security logics puts a stronger focus on the variety of actors that employ and manifest them. It is also particularly suitable for the analysis of the energy security dynamic, which is not only highly practice-oriented, but also marked by multiple actors, understandings and articulations of energy security. Further discussion elaborates how this approach could be applied to the analysis of the energy sector.

Energy security and its logics

When approaching the analysis of security logics in the energy sector, it is not possible to omit a single article that specifically sought to map out energy security logics. Based on the analysis of the main trends and debates in the field of energy studies, Ciută argued that in the case of energy security one could distinguish among its three main logics: the logic of war, the logic of subsistence and the total security logic.[89] According to this typology, these distinct logics "carry different meanings of energy and security, embed political hierarchies, and have distinct vocabularies, policy vehicles and normative consequences."[90]

The first of them, the logic of war, which relates to the patterns of international politics, brings the vocabulary and rationale of conflict to energy security as energy becomes a resource influencing the distribution of capabilities in the international system.[91] The logic of war is therefore characterized by the presence of military planning in the management of natural resources and by the rationale of "hardening, securing and protecting" that permeates the whole domain of energy.[92]

The second logic, the logic of subsistence, shifts energy security concerns closer towards the public policy agenda.[93] It is characterized by the segregation of energy (a type of resources, actors, sectors of activity), multiplication of actors and the rationale of "survival" being replaced by the functional demands of the diverse sectors of activity. Hence, the logic of subsistence implies that "different actors invest to varying degrees political, economic or environmental issues into energy security, and attach different policy instruments to it."[94] As the typology points out, the policy preferences within the logic of subsistence might "signal the hierarchies that govern the interaction between the local and the global (global warming versus cold home versus human security), and broad political orientations (domestic deregulatory versus global deregulatory)."[95]

Finally, the total security logic rests upon the notions of *totality* and *reflexivity* of energy, which stem from the assertion that "energy affects everything, everything affects energy, and, ultimately, everything *is* energy."[96] The latter implies blurring of the distinction between threatening actors and referent objects, as "all the myriad of actual and potential actors acquire simultaneously all possible security roles: they are at the same time referent objects, subjects, threats, vectors and agents of security."[97] Since "security is everywhere" and energy becomes a security problem due to our own actions, the "meaning" or "essence" of security becomes increasingly blurry.

Ciută's take on security logics in the energy sector is a broad one. It builds upon the explicitly "liminal" character of energy security as a "between theory and practice" sphere where multiplication of actors involved in its reformulation result in the diversity of energy security uses, understandings and practices.[98] It avoids giving a single definition of the security logic, but points out that "categories and practices of security cluster contextually according to different meanings produced by situated actors."[99] As such, it outlines the characteristics of the three energy security logics identified. Quite strikingly, though, although Ciută subscribes to or even propagates analytical contextualism, his typology very much reflects Corry's "ideal" types of security grammars. The two typologies exhibit many similarities on the line of: securitization/logic of war, riskification/total security logic and politicization/logic of subsistence.

Hence, although this book conducts a contextualized analysis of German, Polish and Ukrainian energy security, as Corry noted, "even inductivists start from somewhere."[100] The two typologies are contrasted in order to establish an analytical blueprint of the security logics that might be at play across different energy contexts in Europe. Teasing out the elements of both classifications that are relevant to the contextual analysis of energy security is beneficial for two reasons. First, it provides for a more detailed analytical scheme for discerning possible energy security logics in the three case studies. The further discussion outlines such a scheme based on the logics' underlying rationale/imperative, accompanying rhetoric, related practices of the situated actors, possible manifestations as well as the nature and value of security within each logic. Second, they highlight how energy security logics follow similar trajectories to the security logics more broadly, and consequently, how the analysis of energy security could shed light on the dynamics of a wider security phenomenon.

Analytical blueprint of energy security logics

To start with, Corry's depiction of securitization is close to Ciută's energy security logic of war. The logic of war is consistent with the realist-informed understanding of security (focused on the use of force, war and conflict) and with its preoccupation with survival in the face of existential threats. If it is assumed that each security logic has a single underlying rationale, survival underlies the logic of war in the energy sector. The rationale of survival does not equal the war logic, but in favorable background conditions it can serve as a primary imperative around which the logic operates. Here we have state actors as the objects and subjects of energy security and the centralized state control over energy resources—mostly fossil fuels. Since energy is treated as a resource, which affects the distribution of capabilities in the international system, the confrontation and competition over depleting resources often prevail. That can manifest in many forms and range from resource wars in Africa to conflicts around pipeline politics in a geopolitical context. According to Ciută, what the different manifestations of the war logic have in common is the "grammar of conflict" present in the rhetoric of weapons, battles, fear, economic dominance, or lately also in the narrative of the "new Cold War." The very conflict can be framed in terms of a "zero-sum" game. In line with realist thinking, it is always "us" versus "others"—and we either win and ensure the energy supply key to our economic and political survival, or we lose. There is no space for half-measures. Ultimately, as far as this logic is concerned, the nature of security equals either the "absence of war" or, in the case of conflict with an external adversary, it is dependent upon "winning the war." Security within the energy security logic of war that operates in line with survival imperative is therefore exclusive and of a negative value. It is exclusive as we deal here with an external threat in a game, where one's win equals another's loss. It is of a negative value as it is conceived in a threat-based modality and consistent with the realist conceptualization of it.

Given the urgency of the matter, the logic of war might easily translate into energy policies that are put on the immediate political agenda. Corry noted that in the case of securitization a plan of action for defense against threat would be followed by the legitimation of exceptional measures aiming for survival, such as secrecy, no-holds-barred action, no trade-offs with security.[101] In the case of the war logic in the energy sector such exceptional measures could go as far as getting involved in the actual military conflict over energy resources. More frequently, though, they would focus on implementing measures aiming at energy security understood in its traditional terms as the security of supply. The urgency of implementing these measures would trump all the other policy and security considerations at the time—economic, political, societal and environmental. In this sense the logic of war would come close to the Copenhagen School securitization mechanism. However, it remains to be seen how its actual dynamics play out in the local energy contexts. The analysis of the three case studies focuses then not only on the potential rhetoric of conflict in the energy sphere, but investigates to what extent such rhetoric is followed/accompanied by the relevant political actions of the state actors.

The second energy security logic included in Ciută's typology is the logic of subsistence, which corresponds closely to Corry's depiction of the logic of "normal" politics. The logic of subsistence is marked by the multiplication of actors and meanings of energy security. Crucially, the underlying rationale of "survival" from the logic of war is replaced here by "sustenance." Therefore, we have multiple stakeholders, whose different interests and agendas compete to come to the fore of energy policy within domestic sites of contestation. The former might include the political elite, energy companies, expert community, media, environmental groups and civil society. Depending on the context, the relative power standing of different actors within a given constellation might differ—as there are always more mainstream and marginal voices. Consequently, the control over different aspects of energy security is unequally shared among stakeholders and there might be power shifts in relation to various energy security debates and policies. This contesting of energy security within public policy agenda mirrors Corry's politicization, where pros and cons "are weighed more or less evenhandedly so that no-holds-barred and precautionary politics is dropped and marginal utility becomes the dominant logic: will plan A or B do more good than harm?." In "normal" politics goals can be traded off against each other to maximize the overall utility, e.g., healthcare versus education or road-building to be optimized according to preferences.[102] Within the subsistence logic different goals and dimensions of energy security are similarly weighed against alternatives, but the analytical implications of this process are different here. Namely, Corry listed "politicization" in his classification in a typical move to contrast it with "security" and "risk-security" categories. As such "politicization" implies going back to normal politics and de facto desecuritization of an issue. However, the logic of subsistence is still a security logic, as based on the claim that security is contextual, the assertion that actors "speak" security[103] is taken seriously. Hence the contextualized interpretivist analysis has to treat the local conceptualizations and understandings of "energy security" accordingly—as a security issue. Consequently, if actors "speak energy security" in a context of everyday politics, this process should be analyzed on par with other security logics. Such "thick" contextualism also implies that although the logic of subsistence operates within "normal" politics, the definition of "political" is greatly extended here to include less dominant voices of collective and individual actors. Ultimately, the logic revolves around uncovering contextual meanings and understandings of energy security in the shifting constellations of actors. Although sustenance is an underlying rationale here, the imperative that it sets in motion can be achieved in a number of ways as "different actors invest to varying degrees political, economic or environmental issues into energy security, and attach different policy instruments to it."[104] Corry's claim that it is the utility of trade-offs between different policy options that is decisive might be a case in point. Different energy security dimensions could be hierarchized within domestic definitions and policy approaches by the situated actors based on their perceived utility/importance vis-à-vis other options. Crucially, though, as the security logics are contextual, so is the perception of what constitutes a justifiable choice. As such the analysis of the subsistence logic is likely to take us deeper into the specifics of local energy contexts where aspects of energy security are constantly being renegotiated in line with the functional needs of society and current local agendas. Once the outcomes of these contestation processes become sedimented enough, the established understandings and priorities of energy security can be seen across its local policies and definitions.

Security within the subsistence logic is therefore simultaneously "exclusive" and of a "positive" value. It is "exclusive" as we have multiple actors and agendas within domestic sites of contestation and not all energy security dimensions, perspectives and interests would be equally valid at all times when formulating a policy approach. It is not the type of exclusion that we find in the logic of war, though. In the logic of subsistence, the main goal—the fulfillment of functional needs of society in the energy sector—will be met. The exclusionary practice applies then to the extent to which the diverse competing visions are incorporated into the mainstream debate and policy approach to energy security. Security here is of a positive value—as the logic's core imperative revolves around the rationale of sustenance. Therefore, the hierarchies might shift, priorities change over time, but the main goal of fulfilling societal needs in the sphere of energy security remains unaltered.

The last energy security logic in Ciută's classification is the "total security logic," which corresponds to Corry's grammar of riskification. Whereas Ciută's depiction of the logic in the energy sector bears a close resemblance to Beck's world risk society argument,[105] Corry's mechanism of riskification is an attempt to "theorize 'risk logic' at the same level as securitization theory: as an ideal type for rules of action found *across* contexts."[106] Therefore, Corry reviews two main strands of risk literature: One connected to Becksian risk society, which now lives in a "second modernity" and is "increasingly occupied with debating, preventing and managing risks that it itself produced,"[107] and the other inspired by French thinkers Foucault and Bourdieu, which sees risk as a particular rationality of government that works to legitimate certain technologies of power.[108] Based on the perceived similarities between the two schools, Corry outlines a mechanism of "riskification," which "posits risks (understood as conditions of possibility for harm) to a referent object leading to programmes for permanent changes aimed at reducing vulnerability and boosting governance-capacity of the valued referent object itself."[109] A number of elements in Corry's approach could be helpful in tracing the risk logic in the energy sector and discerning it from other logics, with two reservations here. First, a contextual approach would go beyond discursive representations of "riskification," which is operationalized in the same manner as the CS securitization framework. Second, the all-encompassing nature of "energy security" might indeed, similarly to "environmental security," make it a "total" security category as Ciută argues, and as such brings us closer to the risk society dynamics.

Beck first outlined his risk society argument in direct response to the disaster at the Chernobyl nuclear power plant in 1986. According to Beck, we currently live in "reflexive modernity," where societies attempt to prevent and manage risks that they themselves manufactured.[110] Therefore, societal actors continuously monitor themselves while developing new technologies and de facto producing new risks to their own existence. Moreover, advancing globalization makes such risks de-localized and incalculable, with potentially catastrophic consequences for the whole of humanity. Hence, as Beck argues, in the "second modernity," marked by reflexivity and global risks produced by technological change, "the very ideas of controllability, certainty or security—so central to first modernity—collapse."[111] Reflexivity implies that societies can try to assess the level of risks that are produced and attempt to mitigate them, yet the idea of controlling uncertainty is in the Becksian view rather an illusion. Although reflexive retrospection might result in, e.g., increased regulation of the nuclear power industry or ideas of sustainability to be developed, the attempts of control cannot guarantee security in the global risk society.

The risk logic in the energy sector as depicted by Ciută comes close to the above picture. His "total logic of energy security" points to the "totality" and "reflexivity" of energy:

> The totality of energy is inherent in its three key dimensions of growth, the environment and sustenance: energy affects everything, everything affects energy, and, ultimately, everything *is* energy … the reflexivity of energy security draws on the fact that the intersection of the three dimensions makes energy a security problem because of our own actions, rather than, for example, the actions of some threatening actor. To paraphrase Rasmussen … , when faced with the problem of energy, we are facing ourselves.[112]

Therefore, in the total security logic, similarly as in the risk society, energy becomes a security issue due to our own actions, which means that we can ourselves manufacture future energy security risks. Consequently, the distinction between threatening actors and referent objects becomes blurred and, since in an increasingly globalized and interconnected world "energy is everywhere," the scope of such manufactured risks is also likely to be global.

In practical terms this could mean that energy security embraces multiple risks connected to the regional and global energy infrastructure and supply chains—including terrorism, war, brigandage, and natural disasters.[113] Policy manifestations of dealing with such risks could indeed be mostly in line with Corry's mechanism of "riskification." Even assuming that energy security is of "total" and "reflexive" character and that harms can come from virtually everywhere in the energy field, in whichever way, to address such risks the prevention would be an underlying rationale. If internalized enough by the actors on the ground, this security imperative would spark the rhetoric of calculation and precaution as actors would center their efforts on developing strategies for risk alleviation. Given the above examples, the latter could include improvement of technological solutions (e.g., new generation of nuclear power plants), additional safety measures for the transport of energy resources or changing the unstable energy suppliers altogether. Attempting to prepare for the possibilities of harm would then mean to attempt to gain control over the conceivable future "bads" connected to energy production, transportation, exploitation and storage. It is conceivable that under certain circumstances the actors involved could conclude that no amount of precautionary measures could alleviate the perceived risks. However, the totality and reflexivity of energy security would similarly imply here that there is no escape from the global risks. For instance, despite modern advances in nuclear technology, it is not possible to guarantee 100 percent reliability of the nuclear power plants, as, e.g., technical accidents, environmental disasters or terrorist attacks on the nuclear infrastructure could never be fully ruled out. Deciding that nuclear energy is uncontrollable could push decision-makers to opt for alternative energy sources. The policy change itself would serve as a strategy for risk mitigation, but the interconnectedness of global risks would mean that the same actors could still be adversely affected, e.g., by nuclear catastrophes happening elsewhere. Therefore, although security within the total logic of energy security is still about the manageability of risk, the latter more often than not becomes an unattainable goal. The degree to which energy security risks are perceived as "controllable" is therefore likely to be highly context-dependent. Regardless of the motivation or scope of risk mitigation strategies, once the precautionary measures and rhetoric are in place, we can point to the clear manifestation of this logic in the empirical cases. It could then be argued that the risk logic manifesting in the energy sector is inclusive and of a negative value. It is inclusive as risks are of a reflexive nature. It is all of us in the face of risks manufactured through our own agency. As we reflect on the resulting possibilities of harm, the risks could be either managed or they are incalculable and uncontrollable. Such security-risk is also of a negative value, as although we move away from the "existential threat" towards a "possibility of harm," the security mechanism operates here in a similarly antagonistic manner: it is us against adversities that might hit us back from multiple directions.

Table 1.1 summarizes a blueprint for discerning energy security logics based on the above discussion. Each of the discussed logics has an underlying rationale, which once internalized enough serves as an imperative for the respective rhetoric and actions to follow and for the logic to manifest in the given context.

Having established an analytical blueprint for the study of German, Polish and Ukrainian energy security, a critical look back at the two typologies that aided its design raises some questions. The explicit similarities between Ciută's and Corry's classifications might make one wonder whether they do not simply reflect the established theoretical and analytical approaches within the discipline. Valentine, in his criticism of the current state of energy security analysis, used Plato's Allegory of the Cave to suggest that "the assumptions upon which energy

Table 1.1 Energy security logics—a blueprint for analysis

	Rationale/ imperative	*Rhetoric*	*Control*	*Action*	*Manifestation*	*Nature of security*	*Value of security*
Logic of war	Survival	Grammar of conflict	Centralized	Policy moves above "normal politics"	"Zero-sum" energy game	Absence of war/ winning the war	Exclusive negative
Logic of subsistence	Sustenance	Utility of trade-offs	Unequally shared among stakeholders	Hierarchizing energy security dimensions	Establishment of energy security priorities	Fulfillment of needs	Exclusive positive
Risk logic	Prevention	Calculation and precaution	Lack of control/ attempting control	Strategies for alleviating risk	Precautionary measures in place	Manageability of risk	Inclusive negative

security analysis is conducted [shall be taken] out from the ontological caves inhabited by energy security analysts and into the light of day."[114] Given the unique nature of energy security, which—although mirrors some wider patterns of security dynamics—is also likely to open up our boxed understandings of security more broadly, it is tempting to similarly ask here: Are we out of the ontological cave yet?

This question can be fully addressed only through contextual analysis. Whereas the established blueprint for discerning energy security logics can aid in this analysis, the latter should stay open to the possibility of the energy security logics' mutation as well as to uncovering new logics that have not been depicted in the literature so far. Therefore, the three chapters on German, Polish and Ukrainian energy security that follow are narrated in a two-fold manner. First, they trace different logics of energy security along debates and policy developments related to pipeline politics, renewables and nuclear energy. The above analytical blueprint is used to depict and discern possibly occurring logics based on their identified thresholds. The narrative focuses on how diverse meanings of energy security cluster around, and how its practices operate within, different logics according to changing imperatives. The analysis pays attention not only to the political actors, but also to the less mainstream or even marginal voices. As such the analysis provides space for other manifestations of energy security logics by scrutinizing a wide range of actors, rationales, understandings and background conditions against which energy security is conceptualized and practiced contextually. Therefore, similarly to Trombetta's analysis of the securitization of the environment in which she showed how "by securitizing nontraditional sectors, alternative security logics are evoked and practices associated with securitization are challenged and transformed,"[115] the book traces different security logics in the energy sector. However, as opposed to Trombetta, who analyzed the implications of using environmental language for the definition and governance of security,[116] the analysis of the highly practice-oriented energy security field employs even "thicker" contextualism. It does not trace securitizations, but rather conceptualizations of energy security through both their discursive and non-discursive manifestations and allows for the possibility that it is the practice itself that can transform the meanings, understandings and logics of security. Once the logics are depicted, the analysis unpacks the mechanisms of interaction between them. This sheds more light on *how* and *why* certain energy security logics become dominant, whereas others do not, and what the mechanisms of their diffusion and sedimentation are.

Such a broad contextual approach indeed implies that security is what actors make of it, but it does not mean that possibilities are endless here. As Trombetta pointed out: "Suggesting that different security logics interact and coexist does not mean that they can be freely chosen or that other logics, like those based on risk management are without problems."[117] On the contrary, similarly as "we cannot conceptualize a de-contextualized security,"[118] and the notion of "security" will not be stretched endlessly if contextualized, the logics of security that arise from given contexts are limited by the very conditions that let them thrive in the first place. In other words, whereas the contextual thickness of security practices undermines Wæver's logic of security practices,[119] it simultaneously indicates that "both the rules and circumstances that hold security practices are contextually bound."[120] It is then crucial for the analysis to clearly operationalize energy contexts to be studied.

Operationalization of context

Some hints could be obtained here from critical engagements with the CS securitization framework that tackled its contextual dilemma. Three such re-engagements are particularly worth considering. First, it was argued that the analysis of securitization should embrace its "embeddedness" as "security articulations need to be related to their broader discursive contexts from which both the securitizing actor and the performative force of the articulated speech act/text gain the power."[121] Second, as Salter pointed out, the "setting" of a securitization should be taken into account, since the latter "reflects the complex constitution of social and political communities and may be successful and unsuccessful to different degrees, in different settings, within the same issue area and across issues."[122] Third, Balzacq distinguished between two types of context in relation to securitization—proximate context and distal context.[123] Whereas the first type applied to the setting of a securitizing move, the distal context referred to the broader sociocultural context in which securitizing moves were embedded, for example, matters of social class and ethnicity, regional and cultural settings, and the sites of discourse.[124] Certainly, a proper consideration of such sociocultural factors would be crucial to open up the analysis and, as Huysmans previously noticed, a "cultural-historical interpretation of the rhetorical structure would reduce a tendency to universalize a specific logic of security."[125]

The above insights are largely incorporated into the operationalization of context in this book. The "embeddedness" of security articulations that relates to their performative force is directly linked to the strength of the guiding imperative behind the logics' possible manifestations. As the three case studies analyze both the discursive and non-discursive manifestations of the logics, scrutinizing what drives and allows actors in given contexts to employ and express these logics is key. The broad contextual approach also embraces the wider socio-economic, historical and cultural conditions and analyzes how they might enable or hinder certain security logics—as evident in the mainstream and marginal definitions, policy approaches and debates. Lastly, it pays attention to the "setting"/"constellation of actors" within which national energy security dynamics play out. These three elements carry equal weight and are seen in a relational manner (see Figure 1.1).

Therefore, the broad operationalization of context allows us to see how energy security logics interact and compete in the public sphere via diverse mechanisms and within shifting constellations of actors, while both being

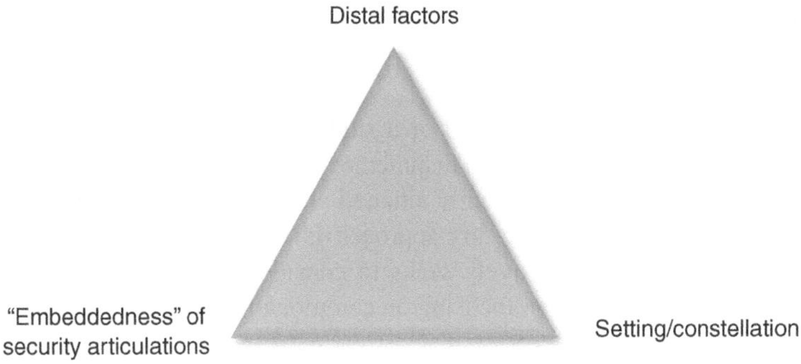

Figure 1.1 The operationalization of context.

influenced by and influencing further the sociopolitical distal context from which they arise. It gives voice to diverse actors and—having in mind their relative standing in a given constellation and background factors that shape their rationale—traces the dynamics of their rhetoric and practice vis-à-vis other rhetoric and practices, which enter that interaction. Such analysis sheds light on both the mainstream and emerging understandings and practices of energy security. As such it can explain the current "state of affairs" as well as point to the new approaches and their potential impact on future energy security scenarios. The contextual analysis grounded in hermeneutics also maneuvers between the theory and practice of energy security and recognizes the embodiment of security in the understandings of theorists and their subjects alike.[126] As Wilkinson pointed out:

> consideration of the distal context of securitizing moves is vital if we are to avoid simply replicating the normative understandings of security inherent in theoretical approaches and instead uncover local understandings of security and how they are created. This is largely the domain of "local knowledge" that is, in contrast to so-called "expert knowledge," experimental, context-specific, tacit, everyday and practice-based.[127]

Therefore, the aim here is not "about challenging scholars to choose between either unhesitatingly imposing their theories upon other people or utterly deconstructing them," but rather that local understandings constitute "a corpus of knowledge and experience that might inform our own."[128] The broadly defined context together with the "liminality" of energy security as an in-between theory, policy and practice category[129] are two hallmarks against which the analysis is conducted. Both points are brought about through an interpretivist methodology and a research practice grounded in hermeneutics.

Methodological approach

As Wilkinson, who conducted a contextual analysis of security dynamics in Kyrgyzstan, noted:

> Moving the local to the foreground of a study permits us to focus on the specificities of, ambiguities in, and disjunctures between theory, method and the field. For the study of inherently situated and context-dependent social phenomenon such as security, this approach is likely to produce a more nuanced account, since it actively seeks to consider multiple perspectives and interpretations rather than focusing on commonalities between empirical cases.[130]

The interpretive methodological approach, which focuses on meaning-making in context by situated actors, is in line with the iterative character of hermeneutic sense-making, where researchers' "initial analytical hunches are continuously contrasted and reassessed vis-à-vis field reality."[131] As such, hermeneutics provides "an interpretive epistemology rooted in the potential for multiple possible meanings of language, acts or physical artefacts" that allows the researcher to access multiple sources in any given context.[132] Consequently, both "theory-based" and "practice-based" knowledge is given high importance as the analysis maneuvers between them in the recursive and reiterative process.[133] The latter implies that the logic of inquiry is not simply inductive (reasoning that begins with observations of the particular phenomenon from which general laws are drawn), but an abductive one—where the researcher is "simultaneously puzzling over empirical materials and theoretical literatures."[134, 135] Such a mode of inquiry continues throughout the entire research process as the theory-informed and fieldwork-informed data generation and analysis are ongoing and intertwined in search of differences, specificities and patterns in/between empirical contexts.[136] This approach is also perfectly suited for the analysis of the liminal phenomenon of energy security.

Unpacking the analytical ground "in-between" energy security theory, policy and practice requires a framework that allows for the established theoretical definitions to be continuously contrasted and re-evaluated vis-à-vis the multiplicity of local understandings and practices. Since multiple meanings of energy security often hide in its everyday practice, such inquiry has the potential to enrich theoretical constructs and frameworks or even challenge them entirely. When analyzed together, the "experimental knowledge of the field" and the "abstract knowledge of theory"[137] aid in uncovering a fuller picture of contextual energy security dynamics. What appears quite challenging for its operationalization, though, is that in a hermeneutic sense-making circle there is not a fixed starting point for an inquiry, but the latter begins "wherever the individual 'is' in her understanding at that moment, with whatever grasp of things she has at that time."[138] How then to account for the liminal sphere of contemporary energy security dynamic and start "from the middle"?

Having in mind the earlier discussion of energy security logics, the book utilizes here for analytical purposes the energy security logic of subsistence. As Ciută pointed out, although energy security logics might operate in different or within the same contexts, it is often the case that they are "simultaneously present in policy documents, academic analyses and business briefs, and their coexistence is marked by a *perpetual politics that organizes them hierarchically*."[139] Here, the logic of subsistence, which constitutes the main site of contestation, could be utilized to approach the energy contexts "from within." As it was argued, the logic of subsistence operates around the three dimensions of growth, sustenance and environment, which drive policy preferences that might "signal the hierarchies that govern the interaction between the local and the global (global warming versus cold homes versus human security), and broad political orientations (domestic deregulatory versus global deregulatory)."[140] If we go one step further, it could appear that the logic of subsistence is not solely confined to the public policy agenda, but goes beyond policy preferences and in a broader sense constitutes an analytical sphere, in which all the energy security logics are reflected. The subsistence logic that is marked by the multiplication of actors and meanings of energy security and replacement of the "survival" rationale by the functional demands of the diverse sectors of activity is the ultimate liminal sphere where the actual hierarchization processes of different energy security dimensions take place. It is within this sphere that the renegotiation processes of what energy security means, as well as the development of rhetoric that is conducive for other security logics to emerge, take place. This is especially so since the broad understandings of energy security, both those underpinning the war logic and those corresponding to the risk logic, are likely to be rooted in the contextual dynamics of the situated actors. In this sense, the logic of subsistence could be seen as an "intermediary logic" or *modus operandi* in the analytical space, where the competing contextual meanings of energy security are mediated and where its diverse logics interact. Approaching it in this way gives the study significant analytical, conceptual and substantive leverage.

To start with, such an approach provides insight into the broadly operationalized context and junctures between its three respective elements. First, identification of multiple relevant actors in a given local setting and their cross-references (actors referring to each other in the debates and semi-structured interviews) shed light on the existing constellations against the background factors ("distal context"). The way in which actors refer to each other also illustrates their relative power/stance within a given constellation and additionally point to the existence of transnational networks of actors and their perceived influence in the domestic energy sphere. Second, attention is paid to the multiple meanings of energy security—both in theory and in practice (local literature and official documentation on the subject and as defined by situated actors). As such, the conceptual analysis is problematized as it points to a key difference between "definition" of energy security versus its "conceptualization." Namely, as opposed to the context-detached definitions based on a set of pre-established indicators, the study uncovers how energy security is conceptualized while entrenched in its empirical and normative dimensions. In this case "starting from the middle" means adhering to *a* key hermeneutic point that "lay actors are concept-bearing beings, whose concepts enter constitutively into what they do."[141] As McSweeney put it: "[It is] a practical implication for professional observers that social science concepts are parasitic on those of the actors under observation. To discover what an actor does logically requires knowing what an actor knows."[142] Consequently, allowing local actors to provide their conceptualizations of energy security takes the contextual analysis further as the latter often reflect and include: (1) different hierarchies and priorities of energy security aspects; (2) the significant "distal factors" in a given context; and (3) the underlying energy security rationales. When considered together, the identified "constellations of actors" and local conceptualizations jointly aid in the exposure of security articulations and logics embedded in a given setting.

Therefore, utilizing the energy security logic of subsistence not only allows analysis of the empirical cases "from within" contexts, but also exploration of the liminal sphere of energy security most effectively: (1) conceptually, as local conceptualizations reflect the intertwinement of practice-based and theory-based understandings; (2) analytically, as such an approach helps to operationalize contextual interactions between actors (What constellations are in place? Do they change in relation to different energy security debates/sources/issues?), meanings (Does rhetoric change over time? Are the hierarchies of energy security dimensions shifting?), and logics (Do they originate/are reflected in/around the subsistence logic?); and (3) substantively, as empirical cases differ in terms of dynamics within the logic of subsistence—across their areas of contestation over the meaning and rationale behind energy security. Hence, analysis framed from this angle sheds light on the diverse empirical energy contexts of Germany, Poland and Ukraine.

This operationalization of the approach is strengthened in practice by adhering to a set of principles for an interpretive inquiry—the mapping techniques for exposure and intertextuality.[143] First, mapping for exposure aims at "maximizing research-relevant field encounters that will provide the researcher with a wide variety of meanings as expressed by situated actors or written records."[144] In this case—since the book employs discourse analysis and semi-structured interviews as its primary research methods—it aims at the selection of diverse written and non-written sources as well as a wide range of interviewees across local energy contexts. The former take into account media outlets, parliamentary debates, official policy documents and public debates. The latter, depending on the possibilities of access, aim to open up the analytical space and to include a wide range of interviewees among: ministerial officials, energy experts, think tank analysts, employees of energy companies, representatives of the green energy movements and NGOs. This broad range of interviewees serves to paint a wider picture of energy security dynamics in each of the analyzed cases, as it scrutinizes both the mainstream and more marginal energy security understandings and practices. The semi-structured interviews follow the criteria of an interpretivist mode of interviewing, as outlined by Soss: (1) prioritization of skepticism about shared meaning (questioning assumptions that particular words, objects, people or events have self-evident or widely shared meanings); (2) placing actors' understandings and sense-making efforts at the forefront of empirical investigation; and (3) treating construction of a coherent account of participants' understandings as a prerequisite for adequate explanation.[145] As such, the interviewees provide their conceptualizations of energy security, list and prioritize its multiple dimensions, and point to key events that in their view had an impact on energy security rationale in a given context. In order to reconcile the use of the interview data with the general tenor of contextualization, the interviewees are asked about their conceptualizations of energy security at the very beginning of the interview process not to plant any "alien"/theoretical conceptual seeds in the local vernacular. Subscribing to the interpretivist methodology—which holds that there are multiple, intersubjective social realities in which the researcher (as well as the researched) is also an interpreter—it is foreseen that the interviewees might provide a variety of answers.[146] However, since empirical cases are not equivalent and even within the same contexts there often exist profound differences in interpretations, it is precisely those differences that might point to what is perceived as significant or meaningful in a given setting.[147] Consequently, it is only through cross-examination of information gathered from such interviews/documents/observations[148] that the study is ultimately able to paint a broader picture of competing meanings, understandings and agendas of energy security in a given context. And here mapping for intertextuality is equally—if not more—important.

The latter aims at "reading across" a number of sources in an intertextual fashion in order to reveal how "different types of data draw on ('cite') material from other kinds of data, such that the researcher can 'read across' them in interpreting meaning" and see " 'intertextual' links across data sources in ways that contribute to … [their] interpretation."[149] Mapping for intertextuality is well suited to the contextual analysis and this book draws on this principle in a broader manner. As the analysis traces both discursive and non-discursive representations of different energy security logics, it does not examine so much the relationship between the texts it refers to, but rather maps out and draws the linkages between diverse meanings, practices and agendas in order to contextualize them. For instance, while the interviewees provide their own narratives, these narratives are contrasted with other accounts of energy security and interpreted to identify unique elements as well as commonalities in reasoning about energy security across sources and empirical cases. The intertextuality is then used to make sense of the multiple accounts, analyze them along with possible energy security logics and contextualize against a broader picture of domestic energy security reasoning and practices. The empirical chapters go into significant depth to "give voice" to a number of different actors in the ongoing debates (from ministerial officials to green energy activists) and to contextualize them by making extensive use of the diversity of sources (including interviews, media coverage, official documents, local energy studies literature and parliamentary speeches). Therefore, the material from interviews is presented as one of the local interpretations that fit into wider discursive patterns. This strategy aims to compose coherent storylines out of the narratives and conceptualizations, which are by default subjective and context-dependent. The principle of intertextuality in its broader application is also useful in establishing what the local constellation of the relevant actors is, e.g., by paying attention to cross-referencing between actors during the interviews.

Both techniques of mapping for exposure and intertextuality are then employed to uncover the main areas of "contestation" over the meaning of energy security in the three discussed countries. The analysis focuses on the public sphere, where multiple understandings are voiced, and on actors that—to a greater or lesser extent—visibly enter this area of interaction. Consequently, the sources that embrace the topic of energy security but do not enter the public debate or do not influence energy security rhetoric and policy to a significant degree (such as legal documents or agendas of insurance companies) are omitted. The entire process is also conducted in a flexible and reflexive manner. Flexible, as an abductive logic of inquiry signifies that "maps" for exposure and intertextuality, which are informed by the researcher's prior knowledge, are likely to be revised during the fieldwork stage.[150] And reflexive, as interpretivist research requires that the researcher constantly checks on their own sense-making until the very completion of the project.[151]

The choice of the methodological approach and its operationalization is reflected in the narrative structure of the three case study chapters. Each chapter starts with a short review of the local conceptualizations of energy security and the rationale behind them is then unpacked further throughout the analysis of a number of debates in the areas of pipeline politics, nuclear energy and renewables. The domestic energy contexts are then explored "from within" those debates. Starting from the logic of subsistence, the latter is utilized to show the main areas of contestation and to illustrate mainstream security understandings operating within typical constellations of actors in a given context (since the latter might shift in relation to other energy issues and logics). The "bargaining" over the priorities of energy security shows different domestic hierarchies of its respective elements (e.g., subsistence vs. sustainable development vs. environment) and, as such, it often points into different directions as far as the conditions conducive for other energy security logics to manifest are concerned.

However, since the cases are not equivalent, the subsistence logic is analyzed around different debates in different national settings: pipeline politics and subsequently "Energiewende" in Germany, EU Climate and Energy package in Poland, and the subsequent drafts of Energy Strategies (2030 and 2035) in Ukraine. Apart from paying attention to the local interactions around the subsistence logic, the book focuses on some "trigger events" in the European energy sphere in the years 2006–2018 that sparked domestic debates on energy security in many European states. These include the Ukrainian gas crises, development of the Nordstream project, the accident at the Japanese Fukushima Nuclear Power Plant, and the expansion of the EU climate agenda. Following an abductive logic of inquiry, the analysis also leaves space for the situated actors and sources to point to other developments that were crucial for reasoning about energy security in a given context, yet which developments could not be easily identified a priori to the analysis. As a result, the empirical narratives include a mixture of debates—those provoked by the same international incidents and those unique for the domestic setting under consideration. Regardless of the expected cross-case differences, such narratives allow comparisons across: significant "distal factors," channels through which particular energy security understandings spread, domestic responses to the "trigger events," dynamics of the main areas of contestation (how are the dimensions of energy security hierarchized?), and most crucially—manifestation of the diverse energy security logics in all three national contexts studied. The following three chapters demonstrate how this methodological approach is utilized for the analysis of the complex and often contradictory German, Polish and Ukrainian energy security approaches.

Notes

1 Buzan, Wæver, and De Wilde, *Security*.
2 Wilkinson, "The Limits of Spoken Words, 95.
3 Ciută, "Conceptual Notes on Energy Security"; Trombetta, "Environmental Security and Climate Change"; Balzacq, *Contesting Security*; Doty, "Immigration and the Politics of Security."
4 Ibid.
5 Corry, "Securitisation and 'Riskification'."
6 Stritzel, "Towards a Theory of Securitization."
7 Balzacq, *Securitization Theory*, 17.
8 Salter, "Securitization and Desecuritization."
9 Claes, "Global Energy Security."
10 Houssin, "Security of Energy Supplies in a Global Market"; Kalicki and Goldwyn, *Energy and Security*; Marquina and Marquina Barrio, *Energy Security*; Moran and Russell, "Introduction," 2–4; Naughten, "Asia's Rising Complex Energy Interdependence"; Toichi, "Energy Security in Asia and Japanese Policy"; Wesley, *Energy Security in Asia*; Yergin, *Energy Security and Markets*; Youngs, "Europe's External Energy Policy."
11 Noël, "Challenging the Myths of Energy Security."
12 D'Agostino et al., "What's the State of Energy Studies Research?"
13 Cherp and Jewell, "The Three Perspectives on Energy Security"; Cherp and Jewell, "The Concept of Energy Security"; McCollum, Krey, and Riahi, "An Integrated Approach to Energy Sustainability."
14 *Green Paper*; *Factsheet: Increasing Our Energy Security*; Sovacool, *Routledge Handbook of Energy Security*, 2.; Sovacool and Brown, "Competing Dimensions of Energy Security"; Sovacool and Mukherjee, "Conceptualizing and Measuring Energy Security"; Kruyt et al., "Indicators for Energy Security"; *Meeting the Energy Challenge*.
15 Ciută, "Conceptual Notes on Energy Security," 126; Sovacool and Lim, "Conclusion," 414.
16 Sovacool, *Routledge Handbook of Energy Security*, 3.
17 Egenhofer et al., "European Energy Security"; Gallis, "NATO and Energy Security"; Luft, "Energy Security"; Mallaby, "What Energy Security Really Means"; Noël, "Is Energy Security a Political, Military or Market Problem?"; Yergin, "What Does 'Energy Security' Really Mean?"
18 Ciută, "Conceptual Notes on Energy Security," 127.

19 Valentine, "The Fuzzy Nature of Energy Security"; Chester, "Conceptualising Energy Security"; Ciută, "Conceptual Notes on Energy Security."
20 E.g., Ansolabehere and Konisky, "Public Attitudes toward Construction of New Power Plants."
21 Ibid.
22 Ciută, "Conceptual Notes on Energy Security."
23 Sovacool, "Diversity."
24 Ciută, "Conceptual Notes on Energy Security."
25 Morgenthau, "Politics among Nations."
26 Walt, "Alliance Formation and the Balance of World Power."
27 Waltz, *Theory of International Relations*, 111–14.
28 E.g., Tennberg, "Risky Business"; Moran, "International Economics and National Security"; Myers, "Environmental Refugees in a Globally Warmed World"; Roberts, "Human Rights and International Security"; Weiner, "Security, Stability, and International Migration."
29 E.g., Campbell, *Writing Security*; Weldes et al., *Cultures of Insecurity*; Huysmans, Dobson, and Prokhovnik, *The Politics of Protection.*
30 Fierke, *Critical Approaches to International Security.*
31 McSweeney, *Security, Identity and Interests*, 21.
32 Ciută, "Conceptual Notes on Energy Security."
33 Lipschutz, *On Security* (Columbia University Press, 1995).
34 Ciută, "Conceptual Notes on Energy Security."
35 Aradau, "Security and the Democratic Scene"; Aradau, "The Perverse Politics of Four-Letter Words"; Balzacq, "The Three Faces of Securitization"; Balzacq, *Securitization Theory*; Hansen, "The Little Mermaid's Silent Security Dilemma"; Stritzel, "Towards a Theory of Securitization"; Williams, "Words, Images, Enemies"; McDonald, "Securitization and the Construction of Security"; McSweeney, "Identity and Security."
36 E.g., Ciută, "Conceptual Notes on Energy Security"; Trombetta, "Environmental Security and Climate Change"; Balzacq, *Contesting Security*; Doty, "Immigration and the Politics of Security."
37 Balzacq, "The Three Faces of Securitization"; McDonald, "Securitization and the Construction of Security"; Ciută, "Security and the Problem of Context."
38 Doty, "Immigration and the Politics of Security"; Trombetta, "Environmental Security and Climate Change." Ibid.
39 McDonald, "Securitization and the Construction of Security."
40 Fierke, *Critical Approaches to International Security*, 103.
41 Buzan, Wæver, and De Wilde, *Security.*
42 Ciută, "Security and the Problem of Context," 306.
43 Ibid.
44 Fierke, *Critical Approaches to International Security*, 103.
45 Ciută, "Security and the Problem of Context," 314. Emphasis added.
46 Buzan and Wæver, *Regions and Powers.*
47 McDonald, "Securitization and the Construction of Security," 563.
48 Ibid.
49 Wilkinson, "The Limits of Spoken Words: From Meta-Narratives to Experiences of Security," 96.
50 Ibid.
51 McDonald, "Securitization and the Construction of Security," 563.
52 Ciută, "Security and the Problem of Context."
53 Ciută, 306–15.
54 Ibid.
55 Ciută, 307.
56 Wæver et al., *Identity, Migration and the New Security Agenda in Europe.*

57 McDonald, "Securitization and the Construction of Security," 579.
58 Ciută, "Security and the Problem of Context," 303.
59 Ciută, "Conceptual Notes on Energy Security," 125; McDonald, "Securitization and the Construction of Security," 579.
60 Wæver, "Securitization and Desecuritization," 51.
61 Doty, "Immigration and the Politics of Security," 79–80.
62 Trombetta, "Environmental Security and Climate Change," 585. Emphases added.
63 Trombetta, 589.
64 Balzacq, *Securitization Theory*.
65 Guzzini, "Securitization as a Causal Mechanism."
66 Elster, "3. A Plea for Mechanisms"; Elster, *Explaining Social Behavior*, 36.
67 Guzzini, "Securitization as a Causal Mechanism," 5.
68 Guzzini, "Securitization as a Causal Mechanism."
69 Balzacq, *Contesting Security*.
70 Hansen, "Conclusion," 225.
71 Aradau, *Rethinking Trafficking in Women*, 72.
72 Van Munster, "Review Essay."
73 Balzacq, "Legitimacy and the 'Logic' of Security," 1.
74 Ibid.
75 Huysmans, "Security!"
76 Balzacq, "Legitimacy and The 'Logic' of Security," 1.
77 Ibid.
78 Ibid.
79 Bourbeau, "Moving Forward Together."
80 Ibid.
81 Ibid.
82 Huysmans, "Security!," 232.
83 *English Oxford Living Dictionaries*.
84 Corry, "Securitisation and 'Riskification'," 237.
85 Ibid., 247.
86 Ibid.
87 Ibid.
88 Ibid.
89 Ciută, "Conceptual Notes on Energy Security."
90 Ibid.
91 Ibid., 130.
92 Ibid.
93 Ibid., 131–2.
94 Ibid., 131–4.
95 Ibid., 133.
96 Ibid., 135.
97 Ibid., 136.
98 Ibid., 127.
99 Ibid., 125.
100 Corry, "Securitisation and 'Riskification'," 241.
101 Corry, 249.
102 Corry, "Securitisation and 'Riskification'."
103 Wæver, "Securitization and Desecuritization," 55.
104 Ciută, "Conceptual Notes on Energy Security," 131–4.
105 Beck, *Risk Society*.
106 Corry, "Securitisation and 'Riskification'," 241.
107 Beck, "Living in the World Risk Society."
108 Bigo, "Security and Immigration"; Huysmans, *The Politics of Insecurity*; Salter, "Securitization and Desecuritization"; Salter, "Imagining Numbers"; Aradau and

Van Munster, "Governing Terrorism Through Risk"; Elbe, "AIDS, Security, Biopolitics."

109 Corry, "Securitisation and 'Riskification'," 248.
110 Beck, "Living in the World Risk Society."
111 Beck, *World Risk Society.*
112 Ciută, "Conceptual Notes on Energy Security," 135.
113 Ibid.
114 Valentine, "The Fuzzy Nature of Energy Security," 70.
115 Trombetta, "Environmental Security and Climate Change," 585.
116 Ibid., 589.
117 Trombetta, "Rethinking the Securitization of Environment," 149.
118 Ciută, "Security and the Problem of Context," 303.
119 Ibid., 311–14.
120 Balzacq, *Contesting Security.*
121 Stritzel, "Towards a Theory of Securitization," 359–60.
122 Salter, "Securitization and Desecuritization," 324.
123 Balzacq, *Securitization Theory*, 17.
124 Ibid.
125 Huysmans, "Revisiting Copenhagen."
126 Ciută, "Security and the Problem of Context," 304.
127 Wilkinson, "The Limits of Spoken Words," 99.
128 Kent, "Reconfiguring Security."
129 Ciută, "Conceptual Notes on Energy Security."
130 Wilkinson, "Not Just Finding What You (Thought You) Were Looking for," 396.
131 Schwartz-Shea and Yanow, *Interpretive Research Design*, 53.
132 Yanow, "Interpretive Political Science."
133 Ibid.
134 Following Schwartz-Shea and Yanow, other characteristics of an abductive logic of inquiry include: bottom–up, *in situ* concept development, constitutive understandings of causality, the relevance of researcher identity in accessing sites and archives, the need to improvise in response to field conditions and data co-generation in field relationships (Ibid., 99).
135 Schwartz-Shea and Yanow, *Interpretive Research Design*, 27.
136 Ibid., 56.
137 Wilkinson, "Not Just Finding What You (Thought You) Were Looking for," 401.
138 Schwartz-Shea and Yanow, *Interpretive Research Design*, 30.
139 Ciută, "Conceptual Notes on Energy Security," 125. Emphasis added.
140 Ibid., 133.
141 Giddens, *New Rules of Sociological Method*, 13.
142 McSweeney, *Security, Identity and Interests*, 146.
143 Schwartz-Shea and Yanow, *Interpretive Research Design*, 79.
144 Ibid., 85.
145 Soss, "Talking Our Way to Meaningful Explanations."
146 Schwartz-Shea and Yanow, *Interpretive Research Design*, 41.
147 Ibid.
148 Yanow and Schwartz-Shea, *Interpretation and Method*, 152.
149 Ibid., 86.
150 Ibid., 88.
151 Ibid.

References

Ansolabehere, Stephen, and David M. Konisky. "Public Attitudes toward Construction of New Power Plants." *Public Opinion Quarterly* 73, no. 3 (2009): 566–77.

Aradau, Claudia. *Rethinking Trafficking in Women: Politics out of Security*. Houndmills: Palgrave Macmillan, 2008.

Aradau, Claudia. "Security and the Democratic Scene: Desecuritization and Emancipation." *Journal of International Relations and Development* 7, no. 4 (2004): 388–413.

Aradau, Claudia. "The Perverse Politics of Four-Letter Words: Risk and Pity in the Securitisation of Human Trafficking." *Millennium: Journal of International Studies* 33, no. 2 (2004): 251–77.

Aradau, Claudia, and Rens Van Munster. "Governing Terrorism through Risk: Taking Precautions, (un)Knowing the Future." *European Journal of International Relations* 13, no. 1 (March 1, 2007): 89–115.

Balzacq, Thierry. *Contesting Security: Strategies and Logics*. London: Routledge, 2014.

Balzacq, Thierry. "Legitimacy and the 'Logic' of Security." In *Contesting Security: Strategies and Logics*, 1–10. London: Routledge, 2015.

Balzacq, Thierry. *Securitization Theory: How Security Problems Emerge and Dissolve*. London: Routledge, 2010.

Balzacq, Thierry. "The Three Faces of Securitization: Political Agency, Audience and Context." *European Journal of International Relations* 11, no. 2 (2005): 171–201.

Beck, Ulrich. "Living in the World Risk Society." Hobhouse Memorial Public Lecture, February 15, 2006. www.lse.ac.uk/collections/sociology/pdf/Beck-LivingintheWorldRiskSociety-Feb2006.pdf.

Beck, Ulrich. *Risk Society: Towards a New Modernity*. London: Sage, 1992.

Beck, Ulrich. *World Risk Society*. Cambridge: Cambridge University Press, 1999.

Bigo, Didier. "Security and Immigration: Toward a Critique of the Governmentality of Unease." *Alternatives* 27 (February 1, 2002): 63–92.

Bourbeau, Philippe. "Moving Forward Together: Logics of the Securitisation Process." *Millennium* 43, no. 1 (2014): 187–206.

Buzan, Barry, and Ole Wæver. *Regions and Powers: The Structure of International Security*. Vol. 91. Cambridge: Cambridge University Press, 2003.

Buzan, Barry, Ole Wæver, and Jaap De Wilde. *Security: A New Framework for Analysis*. Boulder, CO: Lynne Rienner Publishers, 1998.

Campbell, David. *Writing Security: United States Foreign Policy and the Study of Identity*. Minneapolis: University of Minnesota Press, 1998.

Cherp, Aleh, and Jessica Jewell. "The Concept of Energy Security: Beyond the Four As." *Energy Policy* 75 (2014): 415–21.

Cherp, Aleh, and Jessica Jewell. "The Three Perspectives on Energy Security: Intellectual History, Disciplinary Roots and the Potential for Integration." *Current Opinion in Environmental Sustainability* 3, no. 4 (2011): 202–12.

Chester, Lynne. "Conceptualising Energy Security and Making Explicit Its Polysemic Nature." *Energy Policy* 38, no. 2 (2010): 887–95.

Ciută, Felix. "Conceptual Notes on Energy Security: Total or Banal Security?" *Security Dialogue* 41, no. 2 (2010): 123–44.

Ciută, Felix. "Security and the Problem of Context: A Hermeneutical Critique of Securitization Theory." *Review of International Studies* 35, no. 2 (2009): 301–26.

Claes, Dag Harald. "Global Energy Security: Resource Availability, Economic Conditions and Political Constraints." *Panel: Contextualizing Energy Security and Transition.*

Concepts, Framing and Empirical Evidence SGIR 7th Pan-European International Relations Conference 9, no. 11.9 (2010): 2010.

Corry, Olaf. "Securitisation and 'Riskification': Second-Order Security and the Politics of Climate Change." *Millennium: Journal of International Studies* 40, no. 2 (2012): 235–58.

D'Agostino, Anthony Louis, Benjamin K. Sovacool, Kirsten Trott, Catherine Regalado Ramos, Saleena Saleem, and Yanchun Ong. "What's the State of Energy Studies Research? A Content Analysis of Three Leading Journals from 1999 to 2008." *Energy* 36, no. 1 (2011): 508–19.

Doty, Roxanne Lynn. "Immigration and the Politics of Security." *Security Studies* 8, no. 2–3 (1998): 71–93.

Egenhofer, Christian, Leonid Grigoriev, Vladimir Socor, and Alan Riley. "European Energy Security: What Should It Mean? What To Do?" *Working Paper no. 23*. Brussels: Centre for European Policy Studies, 2006. http://shop.ceps.eu/BookDetail.php?item_id=1392.

Elbe, Stefan. "AIDS, Security, Biopolitics." *International Relations* 19, no. 4 (December 1, 2005): 403–19.

Elster, Jon. "3. A Plea for Mechanisms." *Social Mechanisms: An Analytical Approach to Social Theory*, 1998, 45.

Elster, Jon. *Explaining Social Behavior: More Nuts and Bolts for the Social Sciences*. Cambridge: Cambridge University Press, 2015.

English Oxford Living Dictionaries, definition of logic, https://en.oxforddictionaries.com/definition/logic.

Factsheet: Energy Independence and Security Act of 2007. White House, 2007. http://georgewbush-whitehouse.archives.gov/news/releases/2007/12/20071219-1.html.

Factsheet: Increasing Our Energy Security and Confronting Climate Change. White House, 2008. http://useu.usmission.gov/Article.asp?ID=24873062-2BF8-454FB7A8-902BD1976383.

Fierke, Karen. *Critical Approaches to International Security*. Cambridge: Polity, 2007.

Gallis, Paul. "NATO and Energy Security." In *Congressional Research Service Report RS22409*, 2006. www.fas.org/sgp/crs/row/RS22409.pdf.

Giddens, Anthony. *New Rules of Sociological Method: A Positive Critique of Interpretative Sociologies*. London: Hutchinson, 1982.

Green Paper: A European Strategy for Sustainable, Competitive and Secure Energy. Brussels: European Commission (EC), 2006.

Guzzini, Stefano. "Securitization as a Causal Mechanism." *Security Dialogue* 42, no. 4–5 (2011): 329–41.

Hansen, Lene. "Conclusion: Towards an Ontopolitics of Security." In *Contesting Security: Strategies and Logics*, 219–31. London: Routledge, 2015.

Hansen, Lene. "The Little Mermaid's Silent Security Dilemma and the Absence of Gender in the Copenhagen School." *Millennium: Journal of International Studies* 29 (June 2000): 285–306.

Houssin, Didier. "Security of Energy Supplies in a Global Market." In *Speech by IEA Director Office of Oil Markets and Emergency Preparedness to 2nd Energy Forum, Prague*, 4–6, 2007.

Huysmans, Jef. "Revisiting Copenhagen: Or, on the Creative Development of a Security Studies Agenda in Europe." *European Journal of International Relations* 4, no. 4 (1998): 479–505.

Huysmans, Jef. "Security! What Do You Mean? From Concept to Thick Signifier." *European Journal of International Relations* 4, no. 2 (1998): 226–55.

Huysmans, Jef. *The Politics of Insecurity: Fear, Migration and Asylum in the EU.* London: Routledge, 2006.

Huysmans, Jef, Andrew Dobson, and Raia Prokhovnik. *The Politics of Protection: Sites of Insecurity and Political Agency*. London: Routledge, 2006.

Kalicki, Jan H., and David L. Goldwyn. *Energy and Security: Toward a New Foreign Policy Strategy*. Baltimore, MD: Johns Hopkins University Press, 2005.

Kent, Alexandra. "Reconfiguring Security: Buddhism and Moral Legitimacy in Cambodia." *Security Dialogue* 37, no. 3 (2006): 343–61.

Kruyt, Bert, Detlef P. van Vuuren, H.J.M. De Vries, and Heleen Groenenberg. "Indicators for Energy Security." *Energy Policy* 37, no. 6 (2009): 2166–81.

Lipschutz, Ronnie D. *On Security*. New York: Columbia University Press, 1995.

Luft, Gal. "Energy Security: What Does It Really Mean?" In *Energy Security and Security Policy: NATO and the Role of International Security Actors in Achieving Energy Security*. Oberammergau: NATO School, 2007.

Mallaby, Sebastian. "What Energy Security Really Means." *Washington Post* 3 (2006). http://50.57.111.125/revenuewatch_archive/training/Mallaby%20-%20What%20 Energy%20Security%20really%20means.doc.

Marquina, Antonio, and Antonio Marquina Barrio. *Energy Security: Visions from Asia and Europe*. Basingstoke: Palgrave Macmillan, 2008.

McCollum, David L., Volker Krey, and Keywan Riahi. "An Integrated Approach to Energy Sustainability." *Nature Climate Change*, 9 (2011).

McDonald, Matt. "Securitization and the Construction of Security." *European Journal of International Relations* 14, no. 4 (2008): 563–87.

McSweeney, Bill. "Identity and Security: Buzan and the Copenhagen School." *Review of International Studies* 22, no. 1 (1996): 81–93.

McSweeney, Bill. *Security, Identity and Interests: A Sociology of International Relations*. Cambridge: Cambridge University Press, 1999.

Meeting the Energy Challenge: A White Paper on Energy. London: UK Department of Trade and Industry, 2007.

Moran, Daniel, and James A. Russell. "Introduction: The Militarization of Energy Security." *Energy Security and Global Politics: The Militarization of Resource Management*, 2009, 2–4.

Moran, Theodore H. "International Economics and National Security." *Foreign Affairs* 69, no. 5 (1990): 74–90.

Morgenthau, Hans J. *Politics among Nations (1948)*. New York: McGraw-Hill, 1993.

Myers, Norman. "Environmental Refugees in a Globally Warmed World." *Bioscience* 43, no. 11 (1993): 752–61.

Naughten, Barry. "Asia's Rising Complex Energy Interdependence." *International Journal of Global Energy Issues* 29, no. 4 (2008): 400–33.

Noël, Pierre. "Challenging the Myths of Energy Security." *Financial Times*, January 10, 2008.

Noël, Pierre. "Is Energy Security a Political, Military or Market Problem?" *Financial Times*, January 17, 2008.

Roberts, Brad. "Human Rights and International Security." *Washington Quarterly* 13, no. 2 (1990): 65–75.

Salter, Mark B. "Imagining Numbers: Risk, Quantification, and Aviation Security." *Security Dialogue* 39, no. 2–3 (April 1, 2008): 243–66.

Salter, Mark B. "Securitization and Desecuritization: A Dramaturgical Analysis of the Canadian Air Transport Security Authority." *Journal of International Relations and Development* 11, no. 4 (2008): 321–49.

Schwartz-Shea, Peregrine, and Dvora Yanow. *Interpretive Research Design: Concepts and Processes*. London: Routledge, 2013.

Soss, Joe. "Talking Our Way to Meaningful Explanations." In *Interpretation and Method: Empirical Research Methods and the Interpretive Turn*, 127–49. London: Routledge, 2006.

Sovacool, Benjamin K. "Diversity: Energy Studies Need Social Science." *Nature* 511, no. 7511 (July 30, 2014): 529–30.

Sovacool, Benjamin K. *Routledge Handbook of Energy Security*. London: Routledge, 2010.

Sovacool, Benjamin K., and Marilyn A. Brown. "Competing Dimensions of Energy Security: An International Perspective." *Annual Review of Environment and Resources* 35 (2010): 77–108.

Sovacool, Benjamin K., and Tai Wei Lim. "Conclusion: Exploring the Contested and Convergent Nature of Energy Security." In *Routledge Handbook of Energy Security*, 414–27. London: Routledge, 2011.

Sovacool, Benjamin K., and Ishani Mukherjee. "Conceptualizing and Measuring Energy Security: A Synthesized Approach." *Energy* 36, no. 8 (2011): 5343–55.

Stritzel, Holger. "Towards a Theory of Securitization: Copenhagen and Beyond." *European Journal of International Relations* 13, no. 3 (2007): 357–83.

Tennberg, Monica. "Risky Business: Defining the Concept of Environmental Security." *Cooperation and Conflict* 30, no. 3 (1995): 239–58.

Toichi, Tsutomu. "Energy Security in Asia and Japanese Policy." *Asia Pacific Review* 10, no. 1 (2003): 44–51.

Trombetta, Maria Julia. "Environmental Security and Climate Change: Analysing the Discourse." *Cambridge Review of International Affairs* 21, no. 4 (2008): 585–602.

Trombetta, Maria Julia. "Rethinking the Securitization of Environment: Old Beliefs, New Insights." In *Understanding Securitisation Theory: How Security Problems Emerge and Dissolve*, 135–49. London: Routledge, 2010.

Valentine, Scott Victor. "The Fuzzy Nature of Energy Security." In *Routledge Handbook of Energy Security*, 56–73. London: Routledge, 2011.

Van Munster, Rens. "Review Essay: Security on a Shoestring: A Hitchhiker's Guide to Critical Schools of Security in Europe." *Cooperation and Conflict* 42, no. 2 (2007): 235–43.

Wæver, Ole. "Securitization and Desecuritization." In *On Security*. New York: Columbia University Press, 1995.

Wæver, Ole, Barry Buzan, Morten Kelstrup, and Pierre Lemaitre. *Identity, Migration and the New Security Agenda in Europe*. New York: St. Martin's Press, 1993.

Walt, Stephen M. "Alliance Formation and the Balance of World Power." *International Security* 9, no. 4 (1985): 3–43.

Waltz, Kenneth. *Theory of International Relations*. Reading, MA: Addison-Wesley, 1979.

Weiner, Myron. "Security, Stability, and International Migration." *International Security* 17, no. 3 (1992): 91–126.

Weldes, Jutta, Mark Laffey, Hugh Gusterson, and Raymond Duvall. *Cultures of Insecurity: States, Communities and the Production of Danger*. Minneapolis, MN: University of Minnesota Press, 1999.

Wesley, Michael. *Energy Security in Asia*. Vol. 3. London: Routledge, 2007.

Wilkinson, Cai. "Not Just Finding What You (Thought You) Were Looking for: Reflections on Fieldwork Data and Theory." In *Interpretation and Method: Empirical Research Methods and the Interpretive Turn*, 387–405. London: Routledge, 2013.

Wilkinson, Claire. "The Limits of Spoken Words: From Meta-Narratives to Experiences of Security." In *Understanding Securitisation Theory: How Security Problems Emerge and Dissolve*, 94–115. London: Routledge, 2010.

Williams, Michael C. "Words, Images, Enemies: Securitization and International Politics." *International Studies Quarterly* 47, no. 4 (2003): 511–31.

Yanow, Dvora. "Interpretive Political Science: What Makes This Not a Subfield of Qualitative Methods." *APSA Newsletter*, 2003.

Yanow, Dvora, and Peregrine Schwartz-Shea. *Interpretation and Method: Empirical Research Methods and the Interpretive Turn*. London: Routledge, 2015.

Yergin, Daniel. *Energy Security and Markets*. Washington, DC: Woodrow Wilson Press and John Hopkins University Press, 2005.

Yergin, Daniel. "What Does 'Energy Security' Really Mean." *Wall Street Journal* 11 (2006): A12.

Youngs, Richard. "Europe's External Energy Policy: Between Geopolitics and the Market." *CEPS Working Documents*, no. 278 (2007).

2 Germany

Towards a new energy security paradigm

Introduction

The eyes of many are set on Germany's ambitious energy transition. The path of the biggest European economy towards a more sustainable future is not without its ups and downs, which come in the form of fluctuating prices of electricity from renewables, technical setbacks in the form of coal-fired power plants or challenges with promoting its agenda abroad. Energiewende implies much more than a policy change, as it is driven by a multi-layered socioeconomic and political transformation. Understanding the complex forces behind it that might determine its ultimate success or failure is therefore of a wider European and global interest and might have implications for other countries to follow. However, the ongoing energy transition constitutes only one dimension of the broader German energy security dynamics that is rooted in the specific contextual factors and marked by different policy approaches across issue areas. The developments in the German nuclear and gas sectors are a case in point here. Although the historical strength of the anti-nuclear movement and the pro-environmental leanings of the entire German political establishment have been clear for years, making a U-turn policy decision in the aftermath of the nuclear accident in Fukushima still came as a surprise to many. Not consulting key energy businesses on the accelerated nuclear phase-out seemed uncommon for the German context, typically dominated by big industry interests, and raised many questions both domestically and abroad. Simultaneously, the German policy decisions in the area of pipeline politics started to come to the fore of wider security considerations in the CEE region in recent years. The continuous German–Russian energy cooperation on the projects bypassing the transit countries in Central and Eastern Europe (CEE) was neither shaken by the Ukrainian gas crises of 2006 and 2009, nor by the outbreak of the Ukrainian–Russian war in 2014. Whereas this energy policy approach was formerly heavily criticized for its lack of sensitivity towards the eastern neighbors, it started to raise wider questions regarding common values and European solidarity in the face of Russia's aggression in Ukraine.

Shedding light on such complex and at times rather puzzling policy moves requires a detailed analysis of the wider context in which they occur. This chapter unpacks the dynamics of the German energy context along the security logics that drive its different debates and policy sector developments. Following the analytical framework developed in Chapter 1, the narrative starts from the analysis of the logic of subsistence that revolves around economic considerations and that is marked by a multiplicity of actors and meanings of energy security. First, the dilemmas related to the local conceptualizations of energy security are discussed. Second, different competing understandings, interests and agendas that are mirrored in these conceptualizations are scrutinized further at the example of different energy security debates and policy decisions. The chapter begins with discussing German pipeline politics, which is dominated by the subsistence logic, as illustrated by the domestic responses to the Ukrainian gas crises of 2006 and 2009 and the development of the Nordstream project. This set of events highlights the specificities of the traditional energy policy approach in Germany that revolves around big energy businesses and their economic considerations and that is marked by a lack of wider media debate and societal disengagement. The subsequent sections show that the dominance of the sustenance imperative can be challenged in the German context in a two-fold manner. On the one hand, the developments in the aftermath of the nuclear accident at the Japanese nuclear power plant Fukushima illustrate the rapid rise of the risk logic in Germany. The strong imperative of prevention that emerged from a favorable historical and socioeconomic context led to both discursive and policy shifts and to a significant power reshuffle within the domestic constellation of actors. On the other hand, less dramatic yet powerful incremental processes challenge the dominant logic of subsistence, as the gradual re-hierarchization of energy security dimensions and prioritization of the environmental agenda over the years not only change the frame of the economic-centered energy security debate, but set the ground for the emergence of a distinct security logic in the German energy sector. Driven by the imperative of self-reliance, the emerging energy security logic of emancipation is brought about by the gradual diffusion of the centralized energy system, individuals becoming the referent objects of security, reflexive practice of energy production, and a positive notion of energy security. Its rise challenges the dominant sustenance imperative, as the purely economic calculations are overridden by the idea of sustainable development achieved via democratization of energy and turn to green energy solutions by local communities. The rise of this logic has important policy and normative implications and adds yet another layer to the complex German energy security dynamics shaped by the specific historical, political and socioeconomic factors.

Conceptualizing energy security in the German context

Scrutinizing local conceptualizations of energy security provides an insight into the multiplicity of local understandings, interests and agendas that manifest and operate in the German energy context. To start with, the evolution of the concept and its priorities did not follow a single trajectory in Germany, but—similar to many other places—turned out to be a complex and continuous process. As one leading energy expert noted, although the need for "widening" of the security agenda to incorporate other than military dimensions of security was clearly felt in Germany and Europe alike in the 1990s, it proved especially difficult in Germany to operationalize non-militarized meanings of security and to embrace their impact on the concrete security policy and practice at the national and international levels.[1] Regarding energy security, it translated into lack of "security understanding" of the concept in a global context and lack of comprehensive and cross-departmental strategies.[2] The issue of security of supply was for most of the 1990s and 2000s left to private sector energy companies concerned with profits rather than nationwide crisis management in case of emergency.[3] According to local experts, energy security was largely seen as a "settled issue" before 2005—with the debate framed around nuclear phase-out, climate change and price stability.[4] The Ukrainian gas crisis of 2006 changed this dynamic and caused questions of energy security to be raised in Germany for the first time. At the same time, the German Foreign Ministry expressed the belief that energy security constitutes a key issue not only on the twenty-first-century global economic and environmental policy agenda, but also on the security policy one.[5] Consequently, security of energy supply gained prominence at that time, a fact reflected in mainstream definitions of the concept.

Not surprisingly, according to different German energy experts, energy security is consistent with its classical meaning,[6] as they often point to its cost and supply dimension[7] and perceive energy security as achievable through increasing dependencies, energy efficiency and the European market.[8] Such definitions mirror the fact that energy policy is still understood mainly as a part of economic policy in Germany. Although some publications on the subject point to its linkages with numerous other policy areas—such as environment and climate, foreign and security policy as well as with development, transport, housing and social or technology policy—the majority of these interrelated issues are considered to be of secondary importance.[9] Consequently, the dynamic developments, long-term risks and (possible) threats are addressed only marginally in official German energy policy.[10]

Having said that, a look at the wider debates indicates that in the post-2006 period not only the importance of security of supply was highlighted, but that period was also marked by the proliferation of multiple understandings of energy security and its aspects. First, "broader" conceptualizations have emerged as, for example, Caroline Mükusch pointed out:

> Energy policy is a social policy. A competent dealing with the challenge of "energy security" therefore requires values-based and interest-based energy security policies as well as holistic and integrated approaches that combine economic, ecological and socially viable and sustainable development.[11]

Second, the German energy policy trilemma of security of supply, efficiency and environment started to take a new form.[12] As local observers of the domestic energy security debate note, just a few years ago the official energy security discourse in Germany followed the EU-level discourse in emphasizing three key dimensions of energy security—energy efficiency, sustainable development and environmental protection. That trend has recently altered, with more emphasis being put on the "environmental" aspect and some attempts to find a compromise between different dimensions of energy security and different actors in German society.[13] In this respect German "Energiewende," which steers the country away from fossil fuels and atomic energy towards increasingly high reliance on renewable energy, was both accelerated by the alternative views on energy security within German society and is continuously influencing them further. Within the new frame of the debate, the perception of energy security shifts away from the reliance on the energy market and puts more emphasis on how access to different energy resources is guaranteed. The local analysts note that the role of media and government in shaping public attitudes towards various energy security aspects (e.g., energy efficiency) became more appreciated over time.[14] Officials from the German Ministry of the Environment additionally highlight that the continued strong interest and involvement of German society in "Energiewende" will be a decisive factor in the energy transition project's very success.[15] The multiplicity of actors involved in the ongoing energy security debate also marks the multiplication of its understandings. Moreover, the very energy revolution—"Energiewende"—means different things to different groups of actors. Whereas for the public it is largely synonymous with the exit from nuclear and the shift to renewables, the industry follows the cost dimension of the project and a number of complex debates on climate protection, energy efficiency and various aspects of security take place in the background. According to some experts, the often simplified approaches to current energy security debate illustrate that "the debate is too complex, and normal people and even politicians don't have a good understanding of [it]."[16] Indeed, multiple competing understandings interact within different constellations of actors, including energy companies, government, media, energy experts, environmental groups and the general public. These constellations of actors and their relative importance change depending on the energy source to which they relate at any particular moment, with the debates on fossil fuels, nuclear energy and renewables representing different dynamics and following diverse security logics that ultimately influence energy policy developments.

This chapter unpacks this complexity in greater detail—paying special attention to how different notions and logics of energy security play out in the German context across a number of issue areas and debates sparked by some key "trigger" events in the energy sector: the Ukrainian gas crises of 2006 and 2009, the development of both parts of the Nordstream project, the nuclear accident at the Fukushima nuclear power plant, and the ongoing debates on German energy transition.

Pipeline politics: threats in disguise and "business as usual"

The incidents of interrupted gas supplies from Russia in 2006 and 2009 certainly served as one of the most powerful triggers for the issue of the traditionally understood "energy security" to be brought about in the public debates and policy agenda of numerous European states. Germany not only was not an exception here, but the Ukrainian gas crisis of 2006 sparked the most profound debate on German energy security to date. Similar to many states in the CEE region, the gas cut-off episode raised the grammar of conflict and vocabulary very much in line with the realist logic of war in the official rhetoric. However, as opposed to some states of the CEE region, the crisis did not lead to the emergence of the survival imperative in the context of German energy politics. The combination of contextual factors (historically determined perceptions of Russia) and constellation of actors typical for the German energy context (that gives leverage to energy companies and their economic interests) meant that the change in rhetoric was short-lived, as it did not fall on fertile ground and did not put the gas routes' diversification plans at the top of the national security agenda. A closer look at this dynamic scrutinizes how the German context of gas politics driven by the imperative of sustenance is not conducive to the logic of war to thrive in it.

Ukrainian gas crisis 2006

Different German energy experts highlighted that the immediate aftermath of the 2006 gas crisis led to a realization that Ukraine is a really important transit state and caused questions of energy security to be raised for the first time in Germany.[17, 18] If before 2005 the debate on energy security oscillated around the issues of nuclear phase-out, climate change and price stability, the Ukrainian gas crisis deteriorated the reputation of Ukraine and slightly damaged Germany's perception of Russia as a reliable partner—although, as some admit, it was hard to comprehend the actual role of Gazprom in the crisis fully.[19] Crucially, the gas crisis shifted the debate on energy security, and this change in rhetoric was especially visible among the mainstream media, which started to publish opinions and analyses in line with the logic of war. It was therefore noticed that: Putin and his advisers demonstrated a will to use raw materials as a political weapon and engage in energy geopolitics;[20] that more than half of the Leviathan [Gazprom] belongs to the state—which obviously understands energy war as the continuation of politics by other means, as: "Where Khrushchev once rattled missiles, the Kremlin today turns the gas tap";[21] and that Gazprom holds a place of honor in the new superpower conception of Russia as the Kremlin seeks a status of energy superpower that will use the harsh law of supply and demand to reorganize relations in the post-Soviet space.[22] In light of what happened in Ukraine, it was also argued that Russian strategy could be seen as a reformulation of Lenin's slogan of "socialism in one country" into "energism in one hand."[23] Importantly, some analysts also pointed out that whereas energy resources were recognized in Russia as the new currency of power already in the late 1990 (when it was recommended to use gas supplies as a political weapon), these developments were not of interest to the German side prior to the 2006 gas crisis—with the exception of a few analytical outlets.[24] In light of this general approach, the gas cut-off in January 2006 was seen as a "wake-up call"—with some accompanying questions raised at the time: For how long would it be fine to stay so tightly bound to such an authoritarian regime? How vulnerable is the country? And what are the alternatives?[25] Such analyses were limited in number and time-scope, and it was a general perception among local analysts that the German media did not report much about the actual "threat from Russia."[26] Low politicization of the issue also meant that the German debate on Gazprom in the aftermath of the Ukrainian gas crisis was largely an inter-expert debate (as opposed to the multifaceted debate on nuclear energy).[27] Some important expert analyses highlighted how the Ukrainian gas crisis enhanced the importance of security of supply in the target triangle with cost-effectiveness and environment, and how numerous unquestioned assumptions in German energy and foreign policy were demystified as a result.[28] The latter included beliefs that oil and gas are purely economic and non-strategic assets—therefore security of supply is irrelevant and can be left to private energy companies and market rules; that Russia will always be a reliable energy partner for Europe; and that there is a strong and growing interdependence between Europe and Russia in the energy sphere.[29] Especially the latter assumption of "mutual dependence" promoted by the former Chancellor Gerhard Schroder was questioned. Some pointed to the lack of reciprocal behavior on Russia's side—as it was gaining access to European customers via Nordstream, while denying the opening of its energy market to European companies and increasing exports of energy resources to other geographical regions.[30] It is worth highlighting, though, that analyses like the ones above were rather in the minority. According to local energy experts, the majority of their peers continuously saw Russia as more dependent on Europe than vice versa, even in the aftermath of the 2006 gas cut-off episode.[31] As such, there was also a split between the German expert community and the general public that perceived its country as overly dependent on the Russian supplier.

The perception of Russia as a reliable partner was certainly shaken in the eyes of the public, but this fact alone did not have significant repercussions as neither the majority of analysts nor crucial energy businesses shared this view. In the opinion of the representative of the German BDEW (Federal Association of the Energy and Water Industry), the reputation of Russia did not suffer as the energy businesses did not perceive Russia as trying to put pressure on the German market, but saw the gas cut-off episode as a sole result of Russia's conflict with Ukraine.[32] The situation was therefore dealt with in a calm manner, as a representative of E.ON put it in an interview: "We have clearly analyzed this crisis and also consulted with our Russian partners to say: look, it should not happen again."[33]

The above perceptions point to an important difference between Germany and many states of the CEE region when it comes to putting the blame on either side of the 2006 gas conflict. Whereas the latter saw the 2006 gas cut-off episode largely as a Russian dictate, analyses in Germany appeared much more balanced. On the one hand, many voices asked whether Russia, which tried to remotely control the democratically elected government in Kiev by a gas value and discredit the government of President Yushchenko shortly before the parliamentary elections in March, became an unreliable supplier.[34] The Kremlin's decision to put at stake its reputation of a blameless energy provider since the end of the Soviet Union for the sake of a small additional Gazprom revenue was questioned.[35] Some also suggested that Russia's reputation was indeed irreparably damaged.[36] On the other hand, it was pointed out that both parties of the conflict resorted to irresponsible threats: With Ukraine yielding an increase in transit fees for Russian gas to Western Europe and the Russian rent for the naval port of Sevastopol in Crimea, and with Russia threatening to put a stop to the transit of Turkmen gas to Ukraine.[37] Moreover, some media outlets highlighted "ridiculously low" former gas prices for Ukraine while suggesting that:

> The Ukrainians will have to learn now not to regulate the temperature of their overheated rooms in the old Soviet style: by opening a "window" and that it is hard to blame the Russian Finance Minister for saying that "... the times when we almost made our relations with neighboring countries through subsidies come to an end."[38]

The response to the gas crisis in the German context was therefore to a large extent a matter of perceptions. Although the whole event shook Germany's trust in Russia, local observers pointed out that, as opposed to many CEE states, many media and non-media voices in Germany put a lot of blame for the crisis on Ukraine.[39] Consequently, any damage done to the image of Russia as a supplier was short-lived and did not lead to any significant repercussions from the German side. A number of interconnected factors also contributed to this lack of response. First, Germany, because of its high gas reserves, was well covered during the gas cut-off episode and therefore not harmed by the crisis.[40] As an official from one of the four big energy companies in Germany, E.ON, stated: "It was of course not an amusement for the gas industry," but "in essence nothing really happened in Germany for the gas customers, because we had enough storage."[41] Second, the distal context played a role (historically determined perceptions), as in the view of different energy experts Germany had a good experience with gas transits from Russia, with the latter having proved to be a reliable supplier even during the Cold War period.[42] Third, as one Berlin-based analyst pointed out, even with Vladimir Putin as president (or formerly as prime minister), Russia was not perceived as a danger at the time, but rather as a small country due to its small economy.[43] Therefore, even the excessive dependence on a single gas supplier did not constitute a major issue, as the import dependency was perceived in the German context more in economic than security terms and the aspects of energy security related to fossil fuels more in terms of increasing global gas and oil prices rather than import dependency as such.

This dynamic highlights that Germany's pipeline politics is driven by the sustenance imperative that aims at ensuring the security of energy supply with primary focus given to economic considerations. Despite multiple relevant actors here, such as big energy businesses, government, media or the general population, it is the former that have a decisive voice and that steer policy developments in the gas sector. If gas cut-off episodes did not alter this logic, apart from provoking some short-lived debate in the German media, the developments of the Nordstream project made its manifestation even more explicit.

Nordstream

Already in 2005, while writing about the Baltic pipeline project, Cerstin Gammelin from *Die Zeit* noted how the deal was made to please German corporations.[44] With German E.ON/Ruhrgas holding 6.5 percent of Gazprom and with Wintershall aiming at closer ties with the Russian energy monopolist, Nordstream was a clear manifestation of energy companies' interests. However, given that establishing the Baltic pipeline was neither in line with the rule of open competition nor with the lowest possible prices, the newspaper boldly asked: "Why do these developments not interest anybody in Germany?"[45]

A closer look at the constellation of actors in German pipeline politics provides an answer to this question. The establishment of Nordstream was initially set up by a strong alliance between Russia and Germany based on the involvement of two key political figures: former German Chancellor Gerhard Schroeder and Russian President Vladimir Putin. The key players on the German side were energy company E.ON and the Economic Ministry, which pushed forward their economic agenda.[46] However, the German government did not consult any neighboring states at the early stage and, according to local analysts, even the general public was not well aware of the project until the actual deal was signed.[47] Moreover, the political opposition was silent on the issue[48] and some analysts explain this general lack of political debate on Nordstream by the fact that "Energiewende," with its shift to renewable energy, became a new slogan, whereas it started to be politically unpopular to talk about pipeline politics.[49] With a lack of sufficient information in the media, there was also no debate on the project in the German strategic community.[50]

The project appeared therefore as an economically driven "business as usual"—conducted largely away from the scrutinizing eye of the German media and the general public, and not highly politicized. Some local energy experts highlighted that the project's smooth introduction was enhanced not only by the close links between German Social Democrats and Russian politics, but also Gerhard Schroeder's personal and more "behind the scenes" style of politics that enabled the undertaking of the North European pipeline plans, while avoiding much public discussion.[51] After the signing of the deal, Schroeder was criticized for insensitivity to the eastern neighbors, but according to local voices a lot of domestic criticism of his close connections to Russia derived rather from the general critical stance towards Russia and its internal problems (such as respect for human rights), rather than towards the Nordstream pipeline itself.[52] Therefore, although it was admitted even by the representatives of German E.ON that signed the deal that not consulting eastern neighbors (mainly Poland) at the early stage was a mistake,[53] and the entire handling of the situation showed a general lack of sensitivity to the issue of energy security, in the end there was a consensus that Nordstream is good for Germany. Many from German business circles and the expert community alike saw the Baltic pipeline project more as a European venture rather than a nationalistic undertaking.[54] As one of Germany's energy experts put it, "Germany is part of Europe and we are thinking about European security … , Germany doesn't have any important energy security questions."[55] And further: "Most scientists when they think about Germany they think about the government, but here the important decision-makers are energy companies, which are multinational and they work with other European countries," therefore—"there is no national interest, the national interest is the European interest."[56] Going a step further, a representative of E.ON stated in autumn 2012 that Nordstream was not only a European undertaking, but a potential way of closer integration with Russia in general: "People in Western Europe feel too much paranoia vis-à-vis Russia, because [it] tries to come to Europe, [but] … they really need us to modernize [their] country," therefore there is "a need to water down the prejudices to each other … and that requires concrete projects."[57] Against this general trend, opinions that Germany acts like a rich "energy-egoist," as it creates mistrust among its eastern neighbors for the sake of closer ties with Russia and refuses solidarity clause in a crisis that could help weaker EU states, were in the minority.[58]

Interestingly, the 2006 Ukrainian gas crisis, which closely followed initial developments around the Nordstream project, served to justify the venture further. In the opinion of different Berlin-based analysts, the successful finalization of the project was owed to the fact that the gas crisis of 2006 showed the instability of Ukraine and Belarus and the need for alternatives, whereas Russia was still seen as a good, reliable partner—therefore the North European pipeline would provide Germany with "more than less security."[59] In the words of the representative from BDEW, the project illustrated a big trust of Germany in Russia, with the first ending up to be "more secure, because Russians will deliver and no one will interrupt the supply."[60] This rhetoric was also eagerly repeated among the representatives of the German corporations involved in the project, as E.ON CEO Wulf Bernotat stated in an interview with *Der Spiegel* in 2006: "The pipeline is a piece of security of supply," while similarly suggesting that bypassing transit countries like Ukraine might be not so wrong in light of recent developments.[61]

Further gas disputes between Russia and transit states in the following years did not change the dynamics of German pipeline politics, despite some critical media analysis. Media articles repeatedly referred to Gazprom as Putin's gas weapon that he uses to re-establish world power.[62, 63] The rhetoric expressed was also clearly in line with the war logic, as it highlighted its "zero-sum" game dynamics by embracing phrases such as "Gas Putin," "Moscow power games" or cover headlines such as "The state Gazprom: Putin's Energy-Empire."[64] In the aftermath of the next big gas cut-off episode in 2009, *Die Zeit* also rhetorically asked whether Russia is a "false friend."[65] Others pointed out that since the 2006 Ukrainian gas crisis, Germany did nothing to improve the diversification of its gas supplies.[66] However, media articles had little if no impact on the ongoing energy debate and their voices were countered by opinions coming from the political and corporate spheres. Aside from Gerhard Schroeder, who was stating from the start that Nordstream enhances European energy security and is essentially a Russian–European project, a number of executives of the German main energy companies were continuously reassuring that Gazprom is not easy but always a reliable partner. Foreign Minister Frank-Walter Steinmeier even called for the strategic partnership with Russia because of "energy security."[67] With an ongoing argument about "mutual dependency" playing out in the background, and disengagement of other non-corporate actors, the nature of German pipeline politics remained unaltered. The words of the representative of E.ON illustrated it well:

> There is still strategic discussion of course how to diversify sources … which I personally don't like, because there are always some politicians who say "we have to be less dependent on Russia," well … [it is not up to] the politicians to make this diversification of gas supplies.[68]

The change in the political leadership and Angela Merkel's more "transparent" style of politics did not drastically change these dynamics either, as one policy analyst noticed: "Chancellor Merkel never liked the Nordstream project, but will follow whatever is good for economic interests in gas/oil."[69] If a number of German analysts noted as of autumn 2012 that even given the general disillusionment with the pace and direction of political reforms in Russia, and the perception that the country might "switch to chaos," the business-like nature of dealing with the security of gas supply in Germany is likely to stay the same,[70] the development of Nordstream 2 proved them right.

Given the outbreak of the Ukrainian–Russian war in 2014, the plans for yet another gas pipeline bypassing CEE countries raised an alert in the region. A joint letter to the European Commission written by the economy ministers of Poland, Hungary, Romania, Slovakia and the Baltic states highlighted three main issues at stake: Ukraine's transit fees, Europe's increased dependency on Russia and an undermined trust in the planned Energy Union.[71] If the perception in the CEE states was that the recent geopolitical developments in Eastern Europe call for even greater European solidarity, their hopes were dashed, as Germany pushed forward with the project. Some German media outlets even called the development of Nordstream 2 a foreign policy disaster for Germany,[72] as it led to the worsening of already tense German–Polish relations, marginalized Berlin in Europe, angered the US and caused more trouble for Angela Merkel.[73] The German Chancellor sought to reassure Kiev's continuous role as a transit state when in spring 2018 she stated: "This isn't only about an economic project. There are political factors to be considered."[74] However, this rhetoric did not translate into a policy shift. Despite stark opposition to the project in CEE and Brussels, German industry defended the project on the grounds of economic considerations and broader European energy security. As BDI (Federation of German Industries) President Dieter Kempf stated in an interview for the German daily *Süddeutsche Zeitung*: "German industry needs Nordstream 2 to enhance energy supply safety."[75] While alternatives like liquefied gas from the US were dismissed as too costly,[76] energy businesses pointed to 4 billion euros already invested in the project.[77] Some German officials also emphasized a long history of reliable gas supplies from Moscow, since Soviet times, and a necessity of additional energy sources to facilitate the country's transition to renewables.[78] Quite strikingly for the external observers, yet not surprisingly given the specifics of the domestic context of pipeline politics, the development of the Nordstream 2 project is also supported by German society. According to the Forsa poll for N-TV and RTL, 66 percent of respondents believed that its construction should continue, with only 23 percent against it.[79] The main rationale behind the declared support was to "ensure unfettered supply of natural gas to Germany."[80] Therefore, with the Russian side only briefly concluding that gas transits through Ukraine would stay in place as long as they remain economically justified,[81] Nordstream 2 is being developed against the will and interests of the CEE states.

The above subsequent developments in the aftermath of the Ukrainian gas crisis and in relation to the Nordstream project highlight the specificities of German pipeline politics dominated by the subsistence logic. The imperative of sustenance emerges easily within the constellation of actors that gives leverage to big energy businesses, with politicians rarely taking a decisive stance on the developments in the gas sector, media and expert analysis not being strong enough to shift the energy debate or the policy course and the general public remaining largely disengaged. The distal context with historically determined perceptions of Russia and the domination of economic concerns in ensuring energy supply additionally play a role. Although the "grammar of conflict" typical for the logic of war occurs on a number of occasions in the German media outlets reporting on developments in the country's gas sector, it does not fall on fertile ground. Ultimately, German pipeline politics is not conducive to the emergence of the survival imperative and, instead of extraordinary measures, the primary policy focus is on conducting business as usual.

Although such a dynamic illustrates the German mainstream approach to energy security—understood in the traditional terms of security of supply within geopolitical constraints—other energy security logics can emerge and play out differently in relation to other energy sources. The rise of the risk logic in Germany in the aftermath of the nuclear accident in Fukushima demonstrates how this status quo with its traditional constellation of actors and mainstream debate and policy discourse can shift once taken over by the rise of the imperative of prevention in domestic energy affairs.

The accident in Fukushima and accelerated nuclear phase-out: the risk society at its peak

Whereas events in the area of pipeline politics were not able to move the issue of gas dependency on Russia to the higher security agenda, the accident in the Japanese nuclear power plant Fukushima in March 2011 served as a powerful "trigger" for the domestic debate on nuclear energy and further policy developments in Germany. A post-Fukushima "moratorium" given by Chancellor Angela Merkel took the seven oldest of Germany's 17 nuclear power plants off the grid. This decision was quickly followed by the plan agreed between Merkel's Christian Democrats (CDU) and the Free Democrats (FDP) to shut down all the remaining nuclear plants between 2021 and 2022.[82] This sudden political move took place in a shifted constellation of actors—where the government's representative, under immense public pressure fueled by the vivid media debate, made a U-turn policy decision[83] without consulting key energy businesses. This section investigates how the specific distal context favored the emergence of the risk logic in the German nuclear energy sector and how the rise of the prevention imperative both reshuffled the typical power dynamics between different actors and led to a new policy course.

Background of the German nuclear energy debate

No other country fought so bitterly against the nuclear industry and in no other country was the anti-nuclear movement as strong as in Germany.[84] As a representative from the BDEW (German Association of Energy and Water Industries) put it: "Germany is the only country in the world where nuclear energy is such a controversial issue and has been such a controversial issue for over 40 years now."[85] The contextual analysis points to a number of factors that shed more light on this phenomenon.

It seems that one of the main explanations is the anti-nuclear movement, which, as opposed to other states, has been continuously strong in Germany ever since the 1970s.[86] Moreover, the character of this movement was both societal and political—with the very fight against nuclear power serving as the founding myth for the Green Party (since the 1980s).[87] According to some analysts, the roots of the movement itself and the rise of the Greens could be attributed to the public distrust in media (badly covered lies) and the social system itself at the time.[88] In the view of an energy expert from the Berlin-based SWP (Stiftung Wissenschaft und Politik), people from Eastern Germany were skeptical towards governmental statements, therefore they believed that there is a need "to go to the streets," whereas in Western Germany the legacy of the Nazi regime could have played a role—as with a history of being "lied to," there was a general belief that "you can be completely betrayed by the state."[89] This general distrust meant that—even before the rise of the Green movement—the statements of the government had been questioned by the German media already from the 1960s and 1970s.[90] Additionally, some policy analysts specifically link the debate on nuclear power that fueled the fear of nuclear disaster to the German-speaking media at the time, as they point out that similar debates were taking place in Switzerland, Austria and even German-speaking parts of Belgium.[91]

The role of media in shaping the debate on nuclear safety could be traced ever since—especially in the face of big nuclear accidents, such as Chernobyl. The Chernobyl accident contributed to the erosion of trust in science and to the disappearance of technological optimism in Germany, which ultimately led to the political reorientation and decision to phase out nuclear energy by the red–green government in early 2000.[92] As the 2008 article from *Der Spiegel* stated:

> The Chernobyl disaster ... confirmed the suspicion. Now the fear had a real basis. Thousands of people died in Ukraine, some parts of Germany were slightly contaminated.... It was a bad feeling that the doubts about the promised safety of this technology were entitled.[93]

The rhetoric invoked in the German media was therefore in line with Becksian risk society as nuclear energy turned out to be uncontrollable and no precautionary measures could completely alleviate its risks. Consequently, the only conceivable strategy was a policy change. The widely discussed nuclear disaster at the Ukrainian power plant in 1986 directly led to the founding of the first environment ministry in Germany and stopping the plans for building any new nuclear power plants.[94] Later on, it also contributed to the introduction of the first feed-in-tariffs in 1990—the long-term, guaranteed payments for small-scale renewable energy, which ignited the renewables boom two decades later. Moreover, since Chernobyl, the rhetoric, which highlighted the "totality" and unmanageability of nuclear risks in the global age, could be spotted even more clearly across media pieces and expert analysis. On the one hand, there were media articles providing detailed stories about the fate of the local population and workers that took part in eliminating the effects of the Chernobyl disaster, including their radiation-related diseases and continuously harsh living conditions.[95] On the other hand, nuclear risks were highlighted throughout debates on the German future energy mix, as SPD thinker Erhard Eppler stated in 2008 while commenting on a new energy consensus that aimed at the extension of nuclear power plants' operating time: "In a century when states and their monopoly over power decay, while violence is privatized and commercialized and often takes form of the globalized terrorism, nuclear energy is 'lethal carelessness'."[96]

Moreover, even prior to the accident in the Japanese Fukushima nuclear power plant, some analysts spotted how both German politicians and the German media invoked on a number of occasions the rhetoric in line with the risk logic for their own purposes. One such example was the analysis that reconstructed events of the fire accident in the German nuclear reactor Krummel in 2007, with the authors arguing that the regulators played a double game and the incident was "a lesson on the manipulation of public opinion and about opportunism and temptation to engage in the policy of fear."[97] The fire at Krummel provided the

SPD Environment Minister Sigmar Gabriel with the evidence that nuclear energy is a "risk technology" that needs to be abolished as soon as possible, as he called it a "threat reactor" and questioned the reliability of the nuclear industry as a whole.[98] This opinion was echoed by his Parliamentary Secretary Michael Mueller, who put the incident in Krummel at the same level with the Chernobyl catastrophe, as he stated: "In no scenario this incident was obviously intended, and this shows that such accidents can happen not only in the Third World or Eastern Europe, but also in a highly developed country."[99] However, later analysis showed that what happened in the German nuclear power plant would be classified—according to the worldwide standard established by the International Atomic Energy Agency—as 0 on the INES scale[100]—meaning an "event with little or no safety significance."[101] The newspaper investigation also described in detail how the incident had been purposely exaggerated along the way, directly affecting the energy company Vattenfall that owned the plant and causing other energy companies to give up hope that the nuclear phase-out decision could be put once more up for discussion. Therefore, appealing to the prevention rationale served as an effective strategy in the German context to shift the debate from the climate change agenda back to nuclear phase-out and the debate on nuclear energy back to the point where "it has always been after the Chernobyl disaster," while ensuring that the majority of Germans were once again against nuclear power in the opinion polls.[102]

Ironically, once the political mood changed again and Chancellor Angela Merkel tried to extend the operating time of the German nuclear reactors in 2008, *Die Zeit* referred to Ulrich Beck's argument about the risk society, while criticizing Merkel for "trying to hide the risks of nuclear energy in order to save the climate."[103] Speaking of the "competition of major risks," it suggested that the incalculable risks posed by climate change compete with incalculable risks associated with nuclear power plants, therefore:

> Many decisions on major risks are not about choosing between safe and risky alternatives, but of choosing between different risky alternatives, yet since "such considerations are not up to today's forms of scientific and public discourse" Merkel and the CDU/CSU succumb to the temptation of an oversimplification to present the relevant decision as a choice between safe and risky alternatives by displacing the uncertainties of nuclear energy while bringing the risk of the oil crisis and the climate crisis into the center of attention.[104]

As a consequence, *Die Zeit* argued, whoever—like the Greens—denies the revival of nuclear power sins against preventive climate policy, yet this tactic is a "frivolous game played with the security interests of the population," as not all risks are considered equally important in different contexts. Therefore, the Chernobyl experience is valued differently in Germany than in France or Britain, and different contexts represent different "risk cultures."[105]

Both examples point to the relative ease with which the rationale of prevention and the rhetoric of precaution in line with the risk logic are brought up in the German context for strategic purposes. In this case, the ultimate reasoning came closer to the totality of global risks that are out of control and in the face of which the only rational precautionary measure is the drastic policy change of nuclear phase-out. These type of debates and developments coupled with a specific historical background illustrate that the German context has been highly favorable to the emergence of the risk logic in its nuclear energy sector. Not surprisingly, then, the accident at the Japanese power plant in Fukushima gave immediate rise to the imperative of prevention, as this rationale had been well internalized by that time by numerous actors in Germany.

Fukushima and its aftermath in Germany

The 2011 accident in the Japanese NPP Fukushima gave rise to the prevention imperative in the German energy context that reshuffled the traditional power dynamics between different actors and gave new impetus to the anti-nuclear debate. The rhetoric invoked for the most part resembled the dynamics of the global risk society, where the uncontrollable and incalculable risks materialized. With hourly updates and detailed analysis of the newest developments from Fukushima, German media focused on how helplessly the technologically advanced Japan responded in the immediate aftermath of the accident.[106] Issues such as advice for Japanese citizens to stay home and put damp cloths over their mouths illustrated the state of affairs that got out of control. Additionally, German media resorted to strong rhetoric. With articles and headlines declaring "the end of the nuclear age,"[107] "Japan's lesson for the world"[108] and "the end of the atomic dream of mankind that has become a nightmare"[109]—it was "the very existence of millions" at stake that was challenged in Fukushima.[110] Therefore, the nuclear risk materialized in a different way than what is happening in the coal-mining areas, gas fields or oil platforms—it was "invisible," "inescapable," "the curse."[111] The lesson from Fukushima could only be one—"the eleventh commandment for the modern citizen: Thou shalt not play poker—the stakes are too high, too many people are affected."[112] In fact, the very idea that nuclear energy could be made safe turned out to be a "megalomaniac lost bet, with which humanity challenged the forces of nature and physics" and an "arrogant self-assurance."[113] As one journalist put it: "Never again will anyone dare to spread the myth of the safety of reactors with impunity. It proved to be a lie. The reactors were not safe and they will never be."[114] With the frequently repeated argument that if a disaster like this could happen in Japan, then it could also happen in Germany given the appropriate chain of fatal circumstances,[115] German media grandly declared: "Fukushima is everywhere."[116]

Given the specificities of the domestic context, the impact on German nuclear energy policy was immediate. Even if the accident did not challenge the nuclear industry elsewhere in the long run, as some analysts had initially predicted, it surely was the case in Germany. In light of the shifting debate, Chancellor

Merkel stated that the meltdowns proved that even a technologically advanced country like Japan had been unable to shut out the risk of disaster entirely, therefore "Germany must ... rethink and hasten to secure a good and sensible energy supply without atomic power."[117] Many saw that decision as "Merkel's nuclear awakening experience that sealed the fate of nuclear energy in Germany as her scientific mind of a quantum chemist—which told her that according to all the rules of probability nuclear power is viable energy—has been challenged."[118] The extension of modern nuclear power plants' operating time was suddenly seen as irresponsible, whereas the renaissance of the old ones was simply a "dangerous game."[119] In the words of one magazine analysis: "Fukushima should now stand for the end of the dream of the controllable nuclear power, for the admission: over this energy we have no control."[120] The heated nuclear debate shaped by media and a number of politicians illustrated Germany's deeply rooted "fear of nuclear" and began an unprecedented race in German politics with the parties competing over "who wants to get out of this form of energy even faster and more consistently than the other," with even the former pro-nuclear party FDP turning into its opponent.[121] Similarly, even previous supporters of nuclear power among the German population were largely turning against it. In a survey for ARD conducted after the Fukushima accident, 71 percent of Germans declared that they are against nuclear energy (as compared with 51 percent in the autumn of the previous year).[122, 123] However, as many local analysts pointed out, Germany presented rather a "reaction" to Fukushima than a rational action—with the nuclear debate being highly emotional.[124] As a politician from the FDP (Free Democratic Party) noticed, at that time "people in Germany spoke more about that catastrophe [at the Fukushima nuclear plant] than about the tens of thousands of people who had problems or died because of [the tsunami]."[125] The "theme of irrationality" was also undertaken on the part of energy businesses, as a representative from E.ON stated: "In my view this [accelerated nuclear phase-out] is not so rational, Mrs Merkel is a physicist so normally I would say she appears to be a very rational person."[126] Similarly, RWE CEO Juergen Grossmann saw the German debate as irrational, while pointing out that German nuclear energy is produced according to the highest safety standards, which can be additionally reviewed and improved if needed.[127] Yet, the stance of energy businesses regarding what counts as a sufficient precautionary measure to alleviate nuclear energy risks was not shared among other societal actors.

With the German population feeling threatened by the Fukushima accident and afraid of insufficient safety measures at domestic nuclear power plants, as well as the possibility of a similar accident happening in Germany,[128] the debate highlighted multiple security concerns related to nuclear energy. The perceived "irrationality" of such societal fears could have several causes, largely determined by the specifics of the German distal context. The interviewed local energy experts highlighted some of them. Apart from the already mentioned historical factors, some pointed to the possible "psychological aspect of nuclear power" and to the need "to be in control."[129] After all, as even the energy business actors noted, the accident in Fukushima showed that: "At the end of the day we as human beings can clearly see, we are not the master of nature."[130] This fear of the "uncontrollable" was directly linked to the prevailing logic in the German context that "every nuclear reactor adds more risk."[131] Therefore, although the transition from nuclear power to renewables is expensive, in the words of a politician from FDP: "it is of course a question of risks, and if you can afford it—better if there aren't too many."[132] Whereas some questioned the argument that nuclear phase-out "is driven by hysteria, hypochondria and self-pity, in a word—*German Angst*," while arguing that the green German exceptionalism became an incredible success story resulting in a better, healthier nature,[133] others compared German "nuclear fear" with religion, as "faith has nothing to do with facts—unless these facts support the faith."[134] Therefore, even if the possibility of harm caused by a nuclear accident is significantly lower in Germany than Japan (because of its geographical location), this fact ultimately does not matter as "nuclear fear" appears to have numerous deeply rooted causes, which make the German context unique. The specifics of this context also largely explain why it is hard to understand from the German perspective a totally different character of debates on nuclear power in neighboring Poland or Ukraine. As Hans Josef Fell from the Greens put it: "[there are] areas in Belarus and Ukraine that have been completely destroyed by radioactivity … it is completely crazy to go on with this."[135]

According to local observers, the narrative over the last 15 years in Germany also created the belief that nuclear energy will not solve the climate issues, as emissions from nuclear are higher than commonly assumed, therefore nuclear power is not environmentally friendly (although more so than coal).[136] Consequently, many German NGOs working on the issues of environment and climate protection oppose nuclear energy, and this rhetoric came to the very fore of the debate on nuclear energy after Fukushima's accident as a part of a wider societal opposition to the continuation of nuclear power plants' operation. Societal pressure was also one of the key factors influencing the accelerated nuclear phase-out policy decision.

Accelerated nuclear phase-out

The imperative of prevention emerged rapidly in this favorable post-Fukushima context in Germany and the anti-nuclear rhetoric quickly translated into more serious policy moves. Hence, as opposed to the developments in domestic pipeline politics when the grammar of conflict was invoked—but without further policy actions of state actors—the role of media in the aftermath of the Japanese nuclear accident was much more prominent. Not only did the vivid debate further mobilize anti-nuclear sentiments, but various societal actors appeared to have more leverage to influence policy course vis-à-vis energy companies.

The nature and severity of the post-Fukushima nuclear debate in Germany led Chancellor Merkel, who had always been a supporter of nuclear energy—under huge public pressure and with the elections in mind—to make the decision of accelerated nuclear phase-out.[137] Crucially, this decision was taken in what could be seen as a great power reshuffle within the German energy sphere. The policy U-turn was made by the government, driven by the public agenda, backed by the environmental movements and fueled by a vivid debate in the German media, yet quite strikingly, the big four energy companies (E.ON, EnBW, Vattenfall and RWE) were not consulted on that decision.

The more interesting, then, seemed a broad social dialogue launched by the federal government on the issue of the potential nuclear phase-out, which "in a process involving the Ethics Commission on a Safe Energy Supply, reviewed the *risks* posed by nuclear power."[138] Klaus Topfer, the chairman of the Ethics Committee—an energy–ethical council of experts, trade unionists, thinkers and churchmen—stated that Chernobyl was both a disastrous event and an opportunity to move away from a path of destruction, and that the committee wanted to work in that direction "out from the heart of the society."[139] However, some argued that Merkel chose such a solution to, in fact, bypass the debate that could have taken place in the parliament or within wider society instead.[140] Regardless of the motivation, that move showed a significant shift in the German constellation of actors. Whereas the representatives of the Church or academia were asked for an opinion on the issue of accelerated nuclear phase-out as part of this dialogue, the key energy businesses were not—although they were the ones most hit by the change.

As local experts note, before the accident in Fukushima, nuclear companies fully supported "Energiewende," but with the extension of the working time for the nuclear power plants.[141] Yet, the Japanese nuclear disaster at Fukushima and the subsequent debate about nuclear safety have plunged Germany's energy industry into a deep crisis, as the big four's profits started to drastically decrease and its customer base turned to their environmentally friendly rivals—such as Lichtblick and Naturstrom—which offer electricity free of nuclear or coal sources.[142] Moreover, despite the shutdown, the companies had to continue to pay a nuclear fuel tax of around €2.3 billion a year until 2016.[143] In response to these developments E.ON and RWE, concerned about damage to their competitiveness, filed cases with the federal constitutional court claiming that the abrupt closure of nuclear plants is tantamount to expropriation.[144] Additionally, the Economics Ministry—under pressure from the Federation of German Industry—set up an independent process to "monitor" the policy change, with a view to possible course corrections.[145]

The energy businesses saw the companies' moves as necessary steps for protecting their stakeholders' interests, which should not in themselves inhibit the big four energy giants' relations with the German government.[146] However, the accelerated phase-out clearly weakened the energy companies while highlighting the role of other actors in shaping the debate on what the future of the German energy mix should look like. With customers willing to pay more for "clean" energy,[147] and with the idea of "green economy" becoming a prevalent way of thinking in the German context, the companies had no choice but to change their future investment plans. As Oliver Krischer from the Greens stated: "The big energy utilities had ignored that the world was changing for too long" and their losses "were the result of misguided energy policy" and "the logical consequence of an outdated business model that relies on environmentally damaging coal and dangerous nuclear power plants."[148]

In general terms, many policy analysts and energy experts would agree that accelerated nuclear phase-out was a purely political decision on the part of Angela Merkel, as they pointed to a number of factors here.[149] First, with the government trying to ensure its credibility after Fukushima and with 2011 elections in mind, where the CDU could lose a large number of votes to the Conservative Party (anti-nuclear), Merkel "understood that she could not win" otherwise.[150] Second, the initial decision about the nuclear phase-out taken just a few months before the accident in Fukushima played a role. Given strong public support for it, there was also strong public opposition to the extension of the period of operation for nuclear power plants, as reflected by demonstrations at the time.[151] As one energy expert put it:

> Prolonging the phase-out created a strong anti-nuclear resistance so it was a big mistake, because it was only in favor of those four operators,[152] all the other utilities were against it because it also took their chance in covering other power stations on the grid … and in the public there was a big revival of the anti-nuclear movement.[153]

Third, party politics aside, some noted that the disaster in Fukushima created a unique political momentum for a U-turn policy change to be made within such a short period of time.[154] Since the issue of the future of nuclear energy had always divided German society, it was an opportunity to bring all the different social groups together. Therefore, although, as some politicians and ministerial officials admitted, the decision was indeed rushed, it was still "worth doing it" and perhaps could not be done more slowly, as similar to German reunification in the past, expectations were for certain measures to take place immediately.[155] Moreover, since such a conversion of an industrial society did not previously exist, a national effort comparable with the efforts of German reunification was needed.[156] As one member of the Ministry for the Environment put it: "The reason why Germany shifted so fast to the renewables was driven by a huge public support" as the "political agenda regarding those issues in Germany is very much driven by a public agenda"—"now energy companies are coming to terms with that decision."[157]

The question why energy companies were not consulted is less clear. As local experts point out, it was because of the power of the big four energy giants that the German government managed to redo the initial phase-out plans—with Merkel having talks with the big four while "the public was wondering why."[158] This constellation has drastically changed after Fukushima. In some opinions the companies were not consulted because the government wanted to start nuclear phase-out as quickly as possible.[159] Others suggested that Chancellor Merkel decided the policy change on the spot without consulting with anybody except for a coalition partner, as she might have thought that consulting companies would not change anything,[160] or that the chancellor had a new "hammer" in her hand for dealing with the companies after Fukushima.[161] Those who followed the energy businesses–government debate closely also pointed to another reason: The not very diplomatic stance of the former RWE CEO Jürgen Grossmann. Grossmann, former CEO of Germany's second-largest electricity producer, with an enormous responsibility towards both his company and its 70,000-strong workforce,[162] made some confrontational statements while commenting on the government energy policy plans. At the meeting in Düsseldorf he declared that "neither the German government nor Chancellor herself could divert him from his nuclear plans."[163] At another meeting with a group of executives aligned with Merkel's CDU he stated that "government's energy policies were wrong and that Germany is now facing an 'environmental dictatorship'," while also declaring that he needs at least 20 more years for the nuclear power plants to operate.[164] Such declarations created an uneasy atmosphere.[165] In the view of one policy analyst, such statements could be seen as of a "blackmailing" nature—a perception that could not go well with Merkel's personal style of politics and a potential contributor to a further lack of dialogue between energy businesses and the government.[166]

Regardless of the ultimate motive, such a policy move highlighted the weakened position of the German energy big four vis-à-vis other actors. Not consulting energy companies possibly made them also more resistant to cooperate with the government on future investments. That only added to the mounting problems of the policy U-turn, such as insufficient energy grids (with the renewable energy being produced in the north while nuclear in the south), energy market based on fossils, or the increasing cost of the transition and the issue of electricity prices.[167] As such, although the question regarding the operating time of nuclear power plants in Germany was not "if" but "how long" for nearly two decades, the rushed transition into renewables created numerous critics. Some have argued that the "government accelerated nuclear phase-out and now does not know what to do,"[168] while the public and even political debate on the transition is simplified and "nobody has solutions to the problems."[169] Given the multiple dilemmas that have resulted, it is the more significant that the U-turn policy shift took place at the time. The acceleration of the nuclear phase-out highlights therefore how the rise of the prevention imperative in a favorable distal context led to a significant power reshuffle within the domestic constellation of actors that gave more leverage to societal actors and impacted the policy course. These developments highlight that, whereas the rhetoric in line with either the logic of war or the risk logic might periodically occur in Germany—often triggered by external events—it is ultimately the contextual dynamics that determine whether the given logic will manifest in its full spectrum and lead to any tangible outcomes. If domestic pipeline politics is driven by the sustenance imperative, as embraced by the economic calculations and interests of big energy businesses, this imperative can be currently challenged on two grounds. On the one hand, the developments after Fukushima illustrate that the rise of the risk logic led to both discursive and policy shifts that divert from the dominant logic of subsistence in the German energy sector. On the other hand, a number of incremental processes happening in the background give rise to another energy security logic that emerges in a less dramatic fashion. This logic, driven by the imperative of self-reliance, builds upon bottom–up energy initiatives and has been enabled by the gradual re-hierarchization of energy security dimensions over the years. The contestation of the dominant sustenance rationale and prioritization of the environmental and inclusive energy solutions based on the widespread use of renewables set the ground for the emergence of the logic of emancipation in the German energy context. The next sections look at these processes in detail.

Energy–climate nexus: contesting the sustenance rationale

Germany's ambitious energy transition often requires trade-offs and strategies for balancing out different competing dimensions of energy security, as it embraces all levels of actors: from the state to the individual. With all that complexity, the developments around "Energiewende" mark an important shift in approaching energy security—both in terms of conceptualizing it and in developing practical ways via which it can be achieved. The former implies that the environmental aspect of energy security gradually starts to overshadow the mainstream economic agenda that characterizes the dominant subsistence logic, as the societal actors who support alternative solutions gained significant strength over the years vis-à-vis domestic energy businesses. The latter involves the growing number of grassroots citizens' energy initiatives that transform the landscape of the German energy context. Scrutinizing both of these dimensions together makes clear how they ultimately paved the way for the emergence of another security logic in the German energy sphere: the logic of emancipation.

Energiewende: the energy transformation

The first book with the slogan "Energiewende" was published in 1980, but it was not until recently that the term acquired political prominence. "Energiewende"—energy transformation—gained a new impetus after the decision of the accelerated nuclear phase-out was made, with "wende" standing for a sharp turn towards renewable energy. Within the shifted constellation of actors, and with the German public being hostile not only to nuclear power but also "virtually ruling out fracking for shale gas or capturing and burying emissions from fossil fuel plants, renewables and energy efficiency were almost the only options left."[170] Following this reality, the project of energy transformation aims to cut overall energy consumption in Germany by 50 percent by 2050 and electricity consumption by 25 percent, while planning to produce 80 percent of its electricity from renewables by the same date.[171] Despite such ambitious goals, which constitute a big challenge for German society, many analysts consider "Energiewende" a good strategy for the future. The business actors hope that being a forerunner in the project at this scale will enable Germany to develop innovation and technology that would give it leverage in the future energy market.[172] Other voices point out that the support for renewables decreases Germany's dependency on import of fossils.[173] As Milan Nitzschke, CEO of the German Renewable Energy Federation (BEE), put it: "Renewable energy and energy efficiency are the only way out of the price trap of dependency on oil and gas."[174] Similarly, Hans Josef Fell from the Greens stated: "We cannot reach energy security with fossil resources—it already happened that Putin closed the pipeline for a few days"; however, whereas pipeline connections might be uncertain in the future, "the wind will always blow through Germany."[175]

Arriving at this reasoning did not happen overnight, but took significant reshuffles between numerous political players as well as bargaining over the course and priorities of the future energy transition.

Energiewende: the interaction of actors

Many changes in the course of energy policy and commitments to climate protection goals were made in Germany between 1998 and 2002 because of the strength of environmental actors within the domestic environmental policy arena at that time.[176] It was also in 2002 that Schroeder's government took an initial decision about nuclear energy phase-out.[177] Moreover, as some analysts argued, the facts established in that period changed the field of climate and energy policy so effectively that a termination of the chosen path by the next government would have caused serious problems of legitimacy.[178] It could also damage the reputation of the political actors who would try to give up the policy of continuity in the context of the climate agenda.[179] Equally important was the change in political leadership. It was made clear right from the beginning of Merkel's time in office that the social "red rounds" of her predecessor Gerhard Schroeder were finally in the past and that energy policy will no longer be made in any back rooms, but by the federal government.[180] Therefore, even though the industry executives at the time[181] resisted ambitious environmental protection plans, warned of job losses and threatened to emigrate, their sharp criticisms did not have a far-reaching impact.[182] Hence, BASF CEO Juergen Hambrecht complained that "the policy is constantly making new unrealistic targets," E.ON CEO Ulf Bernotat claimed that "the government lacks balance, reason and realism," Vattenfall CEO Klaus Rauscher stated that "the energy policy of this government is an anti-energy policy" and the Federation of German Industry (BDI) raised a question of the "creeping deindustrialization" in one of its papers—all largely in vain.[183] The very next year the CEOs of RWE and E.ON were regularly traveling to Berlin for talks with economics and environment ministers and the chancellor, and "a clean, safe and affordable energy supply" became the new motto of the energy bosses—one that could be achieved only "with and not against each other."[184] The energy "big four" were therefore especially harmed by the U-turn policy shift that happened despite their willingness to cooperate. From the point of view of the energy companies, this decision raised too many doubts. As a representative of E.ON put it, even in the post-Fukushima context, to "say look you have to step out so quickly without answering the question how can we substitute so quickly certain kinds of (volumes) and electricity system—for me it's an open question, hopefully it will work."[185] Although left with no choice, the big energy companies attempt to be a "constructive part of Energiewende," e.g., by investing in offshore energy, they started to make those investments rather late, as like the voices in the industry admit themselves the "business was going too well."[186] In general terms, the developments since the early 2000s show that—aside from the area of pipeline politics—traditional energy businesses lost much of their voice to new actors and agendas in Germany. Although this multiplicity of voices does not make the energy transition any smoother, it shows that "Energiewende" constitutes an intense area of contestation—with various actors entering the debate over the course of energy policy and its priorities.

Starting at the institutional level, the management is split between the often warring ministries of economics (in charge of conventional energy supply, energy efficiency and energy market arrangements) and the environment (responsible for renewable energy and, through health and safety issues, for the nuclear sector).[187] The two ministries hold different opinions on the rationale of the policy shift and cannot agree on targets on climate change and energy saving, differently evaluate the technique of co-generation and disagree on the promotion of renewable energy—with the first supporting and the latter questioning it.[188] This innate tension is additionally strengthened by the fact that in Germany's habitual coalition governments the ministers are usually from different parties, which makes for policymaking that is "openly messy"[189] and creates some uncertainty for the energy industry. Some have even raised concerns that if the "framing of Germany's energy security is a part of an *instrumentalization process*—the governing CDU lost its frame."[190] Indeed, it has been argued that the "current German energy policy is characterized by a high degree of fragmentation, selective intervention and addition of inconsistent and often contradictory aspirations in retail" that takes place within uncoordinated parallel work in different departments and the "government–parties–business" triangle of power, which, because of structural deficits, often works only informally, and is insufficient.[191] Moreover, the growing decentralization of ownership and operation of Germany's energy system complicates the transition further and has far-reaching consequences. It is therefore not only the energy policy that is becoming decentralized, but the entire political context, as "the generation of political and social norms is no longer primarily provided by the state, but increasingly requires a political contribution of other actors such as the economy and the society."[192]

Indeed, "Energiewende" is driven by huge public support. What dominates the public debate is the idea that there will be 100 percent renewables at some point; however, some local analysts point out that other aspects of the debate on the current energy shift are a bit neglected, as the debate appears to be too complex.[193] Consequently, "Energiewende" means different things to different groups of actors, as the public sees it as the "exit from nuclear and shift to renewables," the industry is concerned about the costs of the transition, whereas a number of complex debates on climate protection, energy efficiency and various aspects of security take place in the background.[194] Given that this complexity is often hard to grasp for the societal and political sides alike, it is worth pointing out the role of media and political lobbyists here. In the opinion of some actors from the "green" side, the traditional energy businesses try to exert an influence on German politicians and mainstream media, which in turn protect the interests of big companies by campaigning against renewables, while the pro-environmental debate takes place largely through the Internet and smaller broadcasters.[195] In the opinion of others, the lobby of the companies based on renewable energy sources is even stronger than that of the traditional businesses.[196] These conflicting perceptions show the continuous struggles between different actors in setting the priorities of energy transition project. However, the complexity of issues and the multiplicity of interests involved also create certain contradictions in attitudes—especially on the side of the societal actors. First, whereas there is a need for the reconstruction of the power grid for transporting electricity from the wind-rich north to the industrial south, it is often inhibited by public resistance to new transmission lines in their neighborhoods.[197] Second, the fact that, despite the shift, the energy bridge will be needed in the transition from fossils and nuclear energy to renewables was initially largely ignored in the public debate.[198] Third, rising electricity prices make the "Energiewende" project increasingly expensive and, as an official from the Economic Ministry warned, "a tipping point will come when consumers refuse to pay more for new renewables."[199] Higher electricity prices are a social problem and the government fears the debate on justice and the risk of poverty that could produce social losers.[200] Moreover, the German public complains about expensive energy efficiency regulations,[201] whereas, as some point out, it still consumes too much energy itself, thus not "behaving too exemplary."[202]

Whereas the above issues might be of concern to the German government, the "greens" are rather of an opinion that one must make financial sacrifices for the "ecological transformation of the society."[203] It is therefore no longer strictly economic agenda and fulfillment of societal energy needs at the lowest cost that is a priority, but a higher aim of societal transformation that embraces and protects its own habitat. The fact that the majority of Germans subscribe to this opinion implies that despite the current vivid discussion on increasing prices and many public mood swings, public support for the project remains strong.[204] It is also not likely to change easily, as recent studies reveal that high support for Energiewende among the population (88 percent) occurs across all levels of education, income, political preferences, and in both cities and rural areas.[205] Crucially, though, this change in reasoning was not a sudden one and even given favorable distal context (e.g., history of the Green movement), the changes in the mainstream rhetoric that pointed towards a more "environmentally" oriented energy security agenda could be traced over the years in Germany.

Competing energy security dimensions and changing hierarchies

The competing dimensions of energy security and changes in the prioritization of its different aspects within the debate on Energiewende point to the contestation processes within the logic of subsistence. Interestingly, in this particular case some policy analysts would see different dimensions of energy security as partly competing and partly complementary—especially as "Energiewende" requires a systemic change as "renewables cannot be simply added to the old system."[206] Energy transition has many faces and its long-term impact on the issues such as environment, energy security, competitiveness, technology and prices is not always a straightforward one. In the words of a representative from BDEW: "You have these conflicts: nature protection versus building up more capacities for the renewables … you have the conflict of people living in their villages not wanting these new grids to be put up in their backyards."[207] Moreover, accelerated nuclear phase-out adds to the trade-offs involved in the energy revolution. As Michael Vassiliades, trade union leader and a member of the ethics committee for nuclear power, put it:

> I think it is possible to rename the conflicting goals of energy policy very clear. This allows us to signal to politics and society that hard decisions must be made.… Nuclear energy is cheap—but associated with significant residual risk. Natural gas is relatively environmentally friendly—but must be largely imported. Emissions trading helps the climate—but perhaps sells energy-intensive industries.[208]

However, what seemed crucial for the initial stages of energy transition was a quite common belief that "Energiewende" might in the end bring together and successfully address multiple—and often competing—aspects of energy security better than other options.[209] As the ministerial publication on "Energy concept" stated, the "objectives of energy, climate and budget policy must be harmonized."[210] In the words of Chancellor Merkel: "We want security, affordability and environmental acceptability and I believe we can have all three, as well as creating jobs," and although "Energiewende" might be "a Herculean task … we all can work together on this project to combine future ethical responsibilities with economic success."[211] Similarly, expert analyses, such as those prepared by the Konrad Adenauer Stiftung, saw the triangle of climate change, energy and economy as one in which all the aspects can support the project of "Energiewende."[212] However, as an analyst from KAS noted, although there is no need for conflict between those three dimensions, there is still no ready solution to their harmonization either—with all previous and future attempts being "experimental."[213]

This "experimenting" has been taking place within the energy logic of subsistence: in a changing constellation of multiple actors that hold diverse understandings of energy security and give different importance to its various aspects. In the shift of "Energiewende," "everybody is involved: the federal government, the regional governments, the states, the industry, the consumers." According to some, there are even "too many voices"—especially since different actors understand the current energy transformation differently.[214] Crucially, a certain trend has emerged from this process over recent years—and that trend points to changing energy security priorities in the German context.

Local observers note that just a few years ago the EU-level discourse on energy security, which emphasized its dimensions of sustainable development and environment (in that order), was "replicated" in the German national context.[215] However, that trend gradually started to change with more emphasis being put on the "environmental" aspect of energy.[216] The signs of that shift could be spotted over the years. For instance, as early as in 2007 the German energy industry in a joint statement with the Federation of German Industry (BDI) denounced the completely one-sided energy policy that became subordinated to the "dictates of ecology," while other important issues such as security of supply in Germany suddenly played no role.[217] One year later the Environment Minister Gabriel presented a ten-page paper that described "the thin line on which climate change, nuclear phase-out, affordable electricity prices and security of supply could match."[218] The report presented to the Advisory Council on the Environment of the federal government two years later went a step further with its headline: "Climate compatible, reliable, affordable."[219]

Prioritizing the environmental aspect of energy security could also be traced in the more recent official government documents as well as in the opinions of different policy analysts and politicians. Therefore, in the joint publication of the Federal Ministry for the Environment, Nature Conservation and Nuclear Safety and the Federal Ministry of Economics and Technology from September 2010 titled "Energy concept," one could notice the hierarchization of different energy security aspects. The document stated that the German energy policy aim should be to "ensure an energy supply that is both environmentally sound and at the same time economically viable and secure in the long run, in the interests of industry and consumers alike."[220] Similarly, speaking of the nuclear phase-out plans, the publication argued that: "A limited extension of the operating lives of existing nuclear power plants makes a key contribution to achieving the three energy policy goals of climate protection, economic efficiency and supply security in Germany within a transitional period."[221] The changes made to the document after Fukushima strengthened the above hierarchy even further with "the role assigned to nuclear power in the energy concept [being] reassessed."[222] Another document by the Federal Ministry for the Environment, Nature Conservation and Nuclear Safety, published in the post-Fukushima context and authored by the former Minister for the Environment Peter Altmaier, presented a ten-point program for Germany's future energy and environmental policy. In this document, titled "Moving forward with renewed energy," Altmaier stated that: "Today, environmental protection is of greater importance to most people in Germany than ever before. This applies both to solving global environmental problems and also to people's way of dealing with nature and the environment."[223] Moreover, noticing two years later that the ecological aspect moved down the political agenda because of the debt crisis—despite increasing social awareness—he saw the ongoing debate on energy transition "as an opportunity to bring the ecology forward again."[224]

A number of analysts noticed this hierarchization of energy security dimensions that prioritizes the environmental aspect. According to an expert from SWP in Berlin, the "societal hierarchy of needs" in relation to energy security puts the issue of the environment in the first place, followed by economic competitiveness and security of supply.[225] In a similar manner, Hans Josef Fell—a parliamentarian and a spokesman for energy politics from the Green Party—stated that energy security is primarily about "protecting our climate" and then about securing an energy system independent from rising fossils or nuclear energy prices.[226] Therefore, despite numerous arguments behind "Energiewende" (such as import dependency), many believe, similarly to a representative of BDEW, that "the major reason [behind the transition] is ecological" and related to the goals of climate protection and reduction of CO_2 emissions.[227] As the ministerial publication on "Climate protection and growth" from October 2011 stated: "An ambitious climate and energy policy is also a strategy for innovation and growth. It establishes the conditions that *must be in place* for economic modernization towards a green economy."[228] That statement also points to another important aspect of energy revolution: an attitude towards economic growth. If "growth, sustenance and environment" are the key dimensions of energy security logics,[229] it appears that Energiewende not only reverses this hierarchy and prioritizes the environmental aspect, but also transforms the other two. First, "sustenance" takes a form of "sustainable development" in the environmental discourse. Second, the attitude to economic growth is revisited. As *Die Zeit* argued in 2004: "The energy revolution is crucial for the stabilization of energy costs and for Germany to be modernized ecologically.... Economic development can be drastically decoupled from energy consumption"—and every member of society has to feel responsible for it to work.[230] Similarly, *Der Spiegel* notes in 2011 that such a conversion of industrial society:

> is also the departure from the growth model of the past decade. This model was based on cheap money and cheap energy. It consumed resources that will be lacking in the future, it left a mountain of debt, destroyed the environment and left nuclear waste that will emit for thousands of years.[231]

The argument of decoupling economic growth from energy consumption is typical for the environmental discourse and at the extreme can even call for a "zero-growth economy."[232]

What emerges then from the above is the rhetoric that challenges the dominant logic of subsistence in the German energy context. The analysis of pipeline politics illustrated how the latter is driven by the sustenance imperative that revolves around economic calculations of the big players and how conducting "business as usual" is a permanent characteristic of that dynamic. Whereas the multiple actors here, such as the political elite, media outlets and wider society, would not challenge the imperative guiding the domestic gas and oil sector, their multiple voices and rationales would come more clearly to the fore as far as the contestation over the more sustainable approach to energy security and energy policy is concerned. In this case, the subsequent debates and developments would gradually challenge the subsistence logic and lead to the re-hierarchization of energy security dimensions (see Figure 2.1).

If environment, sustenance and growth are three dimensions of energy security reflected across all its logics,[233] and if the logic of subsistence—with its multiple actors and agendas—is the ultimate area where the hierarchies between energy security dimensions and policy preferences are formed, prioritizing the environmental aspect suggests a certain departure from the underlying sustenance rationale that centers on the fulfillment of societal needs. This reversal of energy security priorities and policy course does not in itself change the nature of the subsistence logic—which remains a site of contestation where further re-hierarchization processes might follow. However, just as the replacement of "sustenance" with the "survival" rationale in the logic of war overshadows other aspects of energy security and points to a distinct security imperative on the rise, similarly prioritization of the environmental aspect and the consequent transformation of other dimensions (sustenance into sustainable development, and growth into a balanced growth) sets the ground for a different security logic to emerge in the energy sphere.

In the German context this re-hierarchization of priorities marks an important shift in thinking about energy security. The emerging approach is not only more

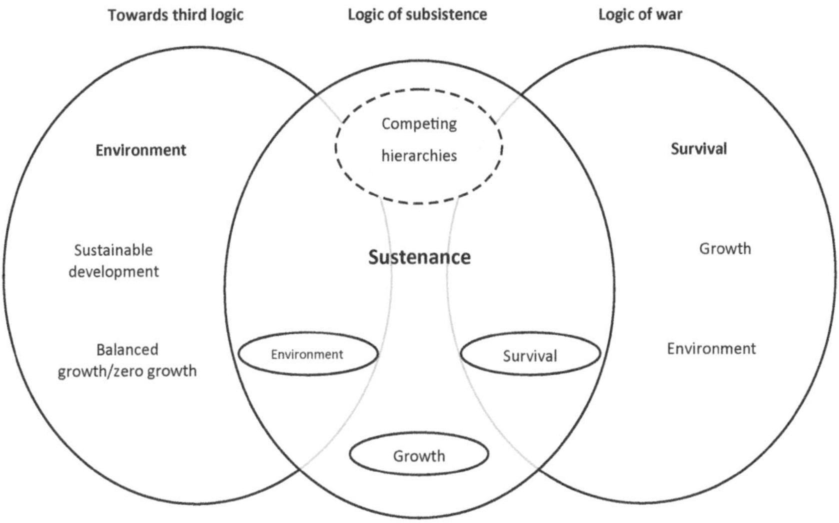

Figure 2.1 Competing energy security dimensions within the logic of subsistence.

environmentally friendly and humanistic, but by its nature is also subdued to the "higher ethical" constraints. Indeed, many Germans regard clean energy as a sort of moral philosophy and this way of thinking seems to permeate the entire German context. Chancellor Merkel explicitly linked financial debt and environmental damage by saying: "Just as we must break even with our finances, so we must [break even] with nature."[234] Crucially, setting new priorities of the energy security agenda both lay the groundwork and goes hand-in-hand with a rise of a distinct imperative of self-reliance. The decentralization of the energy system and an increasing number of local energy initiatives that seek to take their energy affairs "into their own hands" is often accompanied by the rhetoric of social liberation and empowerment. When seen in a broader picture, this changing understanding of energy security into a "positive" and "inclusive" one, based on the local practices of energy production, points to the emerging emancipatory logic in the German energy sector. The next section looks at this phenomenon.

Energiewende—the "energy revolution": from the logic of subsistence to emancipation

The all-encompassing German energy transition is underpinned by the ecological thinking and multiplicity of actors—from state to individuals. As the former Minister of the Environment put it in his *Moving Forward with Renewed Energy*:

> The transformation of our energy system … is the greatest economic policy challenge since post-war reconstruction and the greatest environmental policy challenge ever for the Federal Republic of Germany, … Environmental protection is a principle to be applied across government departments. It is important for all areas of society and policy.[235] … We now have the great opportunity to make the transformation of our energy system a common project that people identify with, … organizing and implementing the transformation of our energy system is a prime responsibility for all of the government and all of the society.[236]

This emphasis on the societal actors highlights how ensuring energy security within the energy transition project shifts the focus towards the level of each individual user.

Indeed, Energiewende has been a great societal project from the start and this re-orientation towards individual citizens was partially enabled by a favorable distal context as—like some analysts pointed out—the seeds of this "people power" revolution lie deep in the soil of German society with its long tradition of collective civic action.[237] This tradition could be traced back to Germany's pre-twentieth-century structure as a collection of city-states as well as to rural cooperatives that brought electricity to the countryside, and it has more recently manifested itself in the form of the anti-nuclear movement of the 1970s and 1980s.[238] As opposed to Denmark, where an interest in cooperatives has decreased despite encouraging legislation, and to the UK, where despite significant government resources a major cooperative movement did not emerge, Germany constitutes an example of "people power" in practice, where the strength of the "green" energy and societal actors can translate into tangible political effects.[239] As Josef Göppel, a former Bavarian forester and a member of the governing CDU/CSU, described it: "The new energy system has a social dimension and if you don't bring it to the people it will not happen."[240] Similarly, the spokeswoman for the Citizens Energy Cooperative Berlin (BEB), which wanted to buy the Berlin power grid, commented in April 2012 that "the design of our future energy system is not just a matter of politics and energy, but a societal problem."[241] Some see this emphasis on the societal dimension of the transition as "an instance of the unmistakable ethical element in the German clean energy policy" and as a "strong moral streak in Germany's cooperative movement, which sometimes involves Protestant Evangelical churches."[242] In this context, the agency clearly shifts towards many local actors and the energy transition became, in the words of H.J. Fell, more of "a grassroots movement in Germany, which is being supported by politics" and "a bottom–up strategy that will come in the next years more and more by positive examples and not influenced by government or the politicians."[243] Such opinions do not seem to be challenged even by the growing costs of Energiewende, as Lower Saxony Prime Minister David McAllister commented on the cost of the energy revolution:

> The energy transition corresponds to the will of the people of Germany. It was based on a cross-party consensus. Now we need to lead them to success together. That this does not work for free was clear to all participants from the outset.[244]

It is therefore an interaction of the grassroots movements and political leadership that is meant to bring about the transformation of the energy system—yet ultimately it is the societal actors that play a more prominent role in this process. Many in German society have benefited from renewable energy and many across all social groups now support the development of the new system.[245] In the words of an official from the Ministry of the Environment:

> All of a sudden you have all those various groups in a society that traditionally wouldn't support the Green agenda, but now they do, because it is in their own personal interest … it is becoming a very bottom–up societal project that people develop their ownership for.[246]

The growing activism of municipal energy companies (Stadtwerke) and citizens' energy cooperatives (Energiegenossenschaften) drive this project, which is also in line with the federal government's goals. According to some analysts, many decision-makers in public utilities and their supervisory bodies have thereby overcome a tangible mental barrier regarding their former opinions about the technical and economic superiority of fossil fuels and nuclear energy.[247] As such, they enabled all potential shareholders to become potential winners of energy transition: the farmers and forest owners, craft shops, planners, energy consultants, sustainably-oriented monetary investors, etc.[248] Speaking in more technical terms, over 850 energy cooperatives were formed between 2006 and 2017 to provide generation and to run local grids.[249] An increasing number of German local authorities are also continuously trying to develop community wind farms, followed by mini-grids.[250] With the aim to become more independent from RWE and other leading energy companies, approximately hundreds of municipal works (which constitute the biggest customers of the big energy providers), have also started the process.[251]

Such local initiatives very often have a strong economic dimension, as some debt-ridden communities, such as Prötzel in Brandenburg, try to modernize with wind turbines by starting a local company that deals directly with the wind power operators.[252, 253] Others are more advanced, such as the 1000-inhabitant town of Dardesheim, which tries to serve as an inspiration to the entire Harz region with its eco-concept.[254] Named as "The City of Renewable Energies," it produces 40 times its own annual electricity needs and transfers the excess energy into the public power grid of E.ON Avacon for a lucrative compensation.[255] Certainly, the fact that the inhabitants of Dardesheim realized the economic benefits involved helped the venture, as the town's mayor noted: "Without the population we couldn't put such project on its feet."[256] With around 50 such projects of "decentralized energy" being at different stages of development in Germany as of 2007, some were already asking whether "energy-autonomous cities" are the future of the German energy supply.[257] Moreover, the individual actors take part not only in energy production, but the participation model is sometimes encouraged in other cases—to lower local resistance. For example, in Schleswig-Holstein the network operator Tennet offered citizens to participate for the first time in the construction of a 150 km power line, and some wondered whether it would soon become a model for the entire country.[258] The participatory solutions meet with greater social acceptance, as citizens are "more willing to accept the argument for more pylons and pipes if it comes from local companies and authorities rather than from a distant private utility."[259]

Crucially, the decentralization of the energy system marks the rise of a distinct imperative of self-reliance in meeting local energy needs. This imperative is often accompanied by the rhetoric of social liberation and empowerment in the energy sphere, as many of the emerging projects aim at empowering people and becoming independent not only from oil and gas, but also from the domestic energy companies.[260] As Josef Göppel from the CDU/CSU described a situation in his local region: "The majority of the population in Bavaria have invested in renewables, so you cannot move back on it now.... They want to be independent in my village, they say *I want to control my own energy*."[261] In the words of an official from the Ministry of the Environment: "The main revolution now is when we are going away from the system where there are only four energy providers to a system where a lot of people produce energy themselves and it is becoming more decentralized."[262] The decentralization of the energy system means that the number of actors involved in and responsible for energy production immensely multiplies and changes the overall dynamics of this system. As Hans Josef Fell from the Greens described the change:

> We are in Germany more progressive, because energy is now not only a business of some big mineral, oil, gas, nuclear, coal companies, it is now a business of millions of people.... We have new cooperatives, societies which make the energy investment in renewables.... People who invested money in the local cooperatives, see it is a *chance for us not a chance for some big companies.*[263]

Indeed, the mayor of Munich, Christian Ude, stated that the big energy corporations are only the "four occupying powers."[264] Munich Stadtwerke, which makes direct investments in projects like drilling in the Norwegian North Sea for gas, has been compared with a "kind of a Gallic village, which still continues to expand its independence from the energy giants," and which tries to serve as a model for many other municipalities.[265] As it strives to become the first major German city in which households can be supplied with green electricity produced in its own facilities, its mayor stated in one interview: "[Formerly] we would only be able to read in the newspaper that a profit-driven company decides [on something] and how much is the price of electricity;"[266] therefore, they decided to invest in their own generating capacity: "We did not want to be just the gas station attendant who is abused by motorists, when gasoline prices rise.... We wanted to be ourselves oil sheiks who earned the right money."[267] This shift in the design of the energy system inherently implies regaining control over energy by local users, a process that gradually leads to breaking up the big energy monopolies.

In this new context private citizens, who know they will get a fixed price for electricity off a solar panel on their roof or a wind turbine on their land, are driving the change, together with municipal power utilities.[268] The latter not only own more than half of the low-voltage distribution, but are often trying to bring local grids, which they had leased to private operators, back under their own management.[269] In light of these developments, energy corporations lose some of their former influence. In fact, it has frequently been repeated that the "big four" have so far "failed" to play their part in Energiewende, but now have a chance to "redeem" themselves in the technically challenging area of offshore wind.[270] Despite their efforts, the ownership structure of the German energy system changes gradually. Whereas the "big four"[271] own 80 percent of the conventional power electricity generation (fossil fuel and nuclear) and all of the high-voltage transmission system,[272] more than half of the 860 low-voltage distribution system operators already belonged to Stadtwerke in 2012.[273] Moreover, 40 percent of the electricity grid in the area of renewables[274] was owned by private individuals and cooperatives as compared with only 7 percent owned by the main energy companies.[275] The majority of energy Stadtwerke also own and run electricity distribution grids.[276]

Therefore, the great changes in the transformation of Germany's energy landscape slowly become clearer—not only for the 200,000 people who work at the four major utilities, but also for the 850,000 employees in agriculture and forestry.[277] The latter see themselves more and more as energy farmers ("Energiewirte" as opposed to "Landwirte"), and for the millions of consumers for whom the cost of electricity became a serious factor in the household budget.[278] This system is also seen as guaranteeing Germany's future energy security. As Ulrich Kelber from the Social Democrats stated: "Many cannot imagine that a decentralized energy system is as secure as a centralized one, yet we are all hooked on a decentralized system called the Internet: that's what we need to do in energy policy."[279] Some also argue that decentralization based on renewables simultaneously means a low-carbon economy that protects the environment and "no more fear of the Arab oil weapon, no problems with the vagaries of Russian gas supplier [and] no fear of nuclear accidents."[280] Ultimately, energy security achieved via such systemic redesign also transforms the meaning of the concept into a positive one—as ensuring energy access no longer depends on struggles for energy supply within the geopolitical context, but is reliant upon diffused energy practices on a local scale.

In a wider perspective this dynamic marks the emergence of a distinct energy security logic of emancipation. The re-hierarchization of the energy security dimensions and a favorable distal context with a long history of grassroots activism in the field of green energy made the rise of the imperative of self-reliance the more likely in Germany. This logic shifts the focus to the local communities and individual users, who become the ultimate referent object of energy security that is achieved via democratic energy production. The diffusion of the energy system is also accompanied by the rhetoric of social liberation and empowerment, as local actors regain control over their energy production and consumption. Within this new paradigm the systemic transformation is largely carried out by the local actors who call for the dismantling of energy monopolies, inclusive solutions, "freeing" from the oppressive system and empowerment through "taking the control over energy back." As the local actors start to engage in the reflexive practices of energy production, their understanding of energy security also transforms into a positive and inclusive one—as it starts to materialize through their own agency and on equal terms where one's gain does not mean another person's loss. The power of this acquired agency can also have far-reaching consequences for sectors other than "energy" and "economic." Whether and how profoundly this transformation continues will depend on numerous factors.

As for now, having reached a consensus that the shift to renewables is a "right decision" with the 2050 prospect in mind, Germany became preoccupied with its national development. The downfall of this focus might be that a project of this type has to be to some extent coordinated with other European states (e.g., the question of grids), yet Germany has no European strategy for the EU-level "Energiewende."[281] As opposed to the debate on climate change, where Germany played a key role in shaping the European discourse on climate protection, energy security poses a bigger challenge for a couple of reasons. First, the issue of energy security remains within the sole power of individual member states. Second, given the economic crisis, the current conditions are not favorable towards triggering deeper debates on EU-level energy security issues. Therefore, although the German government might try to shape the European discourse on energy security together with the EU Commission through the environmental dimension (as it is much harder to do that "through energy"),[282] it seems that the main "strategy" on the German part is to live up to its ambitious goals of "Energiewende." By putting the environmental issues high on its energy agenda while developing a green economy based on renewables, it aims to become a "success case" for other states to follow.

Conclusion

The analysis of the German case sheds light on a number of energy security debates and policy sector developments that are rooted in complex contextual dynamics and driven by a variety of logics. First, this chapter explained how German pipeline politics, which has become a source of increasing tensions in the CEE region in recent years, is driven by the imperative of sustenance that emerges from the interplay of contextual factors (historically determined perceptions of Russia) and the traditional constellation of actors that gives leverage to big energy businesses and economic calculations. Although the "grammar of conflict" re-appears in media coverage in times of crisis, it does not translate into policy moves that would treat the security of energy supply as an emergency issue. Developments in the German gas sector lack the survival or "zero-sum game" reasoning and energy policy is conducted here in a business-like manner, even in the face of key challenges such as the Ukrainian gas crises or the Nordstream project. As such, this context is dominated by the subsistence logic and is not conducive to the logic of war to play an important part in it. However, the former is challenged on both discursive and policy grounds as far as the rise of the risk logic in the German nuclear energy sector and the logic of emancipation in the process of the country's democratic energy transition are concerned. In the first case, the dramatic rise of the prevention imperative after the accident in Fukushima manifested in both the rhetoric of "total" risks and the U-turn policy decision of accelerated nuclear phase-out. The risk logic played out in Germany in full spectrum and was powerful enough not only to alter the policy course, but also to reshuffle a typical constellation of actors in the domestic energy sector. Giving more leverage to societal actors as opposed to big energy businesses in the aftermath of Fukushima also reflects a wider trend of ongoing socioeconomic transformation. If the subsistence logic dominates the German energy context, the contestation over energy security dimensions that accompanies Energiewende makes the multiplicity of voices, interests and agendas most explicit. In Germany the reversal of hierarchies, where environmental concerns start to set the frame of the energy security debate, is coupled with the societal drive towards more sustainable energy solutions. The ongoing decentralization of energy and an increasing number of grassroots projects pave the way for the emergence of the logic of emancipation in the German energy sphere. This logic is driven by the imperative of self-reliance, as taking control over energy back from the big market players by local communities is accompanied by the rhetoric of liberation and social empowerment. Its rise exerts an impact on the domestic energy policy and debate and is likely to be a decisive factor in the country's ongoing energy transition.

Overall, the analysis of the energy security debates and policy developments in Germany proves that energy security is a multidimensional and cross-sectoral phenomenon that involves multiple actors and meanings and that comes to the fore of the public policy agenda through different security logics. Tracing the developments in pipeline politics, the nuclear energy debate and the national project of energy transition highlighted and explained some specificities of the German context. The next two chapters scrutinize the dynamics of energy security logics in two other energy contexts in the CEE region—Poland and Ukraine.

Notes

1 Umbach, "Deutsche Außenpolitik Und Energiesicherheit."
2 Ibid.
3 Ibid.
4 The Nature Conservancy in Europe, Interview.
5 Umbach, "Deutsche Außenpolitik Und Energiesicherheit."
6 SWP II, Interview.
7 Konrad Adenauer Stiftung, Interview.
8 The Nature Conservancy in Europe, Interview; SWP, Interview.
9 Mükusch, "Vernetzte Energiesicherheit."
10 Ibid.
11 Ibid.
12 Ibid.
13 SWP II, Interview.
14 SWP, Interview.
15 BMUB, Interview.
16 Freie Universität Berlin, Interview.
17 The Nature Conservancy in Europe, Interview.
18 Konrad Adenauer Stiftung, Interview.
19 The Nature Conservancy in Europe, Interview.
20 Mayr, "Duell Ohne Leiche."
21 Joffe, "Moskauer Gasmanöver."
22 Voswinkel, "Moskaus Rohrkrepierer."
23 Joffe, "Moskauer Gasmanöver."
24 Thumann, "Viel Wärme von Allen Seiten."
25 Dohmen et al., "Das Ist Ein Weckruf."
26 SWP, Interview.
27 DGAP, Interview.
28 Umbach, "Deutsche Außenpolitik Und Energiesicherheit," 362–3.
29 Ibid.
30 Thumann, "Viel Wärme von Allen Seiten."

31 SWP, Interview.
32 BDEW, Interview.
33 E.ON. Interview.
34 Thumann, "Viel Wärme von Allen Seiten"; "Teure Gasrechnung."
35 Mayr, "Duell Ohne Leiche."
36 Götz, "After the Gas Conflict Economic Consequences for Russia, Ukraine, and Germany."
37 Voswinkel, "Moskaus Rohrkrepierer."
38 Joffe, "Moskauer Gasmanöver."
39 SWP II, Interview; DGAP, Interview.
40 Thumann, "Viel Wärme von Allen Seiten."
41 E.ON., Interview.
42 DGAP, Interview; E.ON., Interview.
43 SWP, Interview.
44 Gammelin, "Die Erdgas-Connection."
45 Thumann, "Wenn Putin Gas Gibt."
46 The Nature Conservancy in Europe, Interview.
47 Ibid.
48 Thumann, "Wenn Putin Gas Gibt."
49 DGAP, Interview.
50 The Nature Conservancy in Europe, Interview.
51 SWP II, Interview.
52 DGAP, Interview; The Nature Conservancy in Europe, Interview; SWP II, Interview.
53 E.ON., Interview.
54 Konrad Adenauer Stiftung, Interview; E.ON., Interview; Freie Universität Berlin II, Interview.
55 Freie Universität Berlin II, Interview.
56 Ibid.
57 E.ON., Interview.
58 Umbach, "Deutsche Außenpolitik Und Energiesicherheit."
59 The Nature Conservancy in Europe, Interview; Konrad Adenauer Stiftung, Interview; SWP II, Interview.
60 BDEW, Interview.
61 Dohmen, "Die Pipeline Ist Ein Stück Sicherheit."
62 Follath and Schepp, "Der Konzern Des Zaren."
63 Beste et al., "Die Waffe Gas."
64 Ibid.; "Der Staat Gasprom: Putins Energie-Imperium."
65 Dohmen, "Die Pipeline Ist Ein Stück Sicherheit."
66 Beste et al., "Die Waffe Gas."
67 Heuser, "Gegenseitig Abhängig"; ibid.
68 E.ON., Interview.
69 Ibid.
70 DGAP, Interview; SWP, Interview.
71 Krupa and Thumann, "Nordstream 2."
72 Thumann, "Nord Stream 2."
73 Krupa and Thumann, "Nordstream 2."
74 "Merkel Casts Doubt on Nord Stream 2 Gas Pipeline."
75 "German Industry Defends Nord Stream 2 Gas Pipeline."
76 Ibid.
77 "Merkel Casts Doubt on Nord Stream 2 Gas Pipeline."
78 "Nord Stream 2 Gas Pipeline."
79 Sputnik News, "Majority of Germans Back Nord Stream 2."
80 Ibid.

81 "Nord Stream 2 Gas Pipeline."
82 Berst, "German Shift to Wind Power Slams Neighboring Grids."
83 After prolonging the lifetime of Germany's nuclear power plants just a few months before Fukushima.
84 Bethge et al., "Energie Krise Kernkraft—Ja Bitte?"
85 BDEW, Interview.
86 "40 Years of German Anti-Nuclear Action."
87 Ibid.
88 SWP II, Interview.
89 SWP, Interview.
90 Ibid.
91 SWP, Interview; SWP II, Interview.
92 Randow, "Von Der Angst Verstrahlt."
93 Bethge et al., "Energie Krise Kernkraft—Ja Bitte?"
94 Freie Universität Berlin, Interview.
95 Mayr, "Pompeji Des Atomzeitalters."
96 Nelles, "Energie Krise Ein Paar Jahre Länger."
97 Fleischhauer and Nelles, "Der Störfall."
98 Ibid.
99 Ibid.
100 International Nuclear Event Scale—a seven-point scale that categorizes failures in nuclear power plants, from "1 disorder," "2 incident" to "7 major accident."
101 Fleischhauer and Nelles, "Der Störfall."
102 Ibid.
103 Beck, "Atomdebatte."
104 Ibid.
105 Ibid.
106 Beste et al., "Fukushima Ist Überall"; Bethge et al., "Der Stromausfall."
107 Ibid.
108 Ulrich, "Atompolitik."
109 Vorholz, "Schluss, Aus."
110 Randow, "In Eine Falle War Ich Getappt."
111 Ibid.
112 Ulrich, "Atompolitik: Japans Lehre Für Die Welt."
113 Bethge et al., "Der Stromausfall"; Beste et al., "Fukushima Ist Überall."
114 Vorholz, "Schluss, Aus."
115 The Nature Conservancy in Europe, Interview; Freie Universität Berlin, Interview; BMUB, Interview; *Climate Protection and Growth.*
116 Bethge et al., "Der Stromausfall"; Beste et al., "Fukushima Ist Überall."
117 Rueter, "Clean Power Benefits from Nuclear Phase Out."
118 Dohmen et al., "Das War's!"
119 Beste et al., "Fukushima Ist Überall"; Bethge et al., "Der Stromausfall."
120 Ibid.
121 Dohmen et al., "Das War's!"
122 And 80 percent additionally agreeing with the moratorium imposed by the government for the old nuclear reactors.
123 Ibid.
124 Konrad Adenauer Stiftung, Interview; DGAP, Interview.
125 FDP, Interview.
126 E.ON., Interview.
127 Hamann, "Wir Können Nur Hoffen."
128 Köcher, "Atemberaubende Wende."
129 DGAP, Interview.
130 E.ON., Interview.

131 SWP, Interview.
132 FDP, Interview.
133 Ulrich, "Ein Land Bleibt Cool."
134 Joffe, "Atomausstieg: 'German Angst'."
135 Fell, Interview.
136 SWP, Interview.
137 Köcher, "Umfrage Für Die F.A.Z. Zur Atomkraft."
138 *Climate Protection and Growth*, 10. Emphasis added.
139 Schwägerl, "Im Töpfer-Kurs."
140 Ibid.
141 Konrad Adenauer Stiftung, Interview.
142 "Business Model at Risk."
143 Berst, "German Shift to Wind Power Slams Neighboring Grids."
144 Ibid.; Dohmen and Neubacher, "Toter Markt."
145 Ibid.
146 E.ON., Interview; BDEW, Interview.
147 Already in 2010 more than half of Germans declared that they would be prepared to pay 10 percent more for electricity from renewables (even among people with low household income of 1000–1500 EUR); source: Brost, "Umfrage Atomausstieg."
148 Becker, "German Energy Firms in Crisis."
149 SWP, Interview; The Nature Conservancy in Europe, Interview; SWP II, Interview; E.ON., Interview.
150 SWP II, Interview; The Nature Conservancy in Europe, Interview.
151 "Protest Gegen Atompolitik."
152 The four big energy companies in Germany: RWE, E.ON., Vattenfall and EnBW.
153 Freie Universität Berlin, Interview.
154 BMUB, Interview; FDP, Interview.
155 FDP, Interview.
156 Frank Dohmen et al., "Das War's!"
157 BMUB, Interview.
158 SWP, Interview.
159 Freie Universität Berlin, Interview.
160 BDEW, Interview.
161 SWP, Interview.
162 "Business Model at Risk."
163 Ibid.
164 Ibid.
165 Ibid.
166 SWP II, Interview.
167 "Nord-Süd-Trasse"; "Teure Noteingriffe Ins Stromnetz Nehmen Zu"; "Welche Auswirkungen hat die Energiewende auf den Strompreis?"
168 DGAP, Interview.
169 FDP, Interview.
170 Berst, "German Shift to Wind Power Slams Neighboring Grids."
171 Ibid.
172 BDEW, Interview.
173 Fell, Interview; Konrad Adenauer Stiftung, Interview.
174 "Energie: Gasprom Droht Der EU."
175 Fell, Interview.
176 Wiesenthal, "Klimawandel Der Umweltpolitik?"
177 Buchan, *The Energiewende—Germany's Gamble*.
178 Wiesenthal, "Klimawandel Der Umweltpolitik?"
179 Ibid.
180 Dohmen, "Missbrauchte Macht."

181 Wulf Bernotat (E.ON), Harry Roels (RWE), Utz Claassen (EnBW) and Klaus Rauscher (Vattenfall).
182 Jung et al., "Der Klima-Handel."
183 Ibid.
184 Dohmen, "Jahr Der Entscheidung."
185 E.ON., Interview.
186 E.ON.; BDEW, Interview.
187 Buchan, *The Energiewende—Germany's Gamble*, 33.
188 Vorholz, "Die Energiewende Zu Babel."
189 Buchan, *The Energiewende—Germany's Gamble*, 33.
190 SWP II, Interview.
191 Mükusch, "Vernetzte Energiesicherheit."
192 Ibid.
193 SWP II, Interview; BMUB, Interview.
194 SWP II, Interview.
195 Fell, Interview.
196 FDP, Interview.
197 Hessler, "RWE Stops Windfarm Projects Amid Energy Policy Dispute"; SWP II, Interview; BMUB, Interview.
198 Ibid.
199 Carrington, "Germany's Renewable Energy Revolution Leaves UK in the Shade."
200 Brost, "Öko Oder Sozial?"; Neubacher and Schröder, "Abgeklemmt."
201 SWP II, Interview; BMUB, Interview.
202 "Zeit Für Eine Revolution."
203 Neubacher and Schröder, "Abgeklemmt."
204 "Polls Reveal Citizens' Support for Energiewende"; Morris, "New Study: Germans Still Support the Energiewende."
205 "Social Sustainability Barometer for the Energiewende."
206 SWP II, Interview.
207 BDEW, Interview.
208 Tenbrock and Vorholz, "Einen Soli Für Das Klima."
209 Freie Universität Berlin, Interview; BMUB, Interview; Fell, Interview.
210 *Energy Concept for an Environmentally Sound, Reliable and Affordable Energy Supply*.
211 Becker, "German Energy Firms in Crisis"; Rueter, "Clean Power Benefits from Nuclear Phase Out."
212 Konrad Adenauer Stiftung, Interview.
213 Ibid.
214 SWP II, Interview; E.ON., Interview.
215 The Nature Conservancy in Europe, Interview.
216 SWP II, Interview.
217 Dohmen, "Missbrauchte Macht."
218 Beste et al., "Auf Schmalem Grat."
219 Bode et al., "Öko Um Jeden Preis."
220 *Energy Concept for an Environmentally Sound, Reliable and Affordable Energy Supply*, 6.
221 Ibid., 15.
222 Ibid.
223 Altmaier, *Moving Forward with Renewed Energy*, 5.
224 Geis and Vorholz, "Coole Aussage, Herr Altmaier."
225 SWP II, Interview.
226 Ibid.
227 BDEW, Interview.
228 *Climate Protection and Growth*, 28. Emphasis added.

229 Ciută, "Conceptual Notes on Energy Security."
230 Vorholz, "Jenseits von Öl Und Atom."
231 Dohmen et al., "Das War's!"
232 Porter, "Imagining a World without Growth."
233 Ciută, "Conceptual Notes on Energy Security."
234 Buchan, *The Energiewende—Germany's Gamble.*
235 Altmaier, *Moving Forward with Renewed Energy*, 5–8.
236 Ibid.
237 Buchan, *The Energiewende—Germany's Gamble*, 8.
238 Buchan, *The Energiewende—Germany's Gamble.*
239 Ibid., 14.
240 Carrington, "Germany's Renewable Energy Revolution Leaves UK in the Shade."
241 Buchan, *The Energiewende—Germany's Gamble*, 14.
242 Ibid.
243 Rueter, "Clean Power Benefits from Nuclear Phase Out"; Fell, Interview.
244 Müller and Sauga, "Nörgeln Ist Keine Tugend."
245 "Social Sustainability Barometer for the Energiewende."
246 BMUB, Interview.
247 Müller, "Erneuerbare Energien Und Regionale Wertschöpfung."
248 Ibid.
249 Die Genossenschaften.
250 Berst, "German Shift to Wind Power Slams Neighboring Grids."
251 Ibid.
252 And according to their own calculation, with 30 to 40 turbines, the community could get rid of the debt.
253 Osang, "Durch Den Wind."
254 Uken, "Die Harzer Stromrebellen."
255 Ibid.
256 Ibid.
257 Ibid.
258 Schröder, "Wenn Anlieger Zu Anlegern Werden."
259 Buchan, *The Energiewende—Germany's Gamble.*
260 Uken, "Die Harzer Stromrebellen."
261 Carrington, "Germany's Renewable Energy Revolution Leaves UK in the Shade." Emphasis added.
262 BMUB, Interview.
263 Fell, Interview. Emphasis added.
264 Rohrbeck, "Das Gallische Dorf."
265 Ibid.
266 Ibid.
267 Ibid.
268 Rueter, "Clean Power Benefits from Nuclear Phase Out."
269 Buchan, *The Energiewende—Germany's Gamble.*
270 Ibid.
271 E.ON, RWE, EnBW, Vattenfall.
272 "Big four" TSOs include: Tennet, Amprion, 50Hertz, Transnetz.
273 Buchan, *The Energiewende—Germany's Gamble*, 8.
274 Except for pumped storage.
275 Other owners: farmers, 11 percent; financiers and project developers, 14 percent; all energy companies, 13.5 percent; banks and investment funds, 11 percent; commercial companies, 9 percent; ibid.
276 With a further 600 doing the same in gas; ibid.
277 Data from 2010; ibid.

278 Bode et al., "Öko Um Jeden Preis"; Berst, "German Shift to Wind Power Slams Neighboring Grids."
279 Berst, "German Shift to Wind Power Slams Neighboring Grids."
280 Bode et al., "Öko Um Jeden Preis."
281 E.ON., Interview; Konrad Adenauer Stiftung, Interview.
282 SWP II, Interview.

References

"40 Years of German Anti-Nuclear Action." *Deutsche Welle*, June 30, 2017. www.dw.com/en/40-years-of-german-anti-nuclear-action/g-39477046.

Altmaier, Peter. *Moving Forward with Renewed Energy*. Federal Ministry for the Environment, Nature Conservation and Nuclear Safety, 2012.

BDEW (Federal Association of the Energy and Water Industry). Interview, Berlin, December 4, 2012.

Beck. "Atomdebatte: Wollen Wir Tschernobyl Wirklich Vergessen?" *Zeit Online*, July 6, 2008. www.zeit.de/2008/28/Risikogesellschaft.

Becker, Andreas. "German Energy Firms in Crisis." *Deutsche Welle*, March 15, 2012. www.dw.com/en/german-energy-firms-in-crisis/a-15809494.

Berst, Jan. "German Shift to Wind Power Slams Neighboring Grids." *Smartgridnews.com* [blog], 2012. www.smartgridnews.com/artman/publish/Technologies_DG_Renewables/German-shift-to-wind-power-slams-neighboring-grids-4373.html#.UPRPO-SZnao.

Beste, Ralf, Philip Bethge, Klaus Brinkbäumer, Dirk Kurbjuweit, Cordula Meyer, René Pfister, Olaf Stampf, Thilo Thielke, and Wieland Wagner. "Fukushima Ist Überall." *Der Spiegel*, March 14, 2011. www.spiegel.de/spiegel/print/d-77435293.html.

Beste, Ralf, Frank Dohmen, Per Hinrichs, Wolfgang Reuter, Monika Scheffler, and Christian Schwägerl. "Auf Schmalem Grat." *Spiegel Online*, April 14, 2008. www.spiegel.de/spiegel/print/d-56574276.html.

Beste, Ralf, Frank Dohmen, Christian Neef, Michael Sauga, Matthias Schepp, and Hans-Jürgen Schlamp. "Die Waffe Gas." *Spiegel Online*, January 12, 2009. www.spiegel.de/spiegel/print/d-63546812.html.

Bethge, Philip, Frank Dohmen, Marco Evers, Frank Hornig, Hans Hoyng, Simone Kaiser, Marion Kraske, et al. "Energie Krise Kernkraft—Ja Bitte?" *Der Spiegel*, July 7, 2008. www.spiegel.de/spiegel/print/d-57970883.html.

Bethge, Philip, Lukas Eberle, Ullrich Fichtner, Raphael Geiger, Fabio Ghelli, Hauke Goos, Veronika Hackenbroch, et al. "Der Stromausfall." *Der Spiegel*, March 21, 2011. www.spiegel.de/spiegel/print/d-77531668.html.

BMUB. (Federal Ministry for the Environment, Nature Conservation and Nuclear safety) Interview, Berlin, December 5, 2012.

Bode, Kim, Frank Dohmen, Alexander Jung, Kirsten Krumrey, and Christian Schwägerl. "Öko Um Jeden Preis." *Der Spiegel*, September 20, 2010. www.spiegel.de/spiegel/print/d-73892376.html.

Brost, Marc. "Öko Oder Sozial?" *Zeit Online*, June 6, 2012. www.zeit.de/2012/24/01-Energiewende.

Brost, Marc. "Umfrage Atomausstieg: Schon Wieder Ärger Mit Dem Volk," *Die Zeit*, n.d., sec. Politik, www.zeit.de/2010/30/Atomausstieg.

Buchan, David. *The Energiewende—Germany's Gamble*. Oxford: Oxford Institute for Energy Studies, June 2012.

"Business Model at Risk: Nuclear Phaseout Could Spell Disaster for German Energy Giants." *Spiegel Online*, June 1, 2011. www.spiegel.de/international/business/business-model-at-risk-nuclear-phaseout-could-spell-disaster-for-german-energy-giants-a-766095.html.

Carrington, Damian. "Germany's Renewable Energy Revolution Leaves UK in the Shade." *Theguardian.com*, May 30, 2012. www.theguardian.com/environment/2012/may/30/germany-renewable-energy-revolution.

Ciută, Felix. "Conceptual Notes on Energy Security: Total or Banal Security?" *Security Dialogue* 41, no. 2 (2010): 123–44.

Climate Protection and Growth: Germany's Path into the Renewable Energy Age. Federal Ministry for the Environment, Nature Conservation and Nuclear Safety, 2011.

"Der Staat Gasprom: Putins Energie-Imperium." *Der Spiegel*, March 5, 2007.

DGAP (German Council on Foreign Relations). Interview, Berlin, October 23, 2012.

Die Genossenschaften, National Office for Energy Cooperatives, www.dgrv.de/en/services/energycooperatives.html.

Dohmen, Frank. "Die Pipeline Ist Ein Stück Sicherheit." *Der Spiegel*, January 9, 2006. www.spiegel.de/spiegel/print/d-45280015.html.

Dohmen, Frank. "Jahr Der Entscheidung." *Spiegel Online*, January 28, 2008. www.spiegel.de/spiegel/print/d-55593295.html.

Dohmen, Frank. "Missbrauchte Macht." *Spiegel Online*, June 25, 2007. www.spiegel.de/spiegel/print/d-52032613.html.

Dohmen, Frank, Dietmar Hawranek, Wiebke Hollersen, Alexander Jung, Armin Mahler, Peter Müller, Gerald Traufetter, Christian Schwägerl, and Christoph Schwennicke. "Das War's!" *Der Spiegel*, April 4, 2011. www.spiegel.de/spiegel/print/d-77855753.html.

Dohmen, Frank, Alexander Jung, Wolfgang Reuter, and Hans-Jürgen Schlamp. "Das Ist Ein Weckruf." *Spiegel Online*, January 9, 2006. www.spiegel.de/spiegel/print/d-45280014.html.

Dohmen, Frank, and Alexander Neubacher. "Toter Markt." *Spiegel Online*, June 11, 2011. www.spiegel.de/spiegel/print/d-78954510.html.

"Energie: Gasprom Droht Der EU." *Die Zeit*, n.d. www.zeit.de/online/2006/17/Gasprom.

Energy Concept for an Environmentally Sound, Reliable and Affordable Energy Supply. Federal Ministry for the Environment, Nature Conservation and Nuclear Safety, and Federal Ministry of Economics and Technology, 2010. www.bmwi.de/English/Redaktion/Pdf/energy-concept,property=pdf,bereich=bmwi,sprache=en,rwb=true.pdf.

E.ON. Interview, Berlin, December 4, 2012.

FDP. Interview, Berlin, November 27, 2012.

Fell, Hans Josef. Interview, Berlin, November 20, 2012.

Fleischhauer, Jan, and Roland Nelles. "Der Störfall." *Spiegel Online*, October 22, 2007. www.spiegel.de/spiegel/print/d-53364516.html.

Follath, Erich, and Matthias Schepp. "Der Konzern Des Zaren." *Der Spiegel*, March 5, 2007. www.spiegel.de/spiegel/print/d-50746908.html.

Freie Universität Berlin. Interview, November 21, 2012.

Freie Universität Berlin II. Interview, November 21, 2012.

Gammelin, Cerstin. "Die Erdgas-Connection." *Zeit Online*, December 15, 2005. www.zeit.de/2005/51/Erdgas.

Geis, Matthias, and Fritz Vorholz. "Coole Aussage, Herr Altmaier." *Zeit Online*, July 26, 2012. www.zeit.de/2012/31/Energiewende-Interview.

"German Industry Defends Nord Stream 2 Gas Pipeline." *Deutsche Welle*, September 24, 2018.www.dw.com/en/german-industry-defends-nord-stream-2-gas-pipeline/a-45611911.

Götz, Roland. "After the Gas Conflict Economic Consequences for Russia, Ukraine, and Germany." *SWP*, March 2006.

Hamann, Götz. "Wir Können Nur Hoffen." *Zeit Online*, March 17, 2011. www.zeit.de/2011/12/Atomenergie-Grossmann.

Hessler, Uwe. "RWE Stops Windfarm Projects Amid Energy Policy Dispute." *Deutsche Welle*, February 2012. www.dw.de/rwe-stops-windfarm-projects-amid-energy-policy-dispute/a-15745965.

Heuser, Uwe Jean. "Gegenseitig Abhängig." *Zeit Online*, January 3, 2008. www.zeit.de/2008/02/Gegenseitig_abhaengig.

Joffe, Josef. "Atomausstieg: 'German Angst'." *Zeit Online*, June 9, 2011. www.zeit.de/2011/24/P-Zeitgeist-German-Angst.

Joffe, Josef. "Moskauer Gasmanöver." *Zeit Online*, January 5, 2006. www.zeit.de/2006/02/01__leit_1_02_06.

Jung, Alexander, Roland Nelles, Alexander Neubacher, Ralf Neukirch, and Wolfgang Reuter. "Der Klima-Handel." *Spiegel Online*, July 2, 2007. www.spiegel.de/spiegel/print/d-52109094.html.

Köcher, Renate. "Umfrage Für Die F.A.Z. Zur Atomkraft: Eine Atemraubende Wende," April 20, 2011. www.faz.net/1.628015.

Köcher Renate. "Atemberaubende Wende." Institut für Demoskopie Allensbach, April 2011. www.ifd-allensbach.de/uploads/tx_reportsndocs/April11_Fukushima.pdf.

Konrad Adenauer Stiftung. Interview, Berlin, November 1, 2012.

Krupa, Matthias, and Michael Thumann. "Nordstream 2: Rohrkrepierer." *Die Zeit*, October 7, 2018. www.zeit.de/2018/41/nordstream-2-konflikt-polen-usa-deutschland-gaspipeline.

Mayr, Walter. "Duell Ohne Leiche." *Spiegel Online*, January 9, 2006. www.spiegel.de/spiegel/print/d-45280058.html.

Mayr, Walter. "Pompeji Des Atomzeitalters." *Spiegel Online*, April 15, 2006. www.spiegel.de/spiegel/print/d-46637177.html.

"Merkel Casts Doubt on Nord Stream 2 Gas Pipeline." *Deutsche Welle*, October 4, 2018. www.dw.com/en/merkel-casts-doubt-on-nord-stream-2-gas-pipeline/a-43328058.

Morris, Craig. "New Study: Germans Still Support the Energiewende." *Energy Transition* [blog], December 18, 2017. https://energytransition.org/2017/12/new-study-germans-still-support-the-energiewende/.

Mükusch, Caroline. "Vernetzte Energiesicherheit–Mehr Chancen Für Deutschlands Zukunft." *Zeitschrift Für Außen-Und Sicherheitspolitik* 5, no. 3 (2012): 425–44.

Müller, Bene. "Erneuerbare Energien Und Regionale Wertschöpfung." In *Energiewirtschaft in Europa*, 47–51. Berlin: Springer, 2010.

Müller, Peter, and Michael Sauga. "Nörgeln Ist Keine Tugend." *Spiegel Online*, April 7, 2012. www.spiegel.de/spiegel/print/d-84789654.html.

Nelles, Roland. "Energie Krise Ein Paar Jahre Länger." *Spiegel Online*, July 7, 2008. www.spiegel.de/spiegel/print/d-57970884.html.

Neubacher, Alexander, and Catalina Schröder. "Abgeklemmt." *Spiegel Online*, June 4, 2012. www.spiegel.de/spiegel/print/d-86109220.html.

"Nord Stream 2 Gas Pipeline—What Is the Controversy About?" *Deutsche Welle*, July 14, 2018. www.dw.com/en/nord-stream-2-gas-pipeline-what-is-the-controversy-about/a-44677741.

"Nord-Süd-Trasse: Wie kommt der Strom von Nord nach Süd?" *Frankfurter Rundschau*, April 6, 2014. www.fr.de/wirtschaft/energie/nord-sued-trasse-wie-kommt-der-strom-von-nord-nach-sued-a-551864.

Osang, Alexander. "Durch Den Wind." *Spiegel Online*, November 21, 2011. www.spiegel.de/spiegel/print/d-81933540.html.

"Polls Reveal Citizens' Support for Energiewende." *Clean Energy Wire*, July 4, 2015. www.cleanenergywire.org/factsheets/polls-reveal-citizens-support-energiewende.

Porter, Eduardo. "Imagining a World without Growth." *New York Times*, December 1, 2015. www.nytimes.com/2015/12/02/business/economy/imagining-a-world-without-growth.html.

"Protest Gegen Atompolitik: Greenpeace Besetzt Dach Der CDU-Zentrale." *Spiegel Online*, October 28, 2010. www.spiegel.de/politik/deutschland/protest-gegen-atompolitik-greenpeace-besetzt-dach-der-cdu-zentrale-a-725787.html.

Randow, Gero von. "In Eine Falle War Ich Getappt." *Zeit Online*, March 24, 2011, sec. Politik. www.zeit.de/2011/13/Neudenken.

Randow, Gero von. "Von Der Angst Verstrahlt." *Zeit Online*, April 20, 2006. www.zeit.de/2006/17/01_leit_1_17.

Rohrbeck, Felix. "Das Gallische Dorf." *Zeit Online*, September 3, 2009. www.zeit.de/2009/37/Stadtwerke.

Rueter, G. "Clean Power Benefits from Nuclear Phase Out." *Deutsche Welle*, March 2012. www.dw.de/clean-power-benefits-from-nuclear-phase-out/a-15790686.

Schröder, Catalina. "Wenn Anlieger Zu Anlegern Werden." *Zeit Online*, March 7, 2013. www.zeit.de/2013/11/Buergerbeteiligung-Stromtrassen-Schleswig-Holstein.

Schwägerl, Christian. "Im Töpfer-Kurs." *Spiegel Online*, March 28, 2011. www.spiegel.de/spiegel/print/d-77745552.html.

"Social Sustainability Barometer for the Energiewende Shows Broad Support along with Doubts about Implementation." *IASS Potsdam*, November 14, 2017. www.iass-potsdam.de/en/news/social-sustainability-barometer-energiewende-shows-broad-support-along-doubts-about.

Sputnik News. "Majority of Germans Back Nord Stream 2, Distrust US Criticism of Project—Poll," July 23, 2018. https://sputniknews.com/europe/201807231066608927-germany-gas-pipeline-poll/.

SWP (German Institute for International and Security Affairs). Interview, Berlin, November 13, 2012.

SWP II. Interview, Berlin, November 16, 2012.

Tenbrock, Christian, and Fritz Vorholz. "Einen Soli Für Das Klima." *Zeit Online*, March 31, 2011. www.zeit.de/2011/14/Energiepolitik-Interview-Vassiliadis.

"Teure Gasrechnung." *Spiegel Online*, January 2, 2006. www.spiegel.de/spiegel/print/d-45168958.html.

"Teure Noteingriffe Ins Stromnetz Nehmen Zu." *Zeit Online*, June 25, 2017. www.zeit.de/wirtschaft/2017-06/energiewende-stromnetze-ausbau-nord-sued.

The Nature Conservancy in Europe. Interview, Berlin, October 31, 2012.

Thumann, Michael. "Nord Stream 2: Ein Außenpolitisches Desaster Für Deutschland." *Zeit Online*, December 7, 2018. www.zeit.de/politik/ausland/2018-12/nord-stream2-pipeline-russland-ukraine-gas.

Thumann, Michael. "Wenn Putin Gas Gibt." *Zeit Online*, September 8, 2005. www.zeit.de/2005/37/Energieprojekte.

Thumann Michael. "Viel Wärme von Allen Seiten." *Zeit Online*, January 12, 2006. www.zeit.de/2006/03/Ressourcen_Headline.

Uken, Marlies. "Die Harzer Stromrebellen." *Zeit Online*, October 30, 2007. www.zeit.de/online/2007/44/Dardesheim.

Ulrich, Bernd. "Atompolitik: Japans Lehre Für Die Welt." *Zeit Online*, March 17, 2011. www.zeit.de/2011/12/japan-kernenergie-leitartikel.

Ulrich, Bernd. "Ein Land Bleibt Cool." *Zeit Online*, March 24, 2011. www.zeit.de/2011/13/German-angst.

Umbach, Frank. "Deutsche Außenpolitik Und Energiesicherheit." In *Deutsche Außenpolitik*, 354–73. Berlin: Springer, 2007.

Vorholz, Fritz. "Die Energiewende Zu Babel." *Zeit Online*, March 1, 2012. www.zeit.de/2012/10/Energiewende.

Vorholz, Fritz. "Jenseits von Öl Und Atom." *Zeit Online*, June 9, 2004. www.zeit.de/2004/25/851_2fAtom.

Vorholz, Fritz. "Schluss, Aus." *Zeit Online*, March 17, 2011. www.zeit.de/2011/12/DOS-Atomausstieg.

Voswinkel, Johannes. "Moskaus Rohrkrepierer." *Zeit Online*, January 5, 2006, sec. Politik. www.zeit.de/2006/02/Ergas.

"Welche Auswirkungen hat die Energiewende auf den Strompreis?" *Lifestrom Magazin* [blog], September 11, 2017. www.lifestrom.de/magazin/welche-auswirkungen-hat-die-energiewende-auf-den-strompreis/.

Wiesenthal, Helmut. "Klimawandel Der Umweltpolitik? Oder: Energiekonzepte Als Identitätskrücke." In *Ökologische Aufklärung*, 173–202. Berlin: Springer, 2010.

"Zeit Für Eine Revolution." *Spiegel Online*, February 12, 2007. www.spiegel.de/spiegel/print/d-50503709.html.

3 Poland

Energy and society at the crossroads

Introduction

Energy security constitutes one of the key political buzzwords as well as concerns of the Polish policy agenda. The developments in the regional pipeline politics marked by the conflictual relations with Russia and projects developed with the omission of the CEE states in particular bring back to the fore the issue of Poland's uneasy geographical location, which was historically a source of its vulnerability. Partially for that reason Poland proved to be an uneasy partner for its European counterparts on a number of occasions; in addition, its habit of making remote historical references in connection with regional energy policy developments might have seemed exaggerated and irrational to the EU side. However, the Polish distal context, with its specific historical, political and socioeconomic factors, impacts not only the country's approach to pipeline politics. On the one hand, Polish plans for the development of nuclear energy raise eyebrows in Germany, which is currently going in the opposite direction with its nuclear energy phase-out. On the other hand, Poland's continuous reliance on coal, coupled with legislation that hinders the development of the renewables sector, does not bring any sympathy either, as it contradicts the common climate protection goals and the wider trend of turning to more democratic energy solutions. The domestic energy security debates and policy approaches across different energy sectors in Poland not only do not reflect the policies of neighboring Germany, but de facto contradict them on multiple levels and are not always easy for external observers to comprehend—especially since both countries are often exposed to similar external triggers and regional energy sector developments.

Utilizing the contextualized approach based on energy security logics developed in Chapter 1, this chapter unpacks the domestic dynamics of the Polish energy context along a number of key debates and policy decisions. Similarly to the German and Ukrainian cases, the analysis is structured according to the variety of energy security logics and starts "from within" the logic of subsistence. As the latter is driven by the imperative of sustenance that prioritizes the economic dimension of energy security, it is the most common energy security logic present in all three states analyzed. However, the logic of subsistence is also marked by the multiplicity of actors, agendas and understandings of energy security and as such constitutes a site of contestation within which other energy security rationales either originate or are reflected and mediated. Its dynamics are explored here first, by unpacking the multiplicity of energy security conceptualizations in the Polish context; and second, by tracing the roots of divergent understandings of energy security as framed by the situated actors across a number of domestic debates and policy developments. By taking the reader through the nuances of the energy security logics driving the debates and policies on the EU Climate and Energy package, nuclear energy plans in the pre- and post-Fukushima period, small-scale renewables, Ukrainian gas crises and the developments of the Nordstream project, this chapter sheds light on the specifics and root causes of Polish approaches to energy security. The subsequent analysis of the debate on the EU Climate and Energy package and the introduction of nuclear energy plans that followed illustrates the workings of the subsistence logic in Poland, which operates within quite an inflexible constellation of actors and a specific distal context, where historical and socioeconomic factors play a crucial role. This dominant imperative of sustenance in energy affairs is only being challenged by two competing logics. On the one hand, there is a still largely marginalized imperative of self-reliance that slowly emerges in the rhetoric of democratic energy transition and the first bottom–up citizens' energy initiatives. Although the Polish distal context is not as favorable as the German one to the rise of the energy security logic of emancipation, its elements are already present here. Moreover, because of the specific distal factors (most importantly Soviet legacy in the area of resource management and centralized political authority), the rise of the emancipatory logic in Poland could be marked by a double transformative character and not only lead to the democratization of the domestic energy system, but, through social empowerment of the so far "silenced" actors, to the democratic transformation of the entire socioeconomic model. On the other hand, the dominant rationale of sustenance in Polish energy policy is periodically overshadowed by the rise of the survival imperative in relation to the country's pipeline politics. As opposed to the hardly visible logic of emancipation, the emergence of the logic of war leads to the significant rhetorical and policy shift at the highest levels, as the issue of energy supply is put on the immediate security agenda and trumps all other policy considerations at the time—economic included.

Analyzing Polish energy context through the prism of security logics sheds light on a number of policy decisions and mainstream energy security debates in recent years. It also outlines why, despite the fact that all four energy security logics identified in the German case are also present in the Polish one, their manifestation and contextual dynamics differ because of the combination of distal factors and a specific constellation of actors.

Conceptualizing energy security in the Polish context

To start with, the multiplicity of energy security understandings in Poland could be most easily spotted among its many definitions. In the Polish energy studies literature, one could point to the dominant tendency to frame energy security in its narrow, economic dimension. Whereas some see energy security as part of broader economic security,[1] others try to establish objective and measurable criteria for evaluating and comparing energy security levels across different states and timeframes.[2] Still others define its multiple dimensions in the typically hierarchical order: price affordability, security of supply and environmental protection.[3] An increasing number of analysts also seem to be more aware of the growing subjectivity in defining contemporary threats and security policies by the diverse actors.[4] This subjectivity is partly reflected in the Polish energy studies literature itself—as energy security becomes defined in much wider terms, therefore reflecting a recent trend of widening moves in relation to the concept. Bartodziej and Tomaszewski,[5] for instance, distinguish among numerous energy security dimensions, which they divide into basic (e.g., sustainable energy balance, diversification of energy sources, access to infrastructure, storage and distribution of fuels) and additional (including economic, ecologic, technological and information security, immunity to intentional and accidental threats). The wider approaches also embrace at times the analyses of actors, who impact energy security dynamics on multiple levels (micro, mezo and macro)[6]—reflecting the multiplication of both actors and meanings within the energy field.

The contextual understandings of energy security seem to be less diverse among Polish ministerial-level officials and energy experts. A number of them have consecutively framed energy security through the hierarchization of its various dimensions along the traditional line: different economic aspects (security of supply, diversification, economic competitiveness, price affordability, energy independence) followed by ecologic concerns.[7] This hierarchy seems to reflect the official stance of the Polish government, which defined energy security as a "state of the economy which covers present and prospective demand for fuels and energy, in a technically and economically justifiable manner, while taking the necessary environmental protection precautions."[8] This hierarchization, which gave priority to the security of supply, as well as economic and technical aspects before environmental security, was further confirmed in the single most important document on the subject—*Polish Energy Policy until 2030*[9]—and is further repeated in the draft of the *Polish Energy Policy until 2050* in progress.[10] Moving away from the ministerial and governmental agenda to the political scene, the disparities in the understandings of what constitutes energy security grow.

In a number of parliamentary debates over the last decade—especially those triggered by the Ukrainian gas crises of 2006 and 2009—many politicians attempted to define energy security in the Polish context. The definitions reflected a wide spectrum of understandings. Most commonly, energy security was framed in economic terms, as security of supply at affordable prices (former Economic Minister Waldemar Pawlak),[11] as a component of wider economic security (Joanna Fabisiak),[12] or as security of supply with the maximum use of domestic energy resources and diversification of supply routes (Jan Kamiński).[13] Still others reflected entirely different understandings, with energy security framed as a matter of Polish self-sufficiency and complete independence from foreign energy companies (Zygmunt Wrzodak),[14] Polish raison d'état (Anna Sobecka),[15] or a matter of reversing dependency, where Poland—being energy self-sufficient—could make other states dependent on its own energy resources (Jan Szyszko from the Law and Justice Party).[16] At the extreme, and in line with the logic of war, energy security was compared with the military security of the Polish state, where the economic aspects of energy (such as price) matter little in the face of national survival. In the words of Jarosław Sellin from the Law and Justice Party: "Of course, we have to move within the limits of common sense, but sometimes we have to prepare—also psychologically—that when it comes to prices, we will bleed—but it will pay off in the end."[17] Interestingly, some conceptualizations also aimed to incorporate the environmental aspect of energy security by pointing to the need for wider use of "green energy" (Andrzej Olechowski),[18] protection of the natural environment (former Prime Minister Donald Tusk),[19] or responsibility to leave an environmentally sound habitat for future generations (Ryszard Zbrzyzny).[20] However, the latter definitions could be seen rather as a footnote to the entire parliamentary debate on the country's energy security priorities. Given the general lack of public debate on the subject, it is worth mentioning a number of actors outside of the official political spectrum, who continuously attempt to involve the wider public in the discussion on Polish energy security and to shift the debate towards a different path.

Therefore, an entirely different view on energy security exists among some societal actors and environmental activists such as Dariusz Szwed, a former leader of the Polish political party "Greens 2004."[21] Szwed defined energy security by distinguishing its three priorities: public participation, competitive energy market and security of state's own energy production—in that order.[22] He also highlighted the importance of the state's own energy production, as in his view only the latter could simultaneously provide for "ecological, societal and economic security."[23] This wide, cross-sectoral approach to energy security was echoed by a number of other interviewees. For instance, an environmental activist and scholar from the Warsaw University of Life Sciences pointed to energy efficiency and development of renewable energy sources based on the culture of prosumers as two key ways of ensuring Poland's energy security.[24] In his view, economic and environmental dimensions of energy security are coherent rather than contradictory.[25] A similar opinion was expressed by a former director of the Warsaw office of the Berlin-based think tank Heinrich Böll Foundation, as he stressed the importance of all economic, ecological and societal aspects in ensuring energy security of the Polish state.[26]

The above inclusive approaches stand in stark contrast to the official definitions, with the latter proving to be similarly diverse. The disparities between conceptualizations reflect not only the multiplicity of meanings of energy security in the Polish context, but also the "liminality" of energy security that indeed functions between theory and practice, as its established definitions in the official documents and analyses continuously clash with the contextual meanings on the ground. The prioritization of different energy security dimensions by different actors also highlights that, whereas there does not exist one unambiguous definition of energy security in the Polish context, its diverse meanings indeed often derive from a "series of assumptions regarding the linkage between growth, sustenance and the environment."[27] From the analytical point of view, it appears that these conceptualizations either differently hierarchize economic and environmental aspects of energy security or give priority to new dimensions—such as social participation. Since different approaches to energy security have different policy and normative consequences, this chapter unpacks those diverse understandings along a number of key debates and policy developments and scrutinizes where they logically lead us regarding the present and future energy security agenda in the Polish context—starting from the analysis of the logic of subsistence.

EU Climate and Energy package through the prism of the subsistence logic

The debate on the EU Climate and Energy package and the introduction of plans for the development of nuclear power plants that followed illustrate well how the dominant imperative of sustenance drives Polish energy affairs within quite an inflexible constellation of actors and a specific distal context, where historical and socioeconomic factors often determine both societal attitudes and policy outcomes.

The EU Climate and Energy package, with its famous "20–20–20" targets,[28] was widely criticized in Poland, as it was perceived by different political and expert circles as damaging to the Polish economy, although the strength of such critiques differed. In the words of a senior official from the Ministry of Environment:

> EU's climate policy has several objectives and, unfortunately, also a few side-effects. In our case what we do not like are the rising costs of energy from coal, which makes our economy less competitive.... Sustainable climate policy should take into account the starting point of each state.[29]

Many expressed much stronger opinions than this. For instance, Professor Szyszko from the Law and Justice Party, a former Minister of the Environment, stated that the EU policy "is boycotted by the entire world" and aimed merely at "making its member states dependent on its technologies."[30] Krzysztof Kilian, a chairman of the Polish Energy Group, stated at the Economic Forum in Krynica that "the climate policy in the times of crisis is a whim, for which the customers will pay."[31] Both views were reflected in the opinion of an energy expert from the conservative think tank *Sobieski Institute*, which supports the Law and Justice Party:[32]

> Professor Staniszkis[33] once talked about *structural violence* or *unbalanced development* ... I think that it is exactly what we have to deal with now: the French want to sell us the nuclear, Germany wants to sell us fans and other elements of the turbine, the same situation is with Danes, who use "ecological" tools as a way of performing their own economic interests ... —and we are quite passively accepting all these 3 x 20 and other whims—I myself question these decisions.[34]

If the diversity of the above voices expressed the doubts of the Polish side regarding the prioritization of environmental concerns over economic interests, a wider debate on the EU package that took place in the Polish Sejm and governmental agencies in 2008 additionally reflected three main themes of the political rhetoric at the time. First, there were concerns regarding the ability of the fast-growing Polish economy to deal with the commitment of CO_2 emissions' reduction in times of economic crisis. Second, some asked to what extent the EU Climate and Energy package is a result of the ideologization and dogmatization of the approach to climate issues and what its true impact could be on the reduction of global CO_2 emissions. And third, it was questioned whether the governmental stance on protecting the domestic coal industry is right and whether some alternative energy sources should not be developed instead.[35]

Overall, one could point to a predominantly economic focus of the debate on the EU Climate and Energy package in Poland. This focus—together with the accompanying economic fears—was additionally fueled by some expert analyses published at the time. For instance, the "EnergSys" report from 2008—ordered and financed by coal energy businesses—predicted that the adoption of the EU Climate and Energy package would lead to 300 percent energy price rises.[36] As one Warsaw-based pro-environmental analyst noted, following this publication some energy experts started to make similar claims, which, coupled with the fears of high CO_2 emissions rights' prices fueled by the big industry lobbies (whereas the actual prices turned out several times lower—6–7 EUR/t in the initial years),[37] succeeded in setting the frame of the public debate in Poland that has prevailed ever since.[38] Local observers noted that the main arguments in that debate include a belief that the EU climate and energy policy will bring losses to Poland and benefit only a few EU states,[39] that it will create a barrier for Poland's development and destroy Polish industry, force the change of the current energy mix and, ultimately, contribute to energy price rises and increased unemployment.[40] Consequently, the EU policy found supporters neither among the Polish government nor the political opposition.

Equally important, the debate on the EU Climate and Energy package was not of public interest either. The majority of the debates that took place occurred among politicians and energy experts as well as some research centers and non-governmental organizations dealing with ecology and sustainable development.[41]

The general public itself did not take a significant part in debating the future of the Polish energy policy approach. This fact raised some postulates for a change of thinking about the issues of national energy and the environment as well as some calls for a more profound public education in these matters.[42] Some therefore asked, why is the issue of "CO_2 emissions," which affects the daily functioning of every human being and which started to function as a slogan on its own (and as such embody all the energy and environmental problems in Poland), treated only as a problem of industry and the government?[43] To many it looked like a missed opportunity. As an analyst from the Warsaw-based think tank demosEUROPA noted:

> Both the EU package and other internal and external factors compel us to a slightly different line of thinking about the way in which we want to produce energy, from what we want to produce it, how we want to distribute it ... [they also have] a very positive influence on thinking about the social model in Poland ... as society has never really been involved in the decisions on the national energy mix.[44]

Despite some signs that social awareness about the issues of climate and energy is rising, continuously low social participation in debates on the subject upholds the centralized character of the decision-making processes in the long run. As an official from the Ministry of the Environment admitted:

> It is a big problem for us as it seems that there is no need for a debate in the society. It seems that [these matters] do not constitute a problem for the Polish citizens that they slip from their agendas. [Therefore] it is hard to establish a negotiating stance or a position of the Polish government if we have no one to talk to. Because of that the governmental position often results from other policies: economic policy, security policies.[45]

He also pointed further to the hierarchization of energy security dimensions in the Polish context that could explain the above phenomenon:

> The awareness of the [environmental] problems is certainly increasing, while the acceptance of the climate policy falls, because people see other problems—such as economic.... Climate policy is high in the Maslow's pyramid while Poland is still in the development stage, therefore people cannot afford the climate policy to constitute some sort of an "issue" to them.[46]

Not much has changed in this respect as far as the subsequent EU Energy and Climate package 2030 is concerned. The new package envisages raising the binding target of reducing CO_2 emissions to 40 percent (43 percent in the Emissions Trading Scheme (ETS) sector as compared with 2005) and increasing the share of renewable energy to a minimum of 27 percent in the final energy balance of the entire EU.[47] Poland remains concerned about how these targets will impact its domestic coal sector and was among five European countries[48] that postulated more careful consideration of the impact of the CO_2 emissions limits for the coal power stations on the industry.[49] Whereas some pro-government news portals reported on the 2030 climate energy package as a "threat" to Poland,[50] Polish Prime Minister Morawiecki stated during the Petersberg Climate Dialogue conference in June 2018 that Poland seeks a golden mean that will allow it to care for the environment while not hampering its economic and social development.[51] However, as the domestic environmental circles point out, finding a middle way is not feasible under the current circumstances. Poland's new program for the domestic coal sector until 2030, with its high targets of coal exploitation and use, runs against the EU climate policy.[52] The new regulations have also failed to provide a strategic impact assessment of the program for the environment, despite a formal requirement to do so. The coming years will show to what extent the agreed targets can be met. As of 2018 Poland was in last place among EU states in its efforts to fight climate change, according to the CAN (Climate Action Network) Europe report, which assesses the role of member states in setting ambitious climate and energy goals and policies, and the progress made in reducing CO_2 emissions and promoting renewables and energy efficiency.[53]

The above dynamics of the ongoing debate and policy developments around the EU Climate and Energy package highlight the specificities of the Polish energy context: strong impact of the distal factors (low environmental awareness), which in turn impacts the constellation of actors (with low mobilization of the society and centralized decision-making), with both of these elements leading to the prioritization of a purely economic agenda within the logic of subsistence. From the analytical point of view, it could be said that this dynamic is driven by a strong imperative of sustenance, as prioritization of economic factors aims here in the most basic sense at affordable energy access for society coupled with protective measures for domestic energy businesses. It is certainly the most common energy security logic generally speaking. The Polish debate on the EU Climate and Energy package shows that in this case the economic agenda prevails, and the preferable means of attaining it is based on a traditional way of thinking and a centralized energy model. The voices that point to alternative solutions are not strong enough to compete with the official agenda and big industry lobbyists, whereas the rest of society remains detached from the debate—which, as some have pointed out, is also lacking. Moreover, Polish economic interests in the energy sector are contrasted here with the "ideologized" and "dogmatized"—and therefore "irrational"—EU agenda. In this light the EU agenda only becomes rational when it is seen as upholding economic interests of its richest and most economically developed states. Consequently, a feeling of being coerced or even taken advantage of, through the invasion of foreign energy technologies, emerges here—reasoning that is quite typical for the Polish context, as it has appeared across other issue areas in the past (e.g., on the eve of Poland's membership of the EU). It is also from within this feeling of coercion that the Polish debate on nuclear energy emerges. The development of nuclear energy plans in Poland is not only similarly driven by the imperative of sustenance in achieving domestic energy security, but the very decision to build nuclear power plants was justified with the EU climate protection goals.

Accident in Fukushima and the Polish nuclear debate: the withering prevention rationale

The nuclear energy debate and its triggers, underlying arguments and policy implications are some of the best examples of the key differences in reasoning about energy security in Poland and Germany—and connected to that manifestation of different security logics in both contexts. Whereas the nuclear accident at Fukushima gave rise to the imperative of prevention and mobilized pro-green German society to exert enormous pressure on the government that led to the acceleration of Germany's nuclear energy phase-out plans and continuation of the more environmentally friendly[54] project of Energiewende, the dominant imperative of sustenance was not shaken in the Polish energy context. Not only did Fukushima do little regarding societal attitudes towards nuclear energy—despite some short-lived debate in the media in its aftermath—but the actual debate on the introduction of the national nuclear energy program and its policy implications was triggered by EU-level policy developments—mostly the EU Climate and Energy package.

The prospects for the development of nuclear energy in Poland have been considered since 2005 by all the subsequent governments. However, only in the aftermath of the debate on the implications of the EU Climate and Energy package was the resolution about starting the Polish nuclear energy program passed on January 13, 2009, by the Council of Ministers.[55] The Commission for Nuclear Security and Radiological Protection was then created—together with the accompanying commissioner office.[56] Given the ambitious goals of CO_2 emissions' reduction, the crucial decision of introducing nuclear energy was justified in the "Polish Energy Policy until 2030" as motivated by security concerns, environmental protection (emphasizing the aspect of CO_2 emissions' ceilings) and independence from the "typical ways of energy production."[57] It is worth emphasizing that the already mentioned justification of the decision hierarchized different energy security dimensions on the line: economic security (security of supplies, prices and diversification of fuel base); environmental aspects (limiting CO_2 emissions); and aspects connected to the broader benefits of the nuclear energy program linked to growth and development (e.g., new employment, new university degrees, development of Polish businesses, and development of regions).[58] The above hierarchy of priorities once again highlighted the dominance of the sustenance imperative in the energy policy agenda focused on the fulfillment of functional needs. Interestingly, although the ecological aspects were given more attention here (taking into account specificities of the Polish context), this development was not echoed in the wider nuclear energy debate in Poland—even among the arguments of the environmental activists.

The very arguments "in favor" and "against" the government's nuclear energy plans differed vastly. Among the propagators of the nuclear energy program one could point to some energy experts (e.g., Teluk, Strupczewski, Kiełbasa, Reński), who supported the development of the nuclear plans in public debates.[59] Both their arguments and prioritization of energy security aspects largely mirrored the official governmental stance. It was therefore noted that the growing demand for electricity makes nuclear energy economically justifiable; that the development of nuclear technology after 1986 makes the repetition of the Chernobyl accident impossible (highlighting the "irrationality" of such fears); and that apart from the economic benefits, nuclear energy would be environmentally friendly (reflecting the hierarchy of energy security priorities).[60] Some energy experts also highlighted the EU context of the Polish decision—"EU policy signifies that Poland has no alternative other than development of the nuclear programme"[61]—while suggesting that if that policy was not in place it could be better to either invest in other energy sources or to continue to rely on Polish coal.[62] As an exception to the rule here, one could see the justification for the nuclear energy program given by an expert on nuclear and radiological safety from the Polish Energy Group:[63] "It is not that we cannot afford renewable energy so we should not follow the German example. The argument here should be rather that the nuclear energy is *green energy*, as it meets all the EU requirements regarding CO_2 emissions."[64] On a similar line, in the opinion of an official from the Ministry of the Environment, the nuclear energy program is mainly "a guarantee for decarbonization and diversification of the energy production portfolio that would help to introduce a new sector of the economy."[65] Interestingly, some of the energy security reports and analyses also pointed to either the competing or complementary character of different dimensions of energy security. For instance, the *Polish Energy Security Report* from 2006 stated that whereas there are inherent trade-offs between the use of cheap energy from coal and environmental protection, other energy security aspects might be complementary in achieving multidimensional energy security (e.g., with nuclear energy being presented as simultaneously economically justifiable, enabling future growth and environmentally friendly).[66] It could be argued that framing the debate in this way sought to eliminate the need for the creation of such hierarchies in the first place—and as such serve as a strategy for alleviating public fears.

While the arguments of energy experts quoted above largely mirrored the governmental stance and were more visible in the public space, they did not represent the whole spectrum of societal opinions. A number of less influential and often more "pro-environmental" voices criticized nuclear energy development plans on several grounds: first, the entire economic rationale behind the nuclear energy plans was questioned; second, it was argued that the development of nuclear energy would result in a triple dependency (building and installation of the nuclear power plants and imports of uranium from Russia)—therefore not contributing to the enhancement of energy security;[67] third, the aspect of further centralization of the Polish energy system was highlighted;[68]

fourth, it was argued that financial resources are being wasted on the nuclear program instead of being invested in the more prospective renewable energy. Here one could point to some criticisms regarding Polish traditionalism in the matters of energy, as one prominent environmentalist noted:

> I think that the Prime Minister and his entourage are very skeptical towards renewables. They still haven't changed their conviction that renewables are merely a hobbyistic solution rather than something that could build Polish energy security. In our context nineteenth-century thinking still dominates.[69]

Fifth, the ethical aspect of leaving nuclear waste to future generations was questioned.[70] Finally, some voices also criticized the predictions made in the *Polish Energy Policy until 2030* document—for its lack of precision and concrete data and lack of evaluation of the environmental impact of the nuclear power plants' building and exploitation.[71]

This multiplicity of criticisms—most of which were never addressed by the governmental side—reflects an uneasy dynamic of the Polish nuclear debate or, as many have pointed out, the lack of it. In the words of an analyst from Warsaw-based think tank demosEUROPA:[72]

> What Poland still did not have is a profound public discussion … about what nuclear energy is, what its costs are, its impact on the environment.… Without the involvement of the civic society it is still various lobbying groups that have the strongest voice, but not the public interest in mind.[73]

Similarly, Dariusz Szwed, a main propagator of "energy democracy" in the Polish context, pointed out that in a given constellation of actors, where different sides have different power, it is not possible to hold an honest pro-democratic and pro-social debate.[74] Subsequent developments in the context of the Polish nuclear policy seem to confirm some of these criticisms. First, even before the decision of the development of nuclear energy was taken, it had been argued that articles in the daily press aimed to manipulate Polish public opinion by their biased propagation of nuclear energy.[75] Second, the very decision of introducing the nuclear energy program was adopted in the *Polish Energy Policy until 2030*—and only then put on hold for three months for some public discussion to take place.[76] Third, the government information campaign on nuclear energy focused solely on its benefits and did not allow for alternative voices to be heard or alternative opinions to be fully confronted. Interestingly, though, as employees of the Nuclear Energy Department in the Polish Ministry of Economy themselves admitted at the time, the campaign was not criticized in the public debate for its explicit one-sidedness, but rather for its low visibility and insufficiently demagogic character.[77] Given the above frame, it is not surprising that the accident at Fukushima did not significantly impact this constellation of actors or the prevailing logic of subsistence in the Polish context.

An accident in Fukushima and the Polish nuclear debate

Similarly to Germany, the accident at the Japanese nuclear power plant caused by the 2011 tsunami received wide media coverage in Poland. Moreover, the Polish media largely exaggerated its scale and impact. In the words of an employee from the Public Relations and Communications Office of the Polish Energy Group (PGE), who closely followed the news coverage because of PGE's involvement in the planned construction of the NPPs in Poland:

> After the accident in the Japanese Fukushima the information about the hundreds of thousands of casualties have been reproduced across Polish media. This number did not apply to the victims of the nuclear power plant, but to the victims of the tsunami. And despite the fact that this error has been corrected many times—it is continuously reproduced, which highlights the sensational character of this information.[78]

Indeed, this search for "sensational" news resulted in the immediate return of the "Chernobyl narrative." One week after the catastrophe in Japan, Polish radio stations, internet news services and TV channels were picking up and highlighting any information about even the slightest changes in nuclear radiation levels in Japan.[79] The press and digital media were saturated at the time with phrases and formulations such as: "nuclear catastrophe," "radiation sickness" or "radioactive cloud."[80] One commentator of the weekly magazine *Polityka* even compared this coverage with the "nuclear show," with "reports from Japan resembling reports from the 'battlefield', where the fate of humankind is being decided."[81] The extent to which the accident at Fukushima dominated information in media at the time was also reflected in the fact that other key issues—mainly the effects of the tsunami itself or bombing of Kadafi's Libya—were moved to the second tier.

This state of affairs led some to argue that Polish democracy is populist-hysteric in character and based on emotions and an atmosphere of fear—fueled by some environmental groups and underpinned by media.[82] It should be noted, however, that although the rhetoric in the immediate aftermath of the Fukushima accident indeed depicted uncontrollable risk of nuclear energy that would resemble the reality of the Becksian risk society, the elements of the risk logic were not as strong as in the German context and they were immediately matched with a counter-narrative. It was then highlighted both by the media and nuclear experts that the rational discussion should not be grounded in anti-nuclear phobia,[83] but that it should take place on a completely different ground—far more technical and substantive rather than emotional.[84] Some also pointed out—referring to the earlier analysis of the nuclear supporters—that although "Chernobyl was primarily a psychological catastrophe as the accident caused a relatively small amount of casualties," its myth is still functioning today.[85] However, not all media sources were equally biased in this respect. Quite interestingly, while one of the tabloids, *Fakt*, was publishing false information about the radioactive cloud coming to Poland, its competitor *Super Express* published at the same time a calming interview with an energy security expert.[86] Such examples illustrate some of the diversity of media voices at the time that served as the diffused centers of legitimacy—formulating their own, often competing rhetoric and constructing the agency of the chosen actors—by providing space for selected voices to be heard.

The government plans and priorities were also not shaken by the crisis at Fukushima. The nuclear energy project started to be framed, though, as a policy option that is based on sound calculations and that is going to be implemented with adequate precaution. A number of statements issued by the government at the time reflected that rhetoric, which aimed to reassure Polish society. It was then stated that the "Polish nuclear power plant will be secure and that security aspects will be one of the major criteria taken into account while choosing technological solutions for its construction and operation."[87] The possibility of natural disasters and potential terrorist attacks was also acknowledged,[88] as the Nuclear Energy Commissioner Trojanowska put it: "The government takes responsibility for protecting the public from eventual negative consequences and for minimizing the risk of accidents. We have to double our efforts not to let nature exceed the boundaries of our imagination."[89] Nuclear energy started to then be presented as a "rational" choice—and by default contrasted with the supposedly "irrational" fears of a large part of the public and environmental groups. A number of themes could be detected here. First, the "rationality" of the nuclear energy option highlighted its economic justification (coal cannot meet future demands and there is no economic alternative to nuclear energy), which fell on fertile ground in the Polish context dominated by the subsistence logic. Second, as opposed to the German context, where in the aftermath of the accident at Fukushima it became a dominant theme that "if such a nuclear disaster could happen in the technologically advanced Japan it could happen everywhere"—the expert voices in Poland pointed rather to the older generation of Japanese nuclear reactors and the specific seismic region, which made this kind of catastrophe unlikely to occur elsewhere.[90] Fifty years of worldwide exploitation of nuclear energy and the fact that six of Poland's neighboring states had nuclear power plants was also quoted as proof that nuclear energy is a sensible policy option.[91] Interestingly, the implication was that even though nuclear energy is safe enough, its risks are "total," as in the case of an accident in the CEE region Poland would be similarly affected—hence it is still rational to invest in nuclear energy. Moreover, the interviewees from the Polish Energy Group in charge of the future NPP in Poland emphasized the EU regulations in guaranteeing a certain level of nuclear waste safety.[92]

Overall, it could be argued that the Polish governing elite at the time portrayed itself as capable of preventing and managing potential risks of nuclear energy. In analytical terms this dynamic could be seen as conscious measures aimed at counteracting the possible rise of the risk logic in the Polish context in its full spectrum. Although it was admitted that the possibilities of harm due to natural disasters or terrorism do exist and might pose risks that are "total" in character, the political elite concluded that adhering to technological safety standards and implementing modern technologies constitute satisfactory precautionary measures and give it sufficient control to manage possibilities of harm deriving from nuclear energy. Crucially, although government actors themselves employed the rhetoric of calculation and precaution, the wider distal context was not favorable to the strong imperative of prevention to emerge and cause a change in the policy course. The societal disengagement certainly played a role here; as opposed to Germany, there is a lack of societal pressure connected to the issue of nuclear energy in Poland.

Putting the stance of Polish public opinion in a wider perspective, it becomes clear that since 1990, when, because of numerous protests of environmental groups and a public referendum (in which 86 percent of respondents voted against nuclear energy plans), the government of Tadeusz Mazowiecki stopped the nuclear power plants in Żarnowiec,[93] public support for the nuclear energy program in Poland has been gradually and steadily growing. Moreover, prior to the accident at Fukushima, the number of nuclear energy supporters has been growing in Poland at the highest rate as compared with other EU states, and was much higher than the European average.[94] The percentage of supporters of nuclear energy for the first time outnumbered its opponents in 2010, yet this trend was reversed after the nuclear accident in Japan the next year.[95] The survey conducted after the Fukushima accident revealed that the shift in perceptions occurred because of increased fears: with 54 percent fearing a nuclear accident, 26 percent recalling the consequences of Chernobyl, and 15 percent pointing to the security risks linked to nuclear waste storage.[96] The opinion poll surveys conducted in the following years additionally show that the accident at Fukushima permanently stopped the trend of growing support for nuclear energy in Poland—although the numbers of both opponents and supporters fluctuate year to year.[97] While a number of supporters of nuclear energy have not reached the all-time high from the pre-Fukushima context, an opinion poll from 2018 estimated the number of opponents at a high of 53 percent.[98] Moreover, 83 percent of the declared opponents pointed to the Fukushima accident as a key factor that lowered their trust in the safety of nuclear energy.[99] Former research into the persistent opponents of nuclear energy in Poland, conducted by a government official from the Department of Nuclear Energy in the Ministry of Economy, additionally distinguished among four such groups: environmentalists; anarchists (motivated by the idea of green capitalism); patriots (against foreign technology or jobs for foreigners); and local communities (expressing mostly economic fears).[100] However, in his opinion, in the Polish context it is not the environmental concerns that fuel most of the opposition towards nuclear energy, but rather the general feeling that Poland "will not manage" to succeed in these plans—therefore pointing to the economic dimension of the project.[101] This lack of public trust underpinned by the economic fears reflects a wider phenomenon of the prioritization of the economic agenda in the Polish context that favors the energy security logic of subsistence. Also for this reason, in both the debate on the EU Climate and Energy package and the nuclear debate, the "green energy" actors tend to appeal rather to the economic dimension of the alternative path of green energy. In the words of one environmentalist:

> I think that it is much better to use economic rather than environmental arguments in the public debate—especially in Poland, because Poland is not a country of people sensitive enough to be ready to protest from the point of view of their threatened environmental interests.[102]

Nuclear energy is also regarded by many of its supporters as "green energy" because of low CO_2 emissions. Hence, many environmental activists in Poland who oppose it, point either to safety concerns related to the operation of nuclear power plants or hint at the alternative solutions altogether. However, although the issue of nuclear safety clearly became important among a high percentage of nuclear energy opponents, as reflected in consecutive opinion polls, it does not in itself lead to a more vivid public debate or have any significant influence on the NPP development plans. The PGE and its daughter company PGE EJ 1 initially planned to build the first nuclear power plant in 2009–2014, which could provide electricity from 2019.[103] This date was postponed several times and, despite significant resources spent on related expert analyses, the construction did not begin.[104] In 2017, however, the Polish government finally made a decision to build the first nuclear power plants.[105] The environmental and location surveys conducted by PGE EJ 1 are to be completed in 2020 and the current plan envisions three nuclear blocks to be constructed between 2040 and 2045.[106]

It appears, then, that the nuclear energy debate in Poland takes place within the same constellation of actors as was the case in the debate on the EU Climate and Energy package: marked by centralized decision-making and general social disengagement. Although in the post-Fukushima context Polish media did play a role in feeding the debate with fear-filled analysis of developments in Japan and the issue of nuclear safety did rise to the fore of public concerns, the specifics of the distal context were not favorable to the imperative of prevention to manifest the risk logic in its full spectrum. The elements of the risk logic in relation to nuclear energy played out in the Polish context similar to the elements of the logic of war in relation to pipeline politics in the German one: the rise of the respective rhetoric stirred an intense, albeit short-lived, debate in the media, but no further policy moves followed. In both cases the domestic contexts were not conducive to the imperatives of survival or prevention, respectively, to raise and drive policy agendas at the time, as in both cases the imperative of sustenance underpinned by the prioritization of economic interests of the dominant actors prevailed.

The dominance of the sustenance rationale is typical for the Polish context and the discursive shifts that would detract from it develop mainly in two directions. First, there is an emerging, yet still marginalized, dynamic of "green" and "democratic" energy promoted by a number of NGOs and activists who refer to the German example of "Energiewende." This dynamic is marked by the reversal of energy security priorities typical for the subsistence logic and shifting attention to aspects such as environmental protection or social participation. The development of renewable energy sources is seen by some of its propagators not only as a means of providing energy security while supporting the climate protection agenda, but also as a way of further democratization of the socio-economic model in Poland. However, despite some emerging rhetoric and the first bottom–up citizens' energy initiatives, the distal context is not conducive to the rise of the imperative of self-reliance in the domestic energy sector on a wider scale. On the contrary, the periodic rise of the survival imperative in the context of Poland's pipeline politics signifies a single most dramatic shift, both in relation to the political rhetoric employed and the consequential energy policy moves. The next sections look at the examples of both dynamics.

Energy democracy in the post-Soviet space: transformation through emancipation

The case of reversed hierarchies

If fulfilling functional needs of society lies at the core of the energy security logic of subsistence, prioritizing any other dimension of energy security would already hint at the ongoing changes in the underlying sustenance rationale—although the basic nature of the logic as a main site of contestation would remain the same. The analysis of the German case showed how such gradual reversal of hierarchies results in much more than a mere alteration of the public policy agenda, as it contributes to the rise of the imperative of self-reliance in wide-scale local energy practices. Having in mind the dynamics of the Polish context, as illustrated by the response to the EU Climate and Energy package and the nuclear debate that followed, it seems that such a shift would be highly unlikely to occur in Poland. However, local voices that call for an alternative way of thinking about the country's energy security are already in place—especially among environmental activists and Warsaw-based NGOs. This emerging agenda gives more weight to the environmental concerns, which not only become one of the policy prerogatives, but which start to set the entire energy security framework. A discussion on the priorities of energy security by Polish environmental activist Professor Andrzej Kassenberg reflects that point:

> First of all, a distinction must be made between energy policy and climate policy. The former involves a traditional way of thinking—that *we need to fulfill the needs*—while the latter is based on the concept of *sustainable development*, where carrying capacity is a starting point. The guiding idea behind strategic documents on energy policy has been to meet the existing requirements, … such as providing a required level of production capacity or ensuring a high degree of fuel and energy security. Within this approach, the question of resource management and nature conservation is confined to increasing resource productivity and minimizing the environmental impact. And the environmental constraints … are all but ignored. But when the

> concept of *sustainable development* is embraced and the global extent of the man-made impact is taken into account, the need arises for incorporating these constraints into strategic documents being drafted. The environmental constraints should then set the framework for energy sector development, thus leading to much increased interest in energy demand management and development of renewable energy sources.[107]

The above discussion points to the energy–climate nexus, yet it reverses the prevailing sequence of priorities within the vast majority of energy security definitions, where environmental protection is put at the bottom of the hierarchy. Pointing to the fact that energy policies are mostly driven by the need to fulfill the functional needs of society—while putting environmental aspects aside—signifies the energy security logic of subsistence driven by the imperative of sustenance. Many definitions of energy security as framed by actors in the Polish context reflect that particular understanding. Theoretically speaking, given that multiple actors attach different meanings to energy security within the subsistence logic, the hierarchy where environmental concerns overthrow the economic agenda is also conceivable. However, as the analysis of the German case showed, and as Kassenberg similarly implies here, once the environmental aspect is prioritized, the remaining dimensions of energy security are not only pushed down on the list of priorities, but transform, too. With the environmental agenda topping the list—the "sustenance" transforms into "sustainable development," while "growth" becomes a "balanced growth" or even gets close to the "zero growth" argument.

Whereas the analysis of the German context showed that reversal of typical hierarchies of energy security dimensions within the subsistence logic lays the groundwork for the incremental processes that give rise to the imperative of self-reliance and the development of the emancipatory logic in the energy sphere, the elements of this logic can also be traced in the Polish context. Moreover, the close cooperation of many "green" actors from the German and Polish sides—with the frequently organized public debates, expert consultations and translation of German-language sources on topics related to energy transition—point to a significant knowledge transfer and the cosmopolitan character of the emancipatory agenda. Several organizations in particular play a key role here, such as Zielony Instytut (Green Institute), Fundacja Przestrzenie Dialogu (Foundation Spaces of Dialogue), Towarzystwo na rzecz Ziemi (Society for Earth), Instytut Energetyki Odnawialnej (Institute for Renewable Energy) as well as the Warsaw offices of the German Heinrich Böll Foundation and Rosa Luxemburg Foundation. The above organizations collaborate on the promotion of energy democracy and the green economy in Poland. Their activities include debates, conferences, training and energy roundtables organized in different parts of Poland, as well as publications and cooperation with some progressive politicians, individual provinces and municipalities. Despite these efforts, the logic of emancipation manifests differently in Poland than in Germany. Although the imperative of self-reliance in local energy affairs is not equally strong due to the mix of different contextual factors, the slowly rising emancipatory rationale could be spotted in the rhetoric of some green energy activists/organizations and in the first bottom–up citizens' energy initiatives. Moreover, the specificity of the Polish context, because of its post-Soviet legacy, implies that the emancipatory agenda in the energy sector has potentially more far-reaching consequences.

To start with, it is worth pointing out that Polish actors who call for change in the dominant approach to energy security often refer to the German example of "Energiewende." Kassenberg's emphasis on the development of renewable energy sources strongly suggests that it is the decentralized and participatory energy system that would take the prioritization of the environmental agenda to its logical conclusion and bring about the change in the way in which we conceptualize and think about energy security. Some energy security definitions given by the environmental actors in Poland similarly reflect that shift in reasoning.

First, many of them point to the cross-sectoral approach to energy security that in their opinion could be realized by the development of renewables. Therefore, Dariusz Szwed, a co-founder of the political party "Greens 2004" and an active member of the Green Institute, suggested that only the state's own energy production based on renewables could simultaneously provide for "ecological, societal and economic security."[108] He later repeated that claim in an important publication on the subject titled "Demokracja energetyczna" (energy democracy), which introduces the concept to the Polish public.[109] Szwed and Maciejewska point out that energy democracy increases social, economic and ecological security.[110] Moreover, the authors mention how newly emerging blogs, websites on social networks and vortals are being created on the Internet to promote energy democracy and to "support one another in building energy security, economic independence and democratic power."[111] These three dimensions are therefore linked for the first time within a single triad. Similar definitions and understandings were expressed by the interviewees from some environmental and academic circles—as energy efficiency and development of renewable energy sources, based on the culture of prosumers, were pointed to as two key ways of ensuring Poland's energy security that would also make the economic, societal and environmental dimensions of energy security compatible.[112]

Second and consequently, the wider conceptualizations and approaches to energy security raise or even prioritize the issue of social participation in energy production that derives from the diffused energy model. The very term "energy democracy" that was initially coined by a number of NGOs and environmental groups highlight the scope of the potential systemic transformation and its underlying logic, where individuals stop being merely the object of the technocratic energy policy and become its subject and sovereign.[113] In the Polish context, a definition of energy security provided by the main propagator of energy democracy, Dariusz Szwed, directly reflected that point. Szwed defined energy security by distinguishing its three priorities: public participation, competitive energy market and security of state's own energy production—in that order.[114] By promoting the development of renewable energy sources and culture of prosumers (simultaneous producers and consumers of energy), he justified his prioritization of societal participation among other energy security dimensions:

> It is quite an unusual approach to this issue, but I would put it as the first priority. Participation might have nothing to do with energy, but it has a lot in common with all other sectors.... [there is a need for] public participation, both at the level of setting the priorities of the state's energy policy, but also at the level of the benefits of its implementation. Society must become a shareholder.[115]

"Demokracja energetyczna" elaborates further on the design of the new system, in which society not only actively participates in the building of an energy model, but also has control over it.[116] The authors argue that this shift implies more than simply an increase in social participation, but more broadly the drive of local communities towards self-sufficiency.[117] Moreover, they note that the diffused energy system based on renewables allows for peaceful energy access (e.g., dispersed energy stores of wind and sun—also home ones). This stands in sharp contrast to the centralized energy system that remains highly dependent on the geopolitical situation and might entail wars over access to energy resources in different geographical locations (and that requires centralized storage facilities for fossil fuels).[118] Therefore, as opposed to the logic of war that involves competition over energy resources within a zero-sum game, the authors of the Polish brochure on energy democracy stress the inclusive character of the alternative energy system, in which energy would be produced in a peaceful and democratic manner.

Third, the agenda of social liberation and emancipation in energy affairs that often accompanies the promotion of energy democracy slowly spreads to new audiences—both in rhetoric and through the practice of the emerging bottom–up citizens' energy initiatives. When it comes to the rhetoric, the slogan "power to the people" was both introduced in "Demokracja energetyczna" publication as referring to energy and power as well as the power of people freeing themselves from monopolies of the twentieth century,[119] and is guiding the activities of some organizations that started to promote the idea of energy democracy, such as the Foundation Spaces of Dialogue—"Power and energy in the hands of people!"[120] As Szwed stated: "We are promoting an entirely different model of energy system ... We are building a grassroots movement for the Polish energy transformation ... Energy companies take energy away from us ... renewable energy will free energy for all the Poles."[121]

The emerging imperative of self-reliance starts to be visible also among some local energy initiatives. For instance, in 2014, the mayor of Brzeziny, Marcin Pluta, announced his intention to make his city of several thousand people independent from external energy sources.[122] The plans for the creation of the first Polish "smart city" in Brzeziny based on the use of renewable energy and electric transport include acquisition of energy using solar screens, construction of a photovoltaic farm, development of wind energy, construction of charging stations for electric cars and building local power transmission lines. The bottom–up initiative started despite the lack of favorable regulations from the government side. As Brzeziny Mayor Marcin Pluta put it:

> The idea for Smart City, as an intelligent city, including self-sufficient energy, was Brzeziny's attempt to act and operate in the area of renewable energy and electronic mobility without the Polish Act on Renewable Energy Sources (RES Act), over which the work lasted for several years. Since we could not wait for official legal regulations, I decided to *take matters into my own hands* and create a set of projects allowing for energy production for the city's needs.... [The] goals are primarily to partially meet energy needs from our own ecological sources and to increase energy independence.[123]

Similar types of initiatives have been slowly emerging in other Polish cities, albeit their scope varies. Bielsko Biała, named the "City of Good Energy" and the winner of the "Eco-City" main prize in the energy efficiency category, has introduced a number of innovative energy solutions over the years.[124] The latter include thermo-modernization of municipal buildings and flats (e.g., ecological heating boilers), promotion of energy efficiency under the "Bielsko Biała protects the climate" program, co-financing of solar collectors on municipal facilities and private homes ($800\,m_2$ of solar collectors installed by 2016), and the recovery of biomass from waste. Among other cities Częstochowa is particularly active in the promotion of energy efficiency measures,[125] Lublin is in the process of installing solar panels on all of the city buses,[126] while Warsaw plans to reach 15 percent share of renewable energy in total energy consumption by 2020 with the help of solar panels, photovoltaic panels, heat pumps, biomass installations and small wind turbines.[127]

The above dynamic, which marks the first stages of the potential democratization of the Polish energy sphere, contains a number of elements that, similarly to the German context, point to the slowly emerging logic of emancipation. First, in theoretical terms we are moving away from the state's centralized control over energy resources (the logic of war), and away from the complex contestation processes within the public policy agenda (the logic of subsistence) towards the level of individual users and local communities. Here the triad of building energy security, local energy independence and democratic power plays out in practice through the reflexive practice of energy production. Energy security is therefore achieved in a peaceful, democratic and inclusive process that ultimately leads to local self-sufficiency and local energy independence. Second, this shift is accompanied by the rhetoric of social liberation and empowerment via participation in the energy system, which stops to be "oppressive" once the power of the energy monopolies breaks down and control over energy becomes diffused. Third and crucially, in the opinion of a number of environmental actors in Poland, its development not only would end the Polish state's omnipotence in the sphere of energy by shifting the responsibility for energy production to citizens,[128] but could also contribute to the transformation of the entire socioeconomic model.[129] In other words, thanks to their scalability and distributed character, renewables not only enable the individuals, cooperatives and local communities to invest and benefit from their development,[130] but social empowerment in the energy sector could lead to further democratization of the entire system—as citizens would become aware of the power of their political agency to bring about the desired changes. This is especially the case in the CEE region, where centralized political power is additionally strengthened by the Soviet legacy of keeping a strict division between the management of resources and societal relations—which impacts both the energy and environmental sectors.[131] For this reason, the introduction of the decentralized energy model based on the renewable energy sources is seen by many as Poland's step into the twenty-first century—as opposed to the "outlived" centralized model that developed mostly in the nineteenth century.[132]

From the analytical point of view, the emancipatory logic could then manifest in the Polish context as strongly transformative on two levels. First, as a growing number of the bottom–up energy initiatives and prosumers (within shifted constellation of actors where they "have a say") would engage in the reflexive practice of energy production (that blurs the lines between referent objects and subjects of security) and lead to the democratic transformation of the energy system (with democratization as the ultimate security mechanism). Second, once that happens, empowered citizens could bring about further changes and transform the entire socioeconomic model ("distal context"). Simultaneously, the changed distal context would further enhance the embeddedness of the security mechanism (democratization of the energy sphere), and strengthen the given constellation of actors (that empowers local communities and individual prosumers). Therefore, such a system would resemble one of the two main models of the energy systems' development: "democratic, participatory and based on the environmentally friendly energy," as opposed to the elitist, centralized energy system that "does not need a large public participation, but … can be realized by a strong central government in collaboration with several large organizations—a view that reflects the traditional industrial thinking."[133]

The advantages of the diffused energy system were highlighted by a number of Polish actors, who claimed that such a system would be more certain in terms of ensuring energy security,[134] have minimal impact on the natural environment because of its reliance on micro-energy installations,[135] and make it extremely hard to carry out a terrorist attack on the national energy infrastructure.[136] Other arguments present in the debates stressed once more the elements that would ultimately show the emancipatory character of such a model. It was then noticed that it would lead to the distribution of profits from energy production among prosumers—as opposed to a few energy companies—and de-monopolize the Polish energy sector,[137] modernize Polish society and lead to its further democratization,[138] increase social awareness regarding environmental and energy issues,[139] or even contribute to the minimization of the areas of social exclusion.[140]

Such an energy system would be compatible with the "high energy culture," as described in the literature on the subject.[141] According to the latter, the energy culture "signifies a humanistic approach to energy issues, both on the part of its producers and consumers, which approach enables solving the social problems."[142] In this understanding, "the less impact on the environment and the smaller the energy loss, the higher the energy culture."[143, 144] High energy cultures are therefore characterized by a high degree of decentralization of the energy systems (dismantling of monopolies), and a highly conscious approach to the issues of energy on the part of the consumers (signifying energy efficiency and reflexive character of energy itself).[145] Most importantly, the process of changing the energy culture from "lower" to "higher" seems to correspond well to the hierarchization processes that take place among multiple actors within the logic of subsistence. In the words of Łucki and Misiak:

> This process takes place in different social spheres that could have an impact on it. These include, among others: scientists, parliament, government agencies, the public, NGOs, investors, energy suppliers, local communities, energy consumers, etc. It is necessary to think in terms of multiple domains and different actors at different levels of scale.[146]

The development of the decentralized energy system in the Polish context faces both regulatory and mental barriers, as well as the constellation of actors that aims at maintaining the status quo. First, the possibility of prioritizing the environmental aspect of energy is hindered by low public awareness of environmental issues. As an official from the Office for Parliamentary Analysis[147] stated:

> Environmental concerns are not perceived as a major problem by Poles. Still more important are the job places and other economic concerns.... As for those who would be potential beneficiaries of the shift to the green economy, they are either not well organized, or do not know about these benefits, or do not perceive of this shift as a potential benefit.[148]

Therefore, whereas issues like "CO_2 emissions are not of the public interest,"[149] it is the economic rationale that guides the general attitudes towards energy in Poland. In this sense, many energy experts doubt that Poles would be willing to "pay twice as much for energy just to have it from the renewable sources."[150] Second, there exist technical and bureaucratic barriers to the development of renewables on a large scale, as the energy infrastructure is lacking, while there are numerous institutional obstacles for individual actors who would like to become energy prosumers.[151] Therefore, many local attempts of creating mini-prosumers cultures often encounter such barriers and result in conflict.[152] Third, there exist traditionally strong links between energy companies and the political sphere in Poland—with the Polish government protecting strong economic interests of the main energy businesses. Moreover, the big energy companies themselves appear highly conservative and avoid innovation. As an analyst from the think tank demosEUROPA noted:

> There is a tendency among energy companies in Poland to do the necessary minimum, but not to expose oneself to the radical changes, not to take risks, not to introduce innovative solutions, because the reward that comes with success is relatively small in comparison to a lack of success.[153]

This rationale reflects wider conservatism typical for the Polish context. Even more important than this conservatism seems to be a deeply rooted conviction among the Polish political elite that it is the state that should define the course and goals of energy security and energy policies. Finally, there are some distal factors specific to the Polish domestic setting. In the words of a prominent Polish environmentalist and scholar:

> I think that Germany is one generation ahead of us. I think that when it comes to us, two important factors play a role. One is the aspect of a certain conservatism of Polish society. The Polish society is in large part a society with rural roots, for whom the environment is something to be transformed, something to be changed, something to be subdued—therefore it is not necessarily seen as something to be admired. Although, of course farmers know that they need to use it in a sustainable way, because if they transform it too much they will not be able to use it in the long run. On the other hand, there exists a right-wing approach additionally reinforced by the Catholic Church—"let us make the earth subjected"—and this voice is much stronger than what John Paul II was saying about the environmental protection.... [Additionally] I think that there is a certain belief ... that environmentalists and pro-green energy movements are some sort of a leftist conspiracy—that they are not true Poles and true patriots.[154]

All the above contextual factors contribute to a certain constellation of actors when it comes to Poland's energy transformation prospects. On the one hand, there is the general public—neither much engaged nor interested in the issues of environment and alternative energy sources, but used to the fact that "these issues are not widely discussed since—given the monopolies—there is not much choice anyway."[155] Some argue that this low public engagement translates into the lack of awareness of one's own best interests and a lack of political representatives that would make the issue of green energy one of their political programs' flagships.[156, 157] On the other hand, there is the Polish government—with the continuously changing strategic energy plans and big energy companies' interests always in mind. This lack of political power on the part of green energy movements means that many environmental activists try to appeal to other than environmental values—since the latter are not especially convincing in the Polish sociopolitical context. Therefore, Dariusz Szwed talks not so much about the ecological aspects, but about the societal, democratic and economic ones. In his words: "What are we doing? We are building a grassroots movement for Poland's energy transformation. And why will we win? Because, people will make a profit out of it."[158] The fact that the above might indeed be the only viable strategy is confirmed by observations made by one Polish environmentalist and researcher:

> I know from the research that I conduct in the rural areas that the prosumers' policy will have a chance to succeed there, because it will be perceived not as an instrument of the climate protection or environment, but as an enhancement of one's own material status.[159]

This strong prioritization of the economic aspect of energy security is taken even further in the opinions of some energy experts. For instance, an analyst from the *Sobieski Institute* sees the ecological discourse in Poland as premature:

> Poland lags behind Western countries when it comes to the issues of security, energy consumption, prosperity, affluence scale … this eco-friendly European project, which is being implemented, would be in my opinion suited for Poland in 20, 30 years—nowadays we cannot afford it.… This [ecological] aspect is at the moment quite abstract to me, and all those demands that come from the European Commission, Germany or Scandinavian countries have nothing to do with the situation in which Poland is today.[160]

From the analytical point of view, the specificities of the Polish context indicate that the ultimate strength of the economically underpinned sustenance rationale also changes the discursive strategies of actors who call for the "green" transformation of the energy system. Appealing to other than environmental issues serves then as a certain "shortcut" that is necessitated by contextual dynamics: unfavorable distal factors (e.g., low environmental awareness), and a traditional constellation of actors (that gives leverage to big industry interests). This dynamic also implies that—as opposed to the German context, the imperative of self-reliance is not strong in the Polish energy context, although as the earlier discussed examples of the emerging rhetoric and first bottom–up practices illustrated, gradual changes are taking place locally.

The Polish energy system is not likely to become diffused anytime soon, though. The ministerial officials working in the departments of renewable energy and the government of former Prime Minister Donald Tusk[161] expressed the view that Poland should aim at a hybrid system—mostly centralized with the development of some additional renewable energy sources as part of widening the energy portfolio. The act on renewable energy sources from February 20, 2015, adopted by the former Civic Platform government, was heading more in that direction, as it introduced tariffs guaranteeing a fixed price for green energy for 15 years and made it easier for potential investors to calculate the costs associated with RES.[162] However, the Law and Justice Party, which came back to power in autumn 2015, changed the existing regulations the following year, first with its act on investments in the field of wind farms from May 20, 2016,[163] and the act on RES adopted on June 22, 2016.[164] The first document has been referred to ever since as an "anti-windmill act," as it introduced regulations de facto preventing the majority of potential wind energy projects from developing.[165] The new RES Act introduced some regulations favoring the development of distributed energy aimed at creating local energy cooperatives and energy clusters that would take part in the auction system. However, it was also criticized, among other things, for its lack of social consultations, elimination of the guaranteed tariff system, unclear regulations regarding contaminated biomass and changes in the auction system towards greater support for energy production from biomass and co-firing (often with coal).[166] Overall, the new regulations favored the bigger players on the market and reflected Law and Justice's preference for a centralized energy system, the strong role of energy companies in cooperation with the government and the use of domestic coal resources. This approach is also starkly visible in the *Polish Energy Policy until 2050* document draft under consideration.[167] The draft has been vividly criticized during public consultations by Polish environmental organizations for serving current political and coal industry interests, while rejecting alternative options for the development of the domestic energy sector with the dominant role of RES and ignoring global trends.[168] According to this critique, favoring the policy variant with a dominant role of fossil fuels condemns Poland to further dependence on the energy resources increasingly imported from the geographical areas prone to conflict. As the "Climate Coalition"—a network of 22 non-governmental organizations involved in climate protection activities in Poland, noted in its critique, the *Polish Energy Policy until 2050* upholds the traditional view of energy security built by large systems, thus limiting the development of distributed prosumer and cooperative installations.[169] However, as its member Professor Kassenberg and founder of the Institute for Sustainable Development argued:

> In many developed countries, the approach that energy security is built by large corporations is abandoned. The importance of individual energy users and local energy systems is growing. We have in Poland 13 million households, nearly 2 million small and medium enterprises and over 900 cities and over 1500 rural municipalities. In them lies the potential of dispersed energy. We must look into the future and not defend the interests of energy magnates all the time. Both energy security and world trends support this.[170]

Theoretically speaking, the two competing approaches described above reflect, on the one hand, a humanistic approach to energy security solutions that relies on the bottom–up democratic practices and on the other, the economic approach that is driven by the imperative of sustenance that in the Polish context is linked to the centralized energy model. The dominance of the sustenance rationale with its economic considerations of big energy players has so far proved to be vulnerable only to the periodic rise of the imperative of survival in relation to national pipeline politics. The next section scrutinizes this dynamic in greater detail.

Pipeline politics: the rise and fall of the logic of war

If the still marginalized emancipatory rationale in Polish energy affairs emerges slowly in the incremental processes of contestation, the imperative of survival can enter the public policy agenda in a dramatic fashion and shift the official rhetoric and policy course within short periods of time triggered by a combination of domestic factors and developments in European pipeline politics.[171] The favorable dynamics of the Polish context with its traditional constellation of actors (centralized decision-making and specific political leadership at the time), and conducive distal context (sociohistorical factors) due to which the notion of "energy security" is equated with "energy sovereignty"—made the rise of the logic of war in the Polish energy sphere especially more likely.

If we consider historical developments, it is clear that the Polish distal context was not always favorable for the imperative of survival to emerge and drive energy affairs. If we trace energy sector developments since the early 1990s, one could notice the predominantly economic reasoning in Poland's energy relations with Russia. To start with, the very issue of energy dependency was not politicized during the Soviet era—as contracts on gas and oil imports were part of the casual relations between states locked within the same economic system. The collapse of the Soviet Union led to the need to renegotiate these contracts, which resulted in signing the agreements on building the infrastructure for gas imports from Russia in 1993 (Yamal pipeline) and on gas imports in 1996.[172] The latter was later harshly criticized for its striking carelessness, as the Polish side contracted more gas for the next 25 years than its expected domestic consumption levels, and agreed to a very unfavorable "take or pay rule," which additionally did not allow Poland to re-export its gas surpluses.[173] Trying to explain this lack of caution one could distinguish between two main factors here: first, centralized decision-making, which meant that the 1996 agreement was not subjected to public scrutiny; and second, the Polish side's preoccupation with maintaining economic ties with the Russian monopolist at any cost. The latter point was illustrated by Janusz Zgórzyński—the director of the Public Relations Office of the Polish Energy Group that signed the 1996 agreement, who, while replying to some criticisms two years later, stated:

> We have to act not only according to the security of supply, but also according to the economy, because we cannot afford the kind of

> diversification that takes place in the rich countries of Western Europe. Russian gas is the cheapest, and now there is no reason for concern about the security of supply from Russia.[174]

However, the unfavorable 1996 agreement led to some politicization of energy supply diversification attempts in Poland. Additionally fueled by former Russian Prime Minister Yevgeny Primakov's explicit statement in the mid-1990s that "in the light of its limited military potential Russia has to use its energy resources as a foreign policy tool,"[175] subsequent Polish governments started to consider alternative routes of gas supply, work to renegotiate the already-signed contracts with Russia and elude the building of the new gas transit system.[176] The multiplicity of different diversification plans introduced by the subsequent cabinets (of Jerzy Buzek, Leszek Miller, Marek Belka and Kazimierz Marcinkiewicz) lacked consistency and proved to be ineffective in the long run. Different governments were coming out with different diversification ideas, while criticizing their predecessors and continuously changing the course of Polish energy policy.[177] To mention just some of the projects, government plans included various diversification routes from: Denmark, Norway, Germany, Central Asia, Ukraine, the building of the LNG Terminal or linking Poland to the Nabucco pipeline.[178] However, despite this variety of efforts, it was not until 2005, when Kaczyńskis' Law and Justice Party won the parliamentary elections, that the imperative of survival emerged in relation to national energy affairs and gave rise to the logic of war.

The rise of the logic of war

Following his election as president in December 2005, and the Ukrainian gas crisis in January 2006, Lech Kaczyński stated the main priorities of his forthcoming presidency:

> Recent Russian moves against Ukraine—and partly also Poland—clearly show that the issue of providing Poland with alternative energy sources is absolutely essential to the national interest.... Poland should take urgent steps in three directions: first, the construction of the LNG terminal; second, the diversification of supply; and third, the increase in gas production from the domestic sources.... One of my first political initiatives as President will be to initiate the adoption of the National Security Act by the Parliament. The Act will be mostly concerned with the issue of energy security.[179]

Kaczyński also took further steps towards expanding the role of the president in the state's energy security policy. The preparation of energy security analysis and action projects became the responsibility of the—subordinate to the president—National Security Agency, a special working group on energy security was established, whereas the issue of energy security itself was included in the National Security Strategy of the Polish Republic, adopted on November

13, 2007.[180] Kaczyński's approach derived from the factors which made it possible for the logic of war to occur: centralized decision-making, the Polish state as a main actor—with energy companies playing a subordinate role—and equating "energy security" with "energy sovereignty," which had further repercussions for national security as a whole.

The logic of war was then set in motion and the policy moves that lifted energy security to the level of the national security agenda were accompanied by the "grammar of conflict" in official political rhetoric. Therefore, the Polish president on numerous occasions referred to the use of oil and gas by Russia as an "energy weapon" and its energy policy conduct as imperialistic.[181] This military rhetoric was echoed by other political actors, who similarly cited "energy weapon" phrase, compared the Nordstream project to the infamous Ribbentrop-Molotov pact, or proposed the "European energy solidarity" project under the slogan of "energy NATO."[182] Sharpening of the rhetoric was not confined to the political sphere only, as for instance one Polish newspaper commented on the Nordstream pipeline:

> Radosław Sikorski is right. Moreover, the comparison of the Russo-German gas pact to the Molotov-Ribbentrop pact looks rather unfavorable for the Putin-Schroeder couple. The gas agreement is in fact more aggressive than the treaty of 1939.... Besides, the objectives of the two documents are the same—to share the influence over the area between Russia and Germany.[183]

The general atmosphere of the energy "Cold War" and the evidence that the imperative of survival entered domestic energy affairs could also be spotted across the headlines of many newspaper articles on energy security at the time, which drew parallels to some historical events, e.g.: *Gas Blitzkrieg?*,[184] *Pipes of War*,[185] *Energy annexation*,[186] *Geopolitical leash*,[187] *Gas encirclement of Poland*.[188] Even more important than the rhetoric, though, were the further policy implications of the above logic.

The new government, supported by the president, announced at the end of 2005 its intention to sign "irreversible" agreements on gas supplies from non-Russian sources.[189] These declarations were followed by consistent efforts at diversification of energy supply—particularly from Central Asia. Favoring that geographical direction motivated Poland to resign from the economically beneficial straight pipeline connection with Germany in order to pursue the much more complicated Odessa-Brody-Gdańsk project.[190] Another important decision was the rejection of the Yamal 2 gas pipeline offered by the Russians, which would enable Poland to transit all the purchased gas.[191] As some analysts noted, the inconsistency of Polish policymaking towards Russia, and its efforts at reducing cooperation, was also one of the reasons why Russia decided to negotiate the Baltic pipeline project with Germany in the first place.[192]

The above policy developments show a changed hierarchization of energy security dimensions quite unusual for the Polish context—with economic concerns being pushed down the hierarchy and replaced with the imperative of survival in the energy policy sphere. Neither the Odessa-Brody-Gdańsk project, nor the rejection of Yamal 2 by Poland had a strong economic justification. The latter was justified mainly by solidarity with Ukraine, whose interests as a transit state to Western Europe could be threatened.[193] One could argue that it was not the economic situation of Ukraine per se that bothered Poland, but rather its geopolitical situation—and a will to remain Ukraine's ally in disputes with Russia. The fact that economic factors were pushed down the list of energy priorities and that energy companies started to be treated as the mere executors of the state's will was also reflected in Kaczyński's decisions regarding diversification of gas supply from Norway and plans for building the LNG terminal (eventually opened in 2015). As some commentators noted:

> The projects of the gas pipeline [from Norway] or LNG terminal are already a foregone conclusion, although experts haven't finished researching the projects' economic and technical feasibility yet.... The same situation applies to the LNG terminal. Prime Minister Kaczyński not only treats this project as a "done deal," but he has even already chosen its location.... Meanwhile, the heads of the PGNiG assure that the works on the project's feasibility are in progress.[194]

The fall of the logic of war

The logic of war started to wane after the Law and Justice Party's defeat in the 2007 parliamentary elections. In their aftermath, many politicians started to distance themselves from the energy policy of their predecessors, while many energy experts criticized the implications of these policies.

Therefore, new Minister of the Economy Waldemar Pawlak stated at the time that any further diversification plans would be verified based on their economic rationale rather than political concerns.[195] Similar rhetoric was expressed a few years later by his successor, Donald Tusk:

> The gas is there to be burned for warming. The government's policy is there to make sure that this gas is not lacking in the case when critical events occur.... Gas should indeed flow from Russia, should not be too expensive and should not become a tool of a political fight.[196]

On the other hand, the energy policy choices of the Law and Justice "era" were criticized for their political and ideological rather than pragmatic motivations and focus on the reduction of relations with Russia rather than potential economic benefits.[197] It was then argued that this lack of political pragmatism derived from the Polish foreign policy being formulated in the historical-ideological frame, underpinned by "mythologized historical politics"; that Polish–Russian relations started to resemble a "Hobbesian state of nature" where the permanent crisis in mutual relations became a normality; and that gas investments looked like country defense preparations, with "politicians deciding everything, while economic matters [were] being taken off the immediate agenda."[198] The critical voices not only distanced themselves from what could be seen as a counterproductive survival rationale, but also pointed to the long-term consequences of such an approach: Poland's undermined position in energy relations with Russia for years to come, continuous lack of alternative supply routes, and a big financial burden for the entire Polish energy sector caused by investments in the LNG terminal.[199] Consequently, further voices that called for diversification grounded their opinions rather in the economic market approach: higher than average prices for Russian gas paid by Poland and the need to lessen dependence on an energy monopolist.[200]

Interestingly, the development of the Nordstream 2 project a few years later did not bring back the rationale of survival, but rather domestic voices focused on highlighting the lack of common values and solidarity within the EU and with Ukraine. Polish president Andrzej Duda, after a meeting with the presidents of the Visegrad Group countries in Slovakia in 2018, brought up the issue of Nordstream 2 and stressed that solidarity and mutual understanding are lacking in the EU.[201] He described the project as a political rather than business undertaking that will result in the dominance of one supplier over the entire EU market and that is being implemented against the interests of several states in the CEE region. As he stated: "We want a solidarity-based European Union that seeks mutual understanding in which every country is treated as equal."[202] This opinion was echoed by the domestic press and politicians. The Polish daily *Rzeczpospolita* noted that Nordstream 2 is likely to bury both the idea of the Energy Union and EU solidarity, as it will de facto prevent the development of the South Stream project and mark the comeback of political realism as reflected by the prevalence of the German national interest over the common one.[203] Whereas some domestic voices highlighted how the project hampers the prospects for the gas pipeline from Norway, increasing the import of liquefied gas and in general creating a competitive gas market in Central Europe,[204] the issue of solidarity emerged as a particularly important one. On the one hand, it was argued that Nordstream has a strong geopolitical dimension and is directly targeted at Ukraine, which will become much more sensitive to blackmail because of possible gas cut-offs.[205] On the other hand, some politicians stated that both the Polish historical experience and the rational evaluation of Putin's policy should encourage the German side to show greater solidarity with the security concerns of the CEE countries.[206] With some energy portals publishing posts under headlines such as "Solidarity in German: Impact of Nord Stream II on Poland, Central Europe and the EU legal order"[207] and the Polish Minister of Foreign Affairs suggesting that Poland would ask the US for support of its policy against the Nordstream 2 project, as the two states "share the same values," the issue of solidarity came to the fore of the political agenda.[208] This perceived lack of solidarity also had another important domestic dimension. As local commentators noted, Polish decision-makers were unpleasantly surprised with the Nordstream 2 project, especially at a time when they were struggling to explain to the domestic population how the adoption of the German proposals of the refugees' allocation would strengthen Poland's position in the EU—also in matters of energy security.[209] Therefore, the development of Nordstream 2 in the face of Russia's expansion in Ukraine not only evoked the worst historic associations, but also made the CEE countries additionally question the need to help Western European states with migration problems.

The Polish responses to the development of the Nordstream project and its extension, Nordstream 2, differed over the years. Does that mean that the occurrence of the logic of war in the Polish context was a one-time event? Arguably, no. Even the relatively calmer response to the construction of the Nordstream 2 pipeline highlighted its geopolitical dimension, framed it as a threat to regional energy security and at times even employed the grammar of conflict, e.g., with *Newsweek Polska* stating that gas pipes are continuously worth more to the Kremlin than infantry divisions and tanks.[210] Moreover, the contextual factors that favor the rise of the logic of war are deeply entrenched in the Polish sociopolitical setting and manifest at different occasions. An interesting example here is the parliamentary debate that took place in the Polish Sejm in the aftermath of the Ukrainian gas crisis in 2009. The profound analysis of the parliamentary speeches from that debate showed the continuously dominant realist logic in the framing of energy security issues, with: first, repetitive use of phrases such as "survival," "national interest" and "security"; second, a state-centric perspective that treats EU and energy companies as secondary actors subordinate to the state's interests; third, only a few voices pointing to the need of relying on the economic rationale in matters of energy policy; and finally, even fewer voices noting the importance of individual citizens in the debate on energy security—as opposed to the state only.[211]

One could therefore conclude that the rise and fall of the logic of war in the Polish context could be easily repeated in the future. Not only do the centralized energy system and low public engagement create an environment that is conducive for the imperative of survival to reappear in the Polish energy sphere, but the same could be said about the distal context (sociohistoric factors), which causes the notions of "energy security" and "energy sovereignty" to be confused and used interchangeably.

Energy security versus energy sovereignty

The confusion of the notions of energy security and energy sovereignty in the Polish context was spotted by one of the academics and propagators of citizens' energy in Poland, Professor Żmijewski. Żmijewski suggested to purposely introduce the term "energy sovereignty" to the public and expert debate on energy security—as one best describing the political and emotional aspects of the energy security problem in the Polish context.[212] According to Żmijewski, "energy sovereignty" could then be described as the ability to independently shape and implement energy policy, including the freedom to shape the foreign purchases' portfolio.[213] A conscious introduction of this term to the debate on energy security could, in his opinion, lead to the rationalization of that debate and the recovery of energy security's original meaning. The latter has been allegedly distorted by the Polish media, which by drawing the parallels to distant historical events, have continuously presented various energy security issues as a matter of Poland's independence and raison d'état. As a result, the possible violation of the Polish state's sovereignty by energy blackmail from Russia became a strong argument in Polish domestic politics and foreign policy alike.[214] However, as Żmijewski pointed out, in all the media coverage of energy security issues, it is the sovereignty of the decision that is questioned and highlighted rather than "energy security" per se, as: "Contrary to fears spread by the media, a complete loss of state's control over the energy sector does not automatically mean the danger to energy security. Yet, it means a symbolic loss of energy sovereignty."[215]

Żmijewski's observation grasps one of the key features underlying the dominant understanding of the energy security concept in the Polish context. This understanding—although most visible during Kaczyński's presidency—has been deeply rooted in the Polish mentality for years. A number of statements that refer both to contemporary and historical developments in Poland's energy policy are a case in point here, as lifting the issue of energy security to the level of the matter of national sovereignty was visible across many policy decisions and their underlying rhetoric over the years. For instance, the "contract of the century" to supply gas from Russia, signed by PGNiG[216] and Gazprom, was termed after closer scrutiny as a "threat to the national energy security … and even to the sovereignty of the Republic."[217] Several years later Poland did not accept Russia's help in developing its nuclear energy project—as similar to the gas supply, the idea was perceived as a "Russia's dictate."[218] Later, the decision to start the works on building the LNG terminal in Gdynia was made by the National Security Agency itself—a development that was compared by some with making an investment in the country's defense system.[219] More recently still, the Law and Justice Party promised to "tear the Polish shale gas out from the foreign hands and make it a national treasure and a true guarantor of energy security" that could "change the geopolitical balance in this part of Europe."[220] Polish "energy sovereignty" rationale also had wider implications as far as the EU energy policy is concerned. Therefore, although Poland has long been a loud advocate of the "energy solidarity" clause among EU member states, it had been simultaneously protecting its domestic monopolies and blocking the entry of other European players on the Polish energy market.[221] As one energy expert noted, it is an ultimate reflection of Polish "ideological dogma that only the state-controlled monopoly PGNiG can ensure our security of gas supply."[222]

Having in mind these developments over the years, the assumption that a conscious introduction of the term "energy sovereignty" to the public debate could alter that contextual understanding seems questionable. Although indeed there is a vast discrepancy between Polish scientific and technical energy studies—which describe energy security by various measurable parameters[223]—and the media rhetoric as well as the political elite's understandings that often confuse the notions of “energy security” and “energy sovereignty”—the raison d’état thinking is deeply rooted also among multiple other actors in the Polish context. Right-wing political scene aside, the arguments repeated by the green energy movements in Poland and the views held by the general public seem to show similar patterns. First, the idea of “freeing” Poland from dependency on Russia has been eagerly repeated by the propagators of the green economy—with the exception that it is renewable sources that would make Poland self-sufficient.[224] Second, similarly, the general public seems to identify “energy security” with “energy sovereignty.” Public surveys conducted by GfK Polonia for Polish daily *Rzeczpospolita* in two consecutive years showed that Poles consider the aspect of energy sovereignty as Poland’s top priority in energy affairs. The first of the surveys was conducted after the Ukrainian gas crisis of January 2009, and in its aftermath 62 percent of respondents saw Poland’s dependency on Russia as a threat to national sovereignty.[225] Even more importantly, 55 percent of respondents claimed that they would be willing to pay higher gas prices if it would help Poland to become independent from Russia regarding energy supplies.[226] The latter response is especially surprising given the Polish context, in which society is usually motivated mainly by economic factors. According to Jacek Kucharczyk, a program director at the Institute of Public Affairs in Warsaw, this response shows that the gas crisis has changed something in the mentality of Poles.[227] However, if we consult opinion polls data from the years preceding the 2009 crisis, a similar long-term pattern emerges. Therefore, Russian gas cut-offs to Ukraine in 2006 and conflicts in the Eastern neighborhood in the states that have been considered by Poland as potential alternative transit routes (Ukraine in 2004 and Georgia in 2008), similarly accelerated public fears.[228] A look at some of the data gathered by the Institute of Public Affairs shows that as much as 62 percent of the Polish population in 2005, and 69 percent in 2008, feared the economic threat from Russia.[229] Having in mind that the economics of energy supplies from Russia was often linked to politics, it might be worth highlighting that the perception of the political threat from Russia among the Polish population was equally high at both times (63 and 66 percent respectively).[230] Given the ongoing Russian–Ukrainian conflict that started in 2013, those historically grounded perceptions of the Poles are only likely to strengthen further. In fact, the domination of the “energy sovereignty” rationale could be recently spotted in the public views on the Polish nuclear energy program. The prioritization of national sovereignty over economic aspects was reflected in a survey concerned with the arguments “for” and “against” development of nuclear power plants, as 66 percent of respondents pointed to energy sovereignty as the main argument in favor of the development of nuclear energy in Poland and only 15 percent to its economic benefits.[231]

The findings of the above discussion have several analytical implications. First, the traditional constellation of actors marked by low social mobilization of Polish society coupled with traditionally centralized energy system and decision-making as well as specific distal factors (sociohistorical), which contribute to the notion of “energy security” to be equated with “energy sovereignty,” make the

Polish context highly conducive for the logic of war to periodically rise in it. When that happens, even the deeply embedded subsistence rationale that aims at the fulfillment of energy needs at the lowest cost possible is overthrown by the rise of the survival imperative in the energy sphere. As such, the logic of war in Poland—similarly to the risk logic in Germany—can be rapidly brought about via congruence of contextual factors, and not only influence the mainstream debate, but the emergent "survival" mode can lead to the policy moves that put the issue of energy supply on the immediate national security agenda. Moreover, the persistent contextual dynamics of the Polish context determine that it is likely to remain conducive to the imperative of survival to periodically re-occur in its energy affairs.

Conclusion

If comprehending some of the political rhetoric or the energy policy moves in Poland could have been challenging for external observers in recent years, the analysis of the security logics that operate in its domestic energy context shed light on the root causes of many of them. Unpacking the specifics of the Polish domestic setting, where historical, cultural and socioeconomic factors play a pivotal role in enabling the rise of certain energy security rationales, while impeding others, allowed the exploration of subsequent debates and policy developments in the renewables, gas and nuclear energy sectors. Although the analysis showed that all four energy security logics of subsistence, risk, emancipation and war identified in the German case are also at play in Poland, their impact and dynamic of operation varied and proved to be highly contextual. First, the imperative of sustenance that prioritizes the economic dimension of energy security and aims at the fulfillment of the functional needs of society appears to largely dominate Polish energy affairs. Its impact was particularly visible in relation to the debates on the EU Climate and Energy package and the development of nuclear energy plans in the pre- and post-Fukushima context. Even the heightened public fears of nuclear energy in the aftermath of the accident at Fukushima did not lead to a higher social mobilization that could give rise to a strong prevention imperative. As such, the risk logic did not manifest in its full spectrum, but the elements of it could be detected, and after a short-lived debate in Polish media, the political actors used the rhetoric of calculation and precaution to assure Polish society about the manageability of risks connected to the national nuclear energy program. The policy focus then shifted towards finding the best technological solutions. However, neither the rhetoric invoked went as far as to paint the gloomy reality of the Becksian risk society, nor did it lead to policy change, as the nuclear energy plans were later confirmed by subsequent governments. Despite multiple voices and interests present, the constellation of actors proved to be rather rigid and the decision-making process centralized. This is typical for the Polish context dynamic and translates into lower prospects for the development of renewables in Poland. Here, however, despite the dominance of the sustenance rationale, a number of actors attempt to change the nature of the Polish debate on energy security and prioritize its environmental and societal aspects. The emerging rhetoric embraces many elements of the emancipatory logic—as it calls for social empowerment and liberation from energy monopolies and for enhancing local energy independence via democratic means. The first local energy initiatives also reflect that reasoning, as they are driven by the growing imperative of self-reliance. Although the energy security logic of emancipation is on the rise, it does not yet constitute a real challenge to mainstream reasoning about energy security in Poland or to the official energy policy approach. Interestingly, though, increasing bottom–up social mobilization is seen by a number of environmentalists as a sign that civic empowerment in the energy sector could translate into further democratization of the entire socioeconomic model in Poland—hence pointing to this logic's transformative nature. Given the typical constellation of actors that, as opposed to Germany, does not change significantly in relation to various energy debates, the very same distal factors that marginalize the emancipatory rhetoric and practices also make the Polish context conducive for the logic of war to rise in it. The centralized decision-making, historical factors and distal context, because of which the notion of "energy security" is confused with "energy sovereignty," make it highly probable for the imperative of survival to rise in the country's energy affairs. The periodic rise of the logic of war in Poland is the single most important mechanism that can change the official rhetoric and practice and overshadow the dominant sustenance rationale. It also leads to the adoption of the confrontational policy stance that makes it harder to achieve regional cooperation in the area of gas politics in cases when historical legacy comes to the fore.

Overall, the analysis of the Polish case illustrates how the operation of different energy security logics within a specific domestic context determines different approaches and policy choices in the energy sector. It also brings further theoretical and empirical insights into the analysis of energy security and its logics. First, the comparison with Germany highlights that energy security logics are *contextual* and do not rise or manifest in the same way across different contexts—even in face of similar "trigger" events. On the one hand, the congruence of contextual factors that play out within the given constellation of actors determines which energy security logics can rise to the fore. On the other hand, the logics that already manifest can follow different trajectories of development (e.g., the transformative character of the logic of emancipation). Second, both the German and the Polish cases show that the logics of subsistence and emancipation appear to be closely linked and "evolutionary" in character, whereas the logic of war and the risk logic can occasionally rise, triggered by key developments in the regional and global energy sector, and cause major discursive and policy shifts.

Notes

1 Chmielewski, *Bezpieczeństwo Energetyczne Państwa*, 8.
2 Świątkowska, *Bezpieczeństwo Energetyczne Państw Grupy Wyszehradzkiej*.

3 Lasoń, "Polska Wobec Wyzwań Bezpieczeństwa Energetycznego," 235.
4 Mickiewicz and Sokołowska, "Bezpieczeństwo Energetyczne Europy Środkowo-Wschodniej," 23.
5 Bartodziej and Tomaszewski, *Polityka Energetyczna I Bezpieczeństwo Energetyczne*,73.
6 Łucki and Misiak, *Energetyka a Społeczeństwo*; Leszczyński, *Teoretyczny Wymiar Bezpieczeństwa Energetycznego*, 27.
7 Sobieski Institute, Interview; Independent energy expert, Interview; Ministry of Economy, Nuclear Energy Department, Interview; Ministry of Economy, Renewable Energy Department, Interview; Ministry of Foreign Affairs, Interview.
8 Płecha, "Powiązania Handlowe Z Rosyjskim Sektorem Paliw Płynnych I Gazu Ziemnego W Świetle Bezpieczeństwa Energetycznego Polski," 56.
9 Where the hierarchization of energy security dimensions followed: energy efficiency, increasing security of energy resources supply, diversification of electricity sources through the development of nuclear energy, development of renewable energy sources (biofuels), development of competitive fuel and energy markets, limiting the negative impact of the power industry on the environment.
10 "Projekt Polityki Energetycznej Polski Do 2050 Roku."
11 Pawlak, "Speech given at the 33rd Parliamentary Session."
12 "Presentation by the Prime Minister."
13 "6th Term of Office, 80th Parliamentary Session."
14 "5th Term of Office, 41st Parliamentary Session."
15 "5th Term of Office, 34th Parliamentary Session."
16 "Presentation by the Prime Minister," 318.
17 "6th Term of Office, 33rd Parliamentery Session."
18 Ibid.
19 "Presentation by the Prime Minister."
20 "6th Term of Office, 80th Parliamentary Session."
21 "Greens 2004" has not succeeded in being elected to the Polish lower chamber of parliament in any of the parliamentary elections so far.
22 Dariusz Szwed, Interview.
23 Szwed.
24 SGGW, Interview.
25 Ibid.
26 Heinrich-Böll-Stiftung Warsaw, Interview.
27 Ciută, "Conceptual Notes on Energy Security."
28 Twenty percent reduction in EU greenhouse emissions, raising the share of EU energy consumption from renewables to 20 percent and 20 percent improvement in the EU's energy efficiency.
29 Ministry of Environment, Interview.
30 Law and Justice, Interview.
31 PAP, "Kilian."
32 Think tank connected to the Law and Justice Party.
33 A Polish sociologist and scientist.
34 Sobieski Institute, Interview.
35 Wylizgała, "Polska a Pakiet Energetyczno Klimatyczny Unii Europejskiej," 225.
36 Jankowski, "Pakiet Energetyczno Klimatyczny Porażką Czy Zwycięstwem Polski I Unii?" 10–14.
37 "2012–02 News-Emisje CO2."
38 SGGW, Interview.
39 Mainly Germany and Denmark.
40 demosEUROPA, Interview; SGGW, Interview.
41 Wylizgała, "Polska a Pakiet Energetyczno Klimatyczny Unii Europejskiej," 224–5.
42 Ibid.

43 Ibid., 225
44 demosEUROPA, Interview.
45 Ministry of Environment, Interview.
46 Ibid.
47 Polski Komitet Energii Elektrycznej, "Komentarz PKEE Do Projektu Pakietu Klimatyczno-Energetycznego 2030."
48 Together with the Czech Republic, Finland, Greece and Great Britain.
49 Szydłowski, "Polska W Koalicji Przeciwko Redukcji Emisji Z Elektrowni."
50 "Pakiet Klimatyczny Zagrożeniem Dla Polski."
51 Kassenberg, "Program Dla Sektora Górnictwa Węgla Brunatnego Czyli Polska W Kontrze Do Polityki Klimatycznej UE."
52 Ibid.
53 "Polska Na Ostatnim Miejscu W UE W Realizacji Celów Klimatycznych."
54 At least in principle, since recent energy sector developments in Germany look less optimistic.
55 Materniak, "Energia Nuklearna W Polsce."
56 Ibid.
57 Przybojewska, "Energetyka Jądrowa W Polskiej Polityce Energetycznej," 64.
58 Przybojewska, "Energetyka Jądrowa W Polskiej Polityce Energetycznej"; Rafał Zasuń, "Dlaczego Energia Jądrowa?"
59 Wierciński, "Energia Nuklearna W Polsce?"
60 Wierciński, "Energia Nuklearna W Polsce?"; Batóg, "Polskie Elektrownie Jądrowe Będą Bezpieczne."
61 Independent energy expert, Interview.
62 Sobieski Institute, Interview.
63 PGE Energia Jądrowa—an energy company that is responsible for the development of the nuclear energy programme in Poland; a part of the bigger Polish Energy Group.
64 PGE, Interview.
65 Ministry of Environment, Interview.
66 Biernat, Mackowicz, and Seremak-Sęk, "Bezpieczeństwo Energetyczne Polski," 26–7.
67 Wierciński, "Energia Nuklearna W Polsce?"
68 Chancellery of the Sejm, Interview; Szwed, Interview.
69 SGGW, Interview.
70 SGGW, Interview; Szwed, Interview.
71 Wierciński, "Energia Nuklearna W Polsce?"; "Ocena Projektu Polityki Energetycznej Polski Do 2030 R."
72 Currently WISE Europa think tank (after merger of WISE Institute and demosEUROPA).
73 demosEUROPA, Interview.
74 Szwed, Interview.
75 Tomiałojć, "Energetyka Obywatelska, Czyli Od Kopalń Do Wiatru I Słońca."
76 Ibid.
77 Ministry of Economy, Nuclear Energy Department, Interview.
78 PGE II, Interview.
79 Rotkiewicz, "Gdzie Ta Apokalipsa?"
80 Ibid.
81 Ibid.
82 Ibid.
83 Polska Agencja Prasowa, "Polska Nie Zrezygnuje Z Programu Nuklearnego."
84 PGE, Interview.
85 Batóg, "Polskie Elektrownie Jądrowe Będą Bezpieczne."
86 Rotkiewicz, "Gdzie Ta Apokalipsa?"

87 Polska Agencja Prasowa, "Niemieckie 'nie' dla Polskich Elektrowni Atomowych."
88 Materniak, "Energia Nuklearna W Polsce."
89 Polska Agencja Prasowa, "Polska Nie Zrezygnuje Z Programu Nuklearnego."
90 "Wybuch W Fukushimie."
91 Materniak, "Energia Nuklearna W Polsce"; Polska Agencja Prasowa, "Polska Nie Zrezygnuje Z Programu Nuklearnego."
92 PGE, Interview.
93 Łazarewicz, "Atom Przechowany W Świerku."
94 PAP, "Polacy Szybko Nabierają Zaufania Do Energetyki Jądrowej."
95 Polska Agencja Prasowa, "CBOS."
96 Materniak, "Energia Nuklearna W Polsce."
97 "Energetyka jądrowa."
98 "Sondaż."
99 Ibid.
100 Ministry of Economy, Nuclear Energy Department, Interview.
101 Ibid.
102 SGGW, Interview.
103 Kosiński, "W Polsce W Końcu Powstanie Elektrownia Atomowa."
104 Ibid.
105 Ibid.
106 Ciepiela, "Polska Elektrownia Jądrowa Powstanie Po 2030 R."
107 Kassenberg, "Climate Policy and Energy Policy," 153. Emphases added.
108 Szwed, Interview.
109 Szwed and Maciejewska, *Demokracja Energetyczna*.
110 Ibid., 5.
111 Ibid., 12.
112 SGGW, Interview; Heinrich-Böll-Stiftung Warsaw, Interview.
113 Szulecki, Ancygier, and Szwed, "Energy Democratization?"
114 Szwed, Interview.
115 Ibid.
116 Szwed and Maciejewska, *Demokracja Energetyczna*, 4.
117 Ibid.
118 Ibid., 9.
119 Ibid., 4.
120 "Demokracja Energetyczna."
121 Szwed, Interview.
122 "Łódzkie/Brzeziny chcą produkować prąd na własne potrzeby."
123 gramwzielone.pl, "Burmistrz Brzezin o budowie pierwszego polskiego Smart City."
124 Olczak, "Bielsko-Biała: Miasto Dobrej Energii."
125 http://czestochowa2.energiaisrodowisko.pl/pl/category/efektywnosc-energetyczna/, City portal
126 Dybalski, "Lublin."
127 Szwed and Maciejewska, *Demokracja Energetyczna*, 19.
128 Szwed, Interview; SGGW, Interview.
129 demosEUROPA, Interview; SGGW, Interview; Chancellery of the Sejm, Interview.
130 Szulecki and Westphal, "The Cardinal Sins of European Energy Policy."
131 Robbins, *Political Ecology*; Jehlicka and Smith, "Out of the Woods and into the Lab."
132 Szwed, Interview; SGGW, Interview.
133 Lund, "Choice Awareness."
134 Ministry of Economy, Renewable Energy Department, Interview; Szwed, Interview.
135 SGGW, Interview.
136 Ministry of Environment, Interview.
137 Szwed, Interview; Chancellery of the Sejm, Interview.

138 Szwed, Interview; SGGW, Interview; Heinrich-Böll-Stiftung Warsaw, Interview; demosEUROPA, Interview.
139 Ministry of Environment, Interview.
140 Szwed, Interview; Chancellery of the Sejm, Interview.
141 E.g., Łucki and Misiak, *Energetyka a Społeczeństwo*.
142 Łucki and Misiak, *Energetyka a Społeczeństwo*, 44–5.
143 The ingredients of the energy culture include: (1) decarbonization of human activity; (2) improving the efficiency of processing of the primary energy; (3) improving the efficiency of energy use; (4) energy conservation by users; (5) providing for cheaper and reliable energy.
144 Łucki and Misiak, *Energetyka a Społeczeństwo*, 44–5.
145 Ibid., 71.
146 Ibid., 71.
147 Biuro analiz sejmowych—an office preparing the analysis and reports for members of the Polish lower chamber of parliament: Sejm.
148 Chancellery of the Sejm, Interview.
149 Ministry of Economy, Nuclear Energy Department, Interview.
150 Sobieski Institute, Interview.
151 demosEUROPA, Interview; Chancellery of the Sejm, Interview; Heinrich-Böll-Stiftung Warsaw, Interview.
152 Ibid.
153 demosEUROPA, Interview.
154 SGGW, Interview.
155 demosEUROPA, Interview.
156 Since the Greens 2004 political party is not in the Polish Sejm.
157 Szwed, Interview; Chancellery of the Sejm, Interview; demosEUROPA, Interview.
158 Szwed, Interview.
159 SGGW, Interview.
160 Sobieski Institute, Interview.
161 Ministry of Environment, Interview.
162 "Ustawa Z Dnia 20 Lutego 2015 R."
163 "Ustawa Z Dnia 20 Maja 2016 R."
164 "Ustawa Z Dnia 22 Czerwca 2016 R."
165 Kukuła, "Nie Ma Miejsca Dla Wiatraków."
166 "Analiza Projektu Nowelizacji Ustawy O OZE."
167 Ministry of Economy, "Polityka Energetyczna Polski Do 2050 Roku," June 2015, http://bip.me.gov.pl/node/24670.
168 gramwzielone.pl, "Polityka Energetyczna Polski Do 2050."
169 Koalicja Klimatyczna, "Stanowisko Koalicji Klimatycznej W Sprawie Projektu 'Polityki Energetycznej Polski Do 2050 Roku'."
170 gramwzielone.pl, "Polityka Energetyczna Polski Do 2050."
171 At least in the European context where it arises mainly in relation to pipeline politics. If considered in line with the original typology, it may also apply to resource wars.
172 Fischer, *Dywersyfikacja Kierunków Dostaw Gazu Do Polski W Latach 1997–2007*, 10–12.
173 Ibid.
174 Pawelczyk and Kudzia, "Skazani Na Gazprom."
175 Fischer, *Dywersyfikacja Kierunków Dostaw Gazu Do Polski W Latach 1997–2007*, 13.
176 Ibid.; Chekaleva-Demidovskaya, "Russian-Polish Relations."
177 Fischer, *Dywersyfikacja Kierunków Dostaw Gazu Do Polski W Latach 1997–2007*, 13; Heinrich, *Poland as a Transit Country for Russian Natural Gas*, 24.
178 Ibid.

179 Nowakowski, "Miotacz Gazu."
180 Lasoń, "Polska Wobec Wyzwań Bezpieczeństwa Energetycznego," 238–45.
181 Heinrich, *Poland as a Transit Country for Russian Natural Gas*, 23.
182 Cohen, "The North European Gas Pipeline Threatens Europe's Energy Security"; Parnes, "Lęk Przed Pustą Rurą"; Heinrich, *Poland as a Transit Country for Russian Natural Gas*, 83.
183 Nowakowski, "Energetyczna Zimna Wojna."
184 Gonchar, "Gazowy Blitzkrieg?"
185 Baliszewski, "Rury Wojny."
186 Piński, "Zabór Energetyczny."
187 Cohen, "Geopolityczna Smycz."
188 Woźniak, Nowakowski, and Sadowski, "Gazowe Okrążenie Polski."
189 Heinrich, *Poland as a Transit Country for Russian Natural Gas*, 25.
190 Łakoma, "Polska Sama Musi Zadbać O Gwarancje Dostaw Surowców."
191 Kubacki, "Nord Stream, Czyli Jak Nie Robi Się Biznesu."
192 Chekaleva-Demidovskaya, "Russian–Polish Relations," 6.
193 Kubacki, "Nord Stream, Czyli Jak Nie Robi Się Biznesu."
194 Grzeszak and Ostrowski, "Taniec Na Rurach."
195 Lasoń, "Polska Wobec Wyzwań Bezpieczeństwa Energetycznego," 252.
196 Naimski and Staniłko, "Gazowa Porażka Polskich Negocjatorów."
197 Bieleń, "Deficyt Realizmu W Polskiej Polityce Zagranicznej," 21–2; Kubacki, "Nord Stream, Czyli Jak Nie Robi Się Biznesu."
198 Bieleń, "Deficyt Realizmu W Polskiej Polityce Zagranicznej"; Grzeszak and Ostrowski, "Taniec Na Rurach."
199 Bieleń, "Deficyt Realizmu W Polskiej Polityce Zagranicznej," 13–14; Szczęśniak, "O Co Chodzi Unii W Sporze Gazowym Między Polską a Rosją?," 43.
200 Kaźmierczak, *Bezpieczeństwo Energetyczne*, 89; Independent energy expert, Interview; Sobieski Institute, Interview.
201 tvn24.pl, "Duda Na Spotkaniu Grupy Wyszehradzkiej."
202 Ibid.
203 Smyrgała, "Co Przyniesie Polsce Nordstream 2?—Opinie."
204 Smyrgała, "LNG to Priorytet—Opinie"; Kublik, "Polska w pułapce Nord Stream 2."
205 Smyrgała, "Co Przyniesie Polsce Nordstream 2?—Opinie"; "Czaputowicz: uważamy, że Nord Stream 2 jest szkodliwy."
206 "Gowin: Oczekuję Od Niemiec Solidarności."
207 "Solidarność Po Niemiecku," 24.
208 "Czaputowicz: USA I Polska Podzielają Te Same Wartości."
209 "Gazprom Kontra Europa."
210 Kacewicz, "Nord Stream II."
211 Kazanecki, "Bezpieczeństwo Energetyczne W Polskiej Debacie Publicznej W Okresie 21.10.2007–9.01.2009 R," 259–63.
212 Bartodziej and Tomaszewski, *Polityka Energetyczna i Bezpieczeństwo Energetyczne*, 129.
213 Ibid.
214 Ibid.
215 Ibid., 131.
216 Polskie Górnictwo Naftowe i Gazownictwo—Polish Oil and Gas Company.
217 Pawelczyk and Kudzia, "Nabici W Rurę."
218 Chmielewski, *Bezpieczeństwo Energetyczne Państwa*, 81.
219 Grzeszak and Walat, "Port Zamiast Rury."
220 Grzeszak, "Świeczki Nie Gaście."
221 Szczęśniak, "O Co Chodzi Unii W Sporze Gazowym Między Polską a Rosją?," 42.
222 Grzeszak, "Gaz Zasmucający."
223 Ibid.

224 Szwed, Interview; SGGW, Interview; Marcin Popkiewicz, Interview.
225 Waszkielewicz, "Droższy Gaz, Byle Nie Z Rosji."
226 Ibid.
227 Ibid.
228 Cohen, "The North European Gas Pipeline Threatens Europe's Energy Security," 3.
229 Institute of Public Affairs, "Ocena Dążeń Rosji I Konfliktu Rosyjsko-Gruzińskiego."
230 Ibid.
231 Kozmana, "Polacy Chcą Debaty O Projekcie Atomowym."

References

"5th Term of Office, 34th Parliamentary Session, Day 2; 'Sprawozdanie Komisji Gospodarki O Stanowisku Senatu W Sprawie Ustawy O Zapasach Ropy Naftowej, Produktów Naftowych I Gazu Ziemnego Oraz Zasadach Postępowania W Sytuacjach Zagrożenia Bezpieczeństwa Paliwowego Państwa I Zakłóceń Na Rynku Naftowym,'" February 15, 2007.

"5th Term of Office, 41st Parliamentary Session, 4th Day; Informacja Ministra Spraw Zagranicznych O Zadaniach Polskiej Polityki Zagranicznej W 2007 R," May 11, 2007.

"6th Term of Office, 33rd Parliamentery Session, 3rd Day; Informacja Prezesa Rady Ministrów Na Temat Bezpieczeństwa Energetycznego Polski W Związku Z Przerwaniem Dostarczania Gazu Ziemnego Z Rosji Przez Terytorium Ukrainy," January 9, 2009.

"6th Term of Office, 80th Parliamentary Session, 3rd Day; Informacja Rządu O Aktualnej Sytuacji I Perspektywach Polskiej Energetyki," December 16, 2010.

"2012–02 News-Emisje CO2." *handel-emisjami.pl*, December 3, 2012. www.handel-emisjami.pl/fileadmin/handel-emisjami/Dateien/News-emisje/2012/02-2012_News_emisje_CO2__PL.pdf.

"Analiza Projektu Nowelizacji Ustawy O OZE." *ClientEarth*, October 5, 2016. http://wiecejnizenergia.pl/wp-content/uploads/2016/05/Publikacje_analiza-projektu-nowelizacji-ustawy-o-oze-coll-pl1.pdf.

Baliszewski, Dariusz. "Rury Wojny." *Wprost*, February 5, 2006. www.wprost.pl/ar/86453/Rury-wojny/.

Bartodziej, Gerhard, and Michał Tomaszewski. *Polityka Energetyczna I Bezpieczeństwo Energetyczne*. Racibórz: Wydawnictwo Nowa Energia, 2009.

Batóg, Patrycja. "Polskie Elektrownie Jądrowe Będą Bezpieczne." *Elektrownia-Jadrowa.pl*, April 26, 2010. http://elektrownia-jadrowa.pl/235.html.

Bieleń, Stanisław. "Deficyt Realizmu W Polskiej Polityce Zagranicznej." *Stosunki Międzynarodowe*, no. 3/4 (t. 38) (2008): 9–29.

Biernat, Monika, Patrycja Mackowicz, and Kinga Seremak-Sęk. "Bezpieczeństwo Energetyczne Polski." In *Bezpieczeństwo Narodowe*, 14–27. 1-2006/1. Biuro Bezpieczeństwa Narodowego, n.d.

Chancellery of the Sejm. Interview, Warsaw, June 7, 2013.

Chekaleva-Demidovskaya, Maria. "Russian–Polish Relations: Need for New Strategic Approach." *Fellowship Program for Young Russian Policy and Opinion Makers*, 2005, 1–5.

Chmielewski, Adam. *Bezpieczeństwo Energetyczne Państwa: Geopolityczne Uwarunkowania*. Wydawnictwo MM, 2009.

Ciepiela, Dariusz. "Polska Elektrownia Jądrowa Powstanie Po 2030 R." *wnp.pl*, March 31, 2018. https://energetyka.wnp.pl/polska-elektrownia-jadrowa-powstanie-po-2030-r,320551_1_0_0.html.

Ciută, Felix. "Conceptual Notes on Energy Security: Total or Banal Security?" *Security Dialogue* 41, no. 2 (2010): 123–44.

Cohen, Ariel. "Geopolityczna Smycz." *Wprost*, December 15, 2006. www.wprost.pl/ar/96425/Geopolityczna-smycz/.

Cohen, Ariel. "The North European Gas Pipeline Threatens Europe's Energy Security." *The Heritage Foundation* 26 (2006). www.massenbach-world.de/media/116800689f529cf2ffff831aac144225.pdf.

"Czaputowicz: USA I Polska Podzielają Te Same Wartości." *Rzeczpospolita*, January 27, 2018. www.rp.pl/Dyplomacja/180129389-Czaputowicz-USA-i-Polska-podzielaja-te-same-wartosci.html.

"Czaputowicz: uważamy, że Nord Stream 2 jest szkodliwy | Surowce." *TVN24 BiS*, August 20, 2018. https://tvn24bis.pl/article/url/862401.

"Demokracja Energetyczna. Projekt Przestrzenie Dialogu." *Sylabus Ekomiasta*, n.d. http://eko.pomyslodalnia.pl/demokracja-energetyczna/.

demosEUROPA. Interview, Warsaw, May 24, 2013.

"Dlaczego Energia Jądrowa?" *elektrownia-jadrowa.pl*, n.d. http://elektrownia-jadrowa.pl/Dlaczego-energia-jadrowa-.html.

Dybalski, Jakub. "Lublin. Wszystkie autobusy MPK będą miały panele fotowoltaiczne." *www.transport-publiczny.pl*, May 26, 2017. www.transport-publiczny.pl/wiadomosci/lublin-wszystkie-autobusy-mpk-beda-mialy-panele-fotowoltaiczne-55324.html.

"Energetyka jądrowa." *Inwestycje Energetyczne*. Accessed January 4, 2019. http://inwestycjeenergetyczne.itc.pw.edu.pl/energetyka-jadrowa/.

Fischer, Konrad. *Dywersyfikacja Kierunków Dostaw Gazu Do Polski W Latach 1997–2007*. Szkoła Główna Handlowa w Warszawie, 2008.

"Gazprom Kontra Europa—Pytania Bez Odpowiedzi." *Rzeczpospolita*, August 10, 2015. https://energia.rp.pl/surowce-i-paliwa/gaz/10139-gazprom-kontra-europa-pytania-bez-odpowiedzi.

Gonchar, Mychail. "Gazowy Blitzkrieg?" *Wprost*, March 26, 2006. www.wprost.pl/ar/88038/Gazowy-blitzkrieg.html.

"Gowin: Oczekuję Od Niemiec Solidarności," April 18, 2017. www.rp.pl/Polityka/304189946-Gowin-Oczekuje-od-Niemiec-solidarnosci.html.

gramwzielone.pl. "Burmistrz Brzezin o budowie pierwszego polskiego Smart City," July 15, 2015. http://gramwzielone.pl/trendy/17152/burmistrz-brzezin-o-budowie-pierwszego-polskiego-smart-city-wywiad.

gramwzielone.pl. "Polityka Energetyczna Polski Do 2050—'Scenariusz Nie Do Przyjęcia,'" September 22, 2015. http://gramwzielone.pl/trendy/18183/polityka-energetyczna-polski-do-2050-scenariusz-nie-do-przyjecia.

Grzeszak, Adam. "Gaz Zasmucający." *Polityka*, October 13, 2009. www.polityka.pl/tygodnikpolityka/rynek/269459,1,zima-wraca-temat-gazu.read.

Grzeszak, Adam. "Świeczki Nie Gaście." *Polityka*, October 12, 2011. http://archiwum.polityka.pl/art/swieczki-nie-gascie,432925.html.

Grzeszak, Adam, and Marek Ostrowski. "Taniec Na Rurach." *Polityka*, October 21, 2006.

Grzeszak, Adam, and Tomasz Walat. "Port Zamiast Rury." *Polityka*, January 14, 2006.

Heinrich, Andreas. *Poland as a Transit Country for Russian Natural Gas: Potential for Conflict*. Koszalin Institute of Comparative European Studies (KICES), 2007.

Heinrich-Böll-Stiftung Warsaw. Interview, June 3, 2013.

Independent energy expert. Interview, May 16, 2013.

Institute of Public Affairs. "Ocena Dążeń Rosji I Konfliktu Rosyjsko-Gruzińskiego," 2008. www.isp.org.pl/files/13327689280252247001221053324.pdf.

Jankowski, Bolesław. "Pakiet Energetyczno Klimatyczny Porażką Czy Zwycięstwem Polski I Unii?" *EnergSys*, November 25, 2008. www.energsys.com.pl/fileadmin/pdf/03_Ekspertyza_Pakiet.pdf.

Jehlicka, Petr, and Joe Smith. "Out of the Woods and into the Lab: Exploring the Strange Marriage of American Woodcraft and Soviet Ecology in Czech Environmentalism." *Environment and History* 13, no. 2 (2007): 187–210.

Kacewicz, Michał. "Nord Stream II. Wielka gra Kremla o bałtycką rurę. Co grozi Polsce?" *Newsweek.pl*, May 5, 2017. www.newsweek.pl/swiat/polityka/nord-stream-ii-o-co-chodzi-w-sporze-o-rosyjski-gazociag/6p5zv38.

Kassenberg, Andrzej. "Climate Policy and Energy Policy: Convergence or Contradiction? The Case of Poland." In *Energy Security and Climate Change*. Warsaw: Polish Institute of International Affairs, 2009.

Kassenberg, Andrzej. "Program Dla Sektora Górnictwa Węgla Brunatnego Czyli Polska W Kontrze Do Polityki Klimatycznej UE." *chronmyklimat.pl*, June 22, 2018. http://chronmyklimat.pl/wiadomosci/polityka-klimatyczna/program-dla-sektora-gornictwa-wegla-brunatnego-czyli-polska-w-kontrze-do-polityki-klimatycznej-ue.

Kazanecki, Wojciech. "Bezpieczeństwo Energetyczne W Polskiej Debacie Publicznej W Okresie 21.10.2007–9.01.2009 R. W Świetle Debat Parlamentarnych." In *Bezpieczeństwo Energetyczne Europy Środkowej*. Toruń: Wydawnictwo Adam Marszałek, 2010.

Kaźmierczak, Tomasz Wojciech. *Bezpieczeństwo Energetyczne—Implikacje Uzależnienia Polski Od Importu Gazu Ziemnego: Zarys Problemu*. Warszawa: Promotor, 2008.

Koalicja Klimatyczna. "Stanowisko Koalicji Klimatycznej W Sprawie Projektu 'Polityki Energetycznej Polski Do 2050 Roku,'" September 18, 2015. www.koalicjaklimatyczna.org/lang/pl/page/stanowiska_koalicji/id/7/.

Kosiński, Dawid. "W Polsce W Końcu Powstanie Elektrownia Atomowa," March 8, 2017. www.spidersweb.pl/2017/08/elektrownia-atomowa-w-polsce.html.

Kozmana, Magdalena. "Polacy Chcą Debaty O Projekcie Atomowym." *Rzeczpospolita*, October 25, 2010. www.rp.pl/artykul/554249-Polacy-chca-debaty-o-projekcie-atomowym.html.

Kubacki, Adam. "Nord Stream, Czyli Jak Nie Robi Się Biznesu." *Newsweek*, November 9, 2009. www.redakcja.newsweek.pl/Tekst/Polityka-Polska/533090,Nord-stream-czyli-jak-nie-robi-sie-biznesu.html.

Kublik, Andrzej. "Polska w pułapce Nord Stream 2. Przed nami wybór jak między dżumą a cholerą." *wyborcza.pl*, September 18, 2017. http://wyborcza.pl/7,155290,22379438,polska-w-pulapce-nord-stream-2.html.

Kukuła, Wojciech. "Nie Ma Miejsca Dla Wiatraków." *chronmyklimat.pl*, June 29, 2016. http://chronmyklimat.pl/projekty/klimapolka/wiadomosci/nie-ma-miejsca-dla-wiatrakow.

Łakoma, Agnieszka. "Polska Sama Musi Zadbać O Gwarancje Dostaw Surowców." *Rzeczpospolita*, December 13, 2007. www.rp.pl/artykul/9211,76410.html.

Lasoń, Marcin. "Polska Wobec Wyzwań Bezpieczeństwa Energetycznego." In *Międzynarodowe Bezpieczeństwo Energetyczne W XXI Wieku*. Kraków: Oficyna Wydawnicza AFM, 2008.

Law and Justice. Interview, Warsaw, June 21, 2013.

Łazarewicz, Cezary. "Atom Przechowany W Świerku." *Polityka*, November 19, 2009. www.polityka.pl/tygodnikpolityka/spoleczenstwo/1500635,2,energia-atomowa-w-polsce.read.

Leszczyński, Tadeusz Zbigniew. *Teoretyczny Wymiar Bezpieczeństwa Energetycznego*. Warsaw: Wyższa Szkoła Informatyki, Zarządzania i Administracji, 2012.

"Łódzkie/ Brzeziny chcą produkować prąd na własne potrzeby." *finanse.wp.pl*, July 29, 2014. https://finanse.wp.pl/lodzkie-brzeziny-chca-produkowac-prad-na-wlasne-potrzeby-6116043114145409a.
Łucki, Zbigniew, and Władysław Misiak. *Energetyka a Społeczeństwo: Aspekty Socjologiczne*. Wydawnictwo Naukowe PWN, 2010.
Lund, Henrik. "Choice Awareness: The Development of Technological and Institutional Choice in the Public Debate of Danish Energy Planning." *Journal of Environmental Policy and Planning* 2, no. 3 (2000): 249–59.
Materniak, Dariusz. "Energia Nuklearna W Polsce." *Portal Spraw Zagranicznych* [blog], April 15, 2011. www.psz.pl/119-energia/energia-nuklearna-w-polsce.
Mickiewicz, Piotr, and Patrycja Sokołowska. "Bezpieczeństwo Energetyczne Europy Środkowo-Wschodniej." *Wydawnictwo Adam Marszałek, Dolnośląska Szkoła Wyższa, Instytut Bezpieczeństwa I Spraw Międzynarodowych, Toruń*, 2010.
Ministry of Economy. "Polityka Energetyczna Polski Do 2050 Roku," June 2015. http://bip.me.gov.pl/node/24670.
Ministry of Economy, Nuclear Energy Department. Interview, Warsaw, May 16, 2013.
Ministry of Economy, Renewable Energy Department. Interview, Warsaw, May 23, 2013.
Ministry of Environment. Interview, Warsaw, June 13, 2013.
Ministry of Foreign Affairs. Interview, Warsaw, June 7, 2013.
Naimski, Piotr, and Jan Staniłko. "Gazowa Porażka Polskich Negocjatorów." *Rzeczpospolita*, June 10, 2010. http://archiwum.rp.pl/artykul/954103-Gazowa-porazka-polskich-negocjatorow.html.
Nowakowski, Jerzy Marek. "Energetyczna Zimna Wojna." *Wprost*, May 14, 2006. www.wprost.pl/ar/90039/Energetyczna-zimna-wojna/.
Nowakowski, Jerzy Marek. "Miotacz Gazu." *Wprost*, January 15, 2006. www.wprost.pl/ar/85836/Miotacz-gazu/.
"Ocena Projektu Polityki Energetycznej Polski Do 2030 R." *Greenpeace*, March 2009. www.greenpeace.org/poland/Global/poland/report/2009/3/polityka-energetyczna-brief.pdf.
Olczak, Katarzyna. "Bielsko-Biała: Miasto Dobrej Energii." *teraz-srodowisko.pl*, July 13, 2016. www.teraz-srodowisko.pl/aktualnosci/Miasto-dobrej-energii-2375.html.
"Pakiet Klimatyczny Zagrożeniem Dla Polski. Do 2030 Roku Będziemy Musieli Zamknąć Wszystkie Elektrownie Węglowe." *Wpolityce.pl*, January 21, 2015.
PAP. "Kilian: Polityka Klimatyczna W Czasie Kryzysu? Fanaberia." *Wprost*, September 2012. www.wprost.pl/ar/346167/Kilian-polityka-klimatyczna-w-czasie-kryzysu-Fanaberia/.
PAP. "Polacy Szybko Nabierają Zaufania Do Energetyki Jądrowej." *Wiadomosci.wp.pl*, May 12, 2010. http://wiadomosci.wp.pl/kat,24915,title,Polacy-szybko-nabieraja-zaufania-do-energetyki-jadrowej,wid,12229612,wiadomosc.html?ticaid=116c16.
Parnes, Jakub. "Lęk Przed Pustą Rurą." *Wiadomosci.polska.pl*, July 15, 2007. http://wiadomosci.polska.pl/specdlapolski/article,Lek_przed_pusta_rura,id,285019.htm.
Pawelczyk, Grzegorz, and Piotr Kudzia. "Nabici W Rurę." *Wprost*, August 15, 1999. www.wprost.pl/ar/5295/Nabici-w-rure/.
Pawelczyk, Grzegorz, and Piotr Kudzia. "Skazani Na Gazprom." *Wprost*, October 25, 1998. www.wprost.pl/ar/6589/Skazani-na-Gazprom/?pg=0.
Pawlak, Waldemar. "Speech given at the 33rd Parliamentary Session," January 9, 2009. http://orka2.sejm.gov.pl/StenoInter6.nsf/main?OpenForm.
PGE (Polish Energy Group). Interview, Warsaw, May 21, 2013.

PGE II. Interview, Warsaw, May 21, 2013.
Piński, Jan. "Zabór Energetyczny." *Wprost*, December 15, 2006. www.wprost.pl/ar/97179/Zabor-energetyczny/.
Płecha, Anna. "Powiązania Handlowe Z Rosyjskim Sektorem Paliw Płynnych I Gazu Ziemnego W Świetle Bezpieczeństwa Energetycznego Polski." Studium Magisterskie. Szkoła Główna Handlowa w Warszawie, 2006. www.cire.pl/praca/pracedyplomowe/praca6/AnnaPlechaPracamagisterska.pdf.
Polska Agencja Prasowa. "CBOS: Większość Polaków Przeciw Budowie Elektrowni Atomowej." *www.pb.pl* [blog], April 28, 2011. www.pb.pl/2416832,63230,cbos-wiekszosc-polakow-przeciw-budowie-elektrowni-atomowej.
Polska Agencja Prasowa. "Niemieckie 'nie' dla Polskich Elektrowni Atomowych." *www.wprost.pl* [blog], March 15, 2011. www.wprost.pl/swiat/235768/Niemieckie-nie-dla-polskich-elektrowni-atomowych.html.
Polska Agencja Prasowa. "Polska Nie Zrezygnuje Z Programu Nuklearnego." *www.forbes.pl*, April 12, 2011. www.forbes.pl/artykuly/sekcje/Wydarzenia/polska-nie-zrezygnuje-z-programu-nuklearnego,13663,1#.
"Polska Na Ostatnim Miejscu W UE W Realizacji Celów Klimatycznych." June 18, 2018. http://chronmyklimat.pl/wiadomosci/polityka-klimatyczna/polska-na-ostatnim-miejscu-w-ue-w-realizacji-celow-klimatycznych.
Polski Komitet Energii Elektrycznej. "Komentarz PKEE Do Projektu Pakietu Klimatyczno-Energetycznego 2030." *www.cire.pl*, January 23, 2014. www.cire.pl/item,88010,13,0,0,0,0,0,komentarz-pkee-do-projektu-pakietu-klimatyczno-energetycznego-2030.html.
Popkiewicz, Marcin. Interview, Warsaw, June 10, 2013.
"Presentation by the Prime Minister of the Action Plan of the Council of Ministers with a Request for a Vote of Confidence at the 2nd Parliamentary Session, Day 1," November 23, 2007. http://orka2.sejm.gov.pl/Debata6nsf/91668423b136667cc12573930043a099/c2f0913296a12fedc12573ad0041f851?OpenDocument.
"Projekt Polityki Energetycznej Polski Do 2050 Roku." Ministry of Energy, August 2014. http://gramwzielone.pl/uploads/files/Projekt%20PEP%202050.pdf.
Przybojewska, Ilona. "Energetyka Jądrowa W Polskiej Polityce Energetycznej—Uwarunkowania Prawne I Faktyczne." In *Polska Polityka Energetyczna—Wczoraj, Dziś, Jutro*. Warsaw: Prezes Urzędu Regulacji Energetyki, 2010.
Robbins, Paul. *Political Ecology: A Critical Introduction*. Oxford: Oxford University Press, 2004.
Rotkiewicz, Marcin. "Gdzie Ta Apokalipsa?" *Polityka*, March 28, 2011. www.polityka.pl/tygodnikpolityka/nauka/1514220,1,media-a-sprawa-elektrowni-w-fukushimie.read.
SGGW (Warsaw University of Life Sciences). Interview, Warsaw, June 12, 2013.
Smyrgała, Dominik. "Co Przyniesie Polsce Nordstream 2?—Opinie." *Rzeczpospolita*, September 9, 2015. www.rp.pl/Opinie/309099933-Co-przyniesie-Polsce-Nordstream-2.html.
Smyrgała, Dominik. "LNG to Priorytet—Opinie." *Rzeczpospolita*, November 9, 2015. www.rp.pl/Opinie/309119824-LNG-to-priorytet.html.
Sobieski Institute. Interview, Warsaw, May 22, 2013.
"'Solidarność Po Niemiecku.' Wpływ Nord Stream II Na Polskę, Europę Środkową I Porządek Prawny UE." *Energetyka24*, May 9, 2015. www.energetyka24.com/solidarnosc-po-niemiecku-wplyw-nord-stream-ii-na-polske-europe-srodkowa-i-porzadek-prawny-ue.
"Sondaż: Polacy znów przeciw atomowi." *Newsweek.pl*, April 28, 2011. www.newsweek.pl/polska/sondaz-polacy-znow-przeciw-atomowi/x55yt3l.

Świątkowska, Joanna (ed.). *Bezpieczeństwo Energetyczne Państw Grupy Wyszehradzkiej. Jak Zmieniają Się Relacje Energetyczne W Europie*. Kraków: Instytut Kościuszki, 2011.

Szczęśniak, Andrzej. "O Co Chodzi Unii W Sporze Gazowym Między Polską a Rosją?" In *Bezpieczeństwo Energetyczne—Rynki Surowców I Energii*. Poznań: Wydawnictwo Wyższej Szkoły Bezpieczeństwa, 2011.

Szulecki, Kacper, Andrzej Ancygier, and Dariusz Szwed. "Energy Democratization? Societal Aspects of de-Carbonization in the German and Polish Energy Sectors." *Environmental Studies and Policy Research Institute: Wroclaw*, March 9, 2015.

Szulecki, Kacper, and Kirsten Westphal. "The Cardinal Sins of European Energy Policy: Nongovernance in an Uncertain Global Landscape." *Global Policy* 5, no. s1 (2014): 38–51.

Szwed, Dariusz, and Beata Maciejewska. *Demokracja Energetyczna*. Warsaw: Zielony Instytut, 2014.

Szwed, Dariusz. Interview, Warsaw, May 27, 2013.

Szydłowski, Kamil. "Polska W Koalicji Przeciwko Redukcji Emisji Z Elektrowni." *chronmyklimat.pl*, October 25, 2016. http://chronmyklimat.pl/wiadomosci/polityka-klimatyczna/polska-w-koalicji-przeciwko-redukcji-emisji-z-elektrowni.

Tomiałojć, Ludwik. "Energetyka Obywatelska, Czyli Od Kopalń Do Wiatru I Słońca." *Czysta Energia* 80, no. 6 (2008): 20–3.

tvn24.pl. "Duda Na Spotkaniu Grupy Wyszehradzkiej," December 10, 2018. www.tvn24.pl/wiadomosci-ze-swiata,2/duda-na-spotkaniu-grupy-wyszehradzkiej,875629.html.

"Ustawa Z Dnia 20 Lutego 2015 R. O Odnawialnych Źródłach Energii." Sejm, February 20, 2015. http://prawo.sejm.gov.pl/isap.nsf/DocDetails.xsp?id=WDU20150000478.

"Ustawa Z Dnia 20 Maja 2016 R. O Inwestycjach W Zakresie Elektrowni Wiatrowych." Dziennik Ustaw Rzeczypospolitej Polskiej, 2016. http://dziennikustaw.gov.pl/du/2016/961/1.

"Ustawa Z Dnia 22 Czerwca 2016 R. O Zmianie Ustawy O Odnawialnych Źródłach Energii Oraz Niektórych Innych Ustaw." Sejm, June 22, 2016. http://prawo.sejm.gov.pl/isap.nsf/DocDetails.xsp?id=WDU20160000925.

Waszkielewicz, Bernadeta. "Droższy Gaz, Byle Nie Z Rosji." *Rzeczpospolita*, January 17, 2009. www.rp.pl/artykul/249551-Drozszy-gaz-byle-nie-z-Rosji-.html.

Wierciński, Jacek. "Energia Nuklearna W Polsce? Debata Polskiej Racji Stanu." *wybrzeze.24.pl*, April 11, 2011. http://wybrzeze24.pl/aktualnosci/energia-nuklearna-w-polsce-debata-polskiej-racji-stanu.

Woźniak, Piotr, Jerzy Marek Nowakowski, and Grzegorz Sadowski. "Gazowe Okrążenie Polski." *Wprost*, 2005.

"Wybuch W Fukushimie. Uszkodzony Reaktor Nr 2." *TVN24.pl*, March 15, 2011. www.tvn24.pl/r/213144.

Wylizgała, Hanna. "Polska a Pakiet Energetyczno Klimatyczny Unii Europejskiej." In *Bezpieczeństwo Energetyczne Europy Środkowej*. Toruń: Wydawnictwo Adam Marszałek, 2010.

Zasuń, Rafał. "Dlaczego Energia Jądrowa?," *Elektrownia-Jadrowa.pl*, n.d., http://elektrownia-jadrowa.pl/Dlaczego-energia-jadrowa-.html.

4 Ukraine

Energy policy within geopolitical constraints

Introduction

The developments in the Ukrainian energy sector have a crucial influence on the country's political stability and the issue of energy security that gained prominence during the gas disputes with Russia in 2006 and 2009, became intertwined with the national security agenda after the outbreak of the Russian–Ukrainian military conflict in 2014. Although it became clear that after years of Ukraine's maneuvering between Western and Eastern policy influences the country had to make a clear shift towards the former, Ukrainian domestic energy policy is anything but less complicated as a result. The increase in gas prices due to the strained relations with the Russian supplier tends to dominate the current political agenda and gives rise to the right-wing political populism. The logic of war that literally plays out in the persistent conflict in the East also permeates to Ukraine's energy affairs, where it frequently gives rise to sharp rhetoric and confrontational policy stances in the energy sector. Additionally, the idea of energy independence emerges not only in relation to pipeline politics, but started to serve as a justification for a number of energy policies that were traditionally driven by pure economic calculations, such as nuclear. If the further development of nuclear energy in Ukraine, despite its Chernobyl legacy, is rather surprising, it continues within a specific distal context where the need for "energy sovereignty" increasingly plays a role. At the same time, the outbreak of war with Russia shook the domestic status quo in Ukrainian energy affairs and gave a new impetus to much-needed energy-efficiency reforms as well as social mobilization in energy-related initiatives. Although a number of local NGOs have been trying to promote progressive solutions based on small-scale renewables and energy efficiency measures for years, their voice was not heard—partly because of their own shortcomings and partly because of the domestic context where the mainstream public discourse and policy remain dominated by oligarchic interests. The ongoing conflict led to a significant reshuffle within the domestic constellation of actors and gave more advantage to the societal actors.

This chapter takes the reader through the nuances of the currently complicated energy security reasoning in Ukraine. It makes sense of it by analyzing the energy security logics that play a crucial role in the Ukrainian context of nuclear, fossil fuel and renewable energy/energy-efficiency debates and policy developments. Similarly to the German and Polish cases, the analysis starts "from within" the logic of subsistence marked by the multiplication of actors and understandings of energy security. First, its various definitions and conceptualizations in Ukraine are scrutinized. Then the discussion moves to the contestation over the changing policy directions and priorities of energy security in Ukraine. The latter is best illustrated through the example of the workings on subsequent drafts of the national energy strategies (2030 and 2035)—prior to the outbreak of the military conflict with Russia and in its aftermath. The dynamic of the development of both documents illustrates the specifics of the Ukrainian energy context with its multiple actors, oligarchic interests, centralized decision-making and the dominant imperative of sustenance that drives energy security policy with a focus on the use of domestic energy resources. The workings of the National Energy Strategy 2035 in the post-2014 context also mark a domestic power reshuffle towards a more climate-friendly energy agenda and greater inclusion of societal actors. Although the wider prospects for the gradual democratization of the domestic energy sector remain out of reach because of both technical and societal aspects, first initiatives are gradually emerging and add yet another nuance to the complex Ukrainian energy affairs. However, as further discussion explores, green actors struggle to promote the democratic ideals of self-reliance in a country that remains at war. The imperative of survival manifested in Ukraine's pipeline politics in the aftermath of the 2006 and 2009 gas crises, but the developments of 2014 caused it to become entrenched in the entire policy scene, where it leads to discursive shifts in the framing of energy policy on multiple levels—including local. In this light, the virtually non-existent debate on nuclear energy safety is just a footnote. The puzzling lack of the risk logic in a country that had to deal with the consequences of the Chernobyl catastrophe was also visible in the post-Fukushima context. Yet, the absence of the imperative of prevention and the current plans to develop nuclear power plants could be further explained by context-determined societal disengagement coupled with the dominance of the subsistence logic that is increasingly underpinned by the idea of energy independence at all costs.

Around the subsistence logic

Conceptualizing energy security in the Ukrainian context

Similarly to the German and Polish contexts, definitions of energy security in Ukraine vary, as depending on the actors who frame them, different aspects come to the fore of the energy security agenda. Not surprisingly, given the pressing problems of the Ukrainian energy sector, the majority of actors over the years pointed either to energy efficiency,[1, 2] or energy market reforms that would lead to increased competitiveness and transparency,[3] as main priorities in ensuring Ukraine's energy security. The first aspect is important not only for the Ukrainian companies that need to modernize in order to save energy, but also for the Ukrainian communal branch, where old water systems and heating devices—and often entire buildings—should be reconstructed. Prior to the conflict with Russia aspects that were frequently present in energy security definitions included: diversification of energy supply, investment in Ukraine's own fossil fuel resources and extraction technologies, sustainability of the domestic coal sector, consolidation of energy networks,[4] increasing innovation of energy companies, increase of energy fuels' reserves or finally the development of renewables.[5] Although even before 2014 it was generally acknowledged that maintaining good cooperation with Russia regarding gas supplies was strategically important for Ukraine,[6] the economic and political costs of overdependence on a gas monopolist already constituted a primary policy concern. The outbreak of the war significantly changed the situation in the Ukrainian gas (increased prices) and coal (occupation of the Donbas region) sectors, and the reasoning about domestic energy policy shifted towards limiting Ukraine's energy dependence on Russia to the absolute minimum. The new energy policy agenda focused on diversification plans that would include investments in the LNG terminal, shale gas and further development of the nuclear energy sector. Therefore, whereas similarly to the Polish context the notions of "energy security" and "energy sovereignty" used to be confused and used interchangeably in Ukraine, currently the former is often understood as an outright "energy independence." This "island thinking" clearly contradicts the more market-oriented approach to energy security that was typical for the German context.

The outbreak of the Russian–Ukrainian conflict and the resulting energy policy shift also gradually impacted Ukraine's approach to energy security dimensions that relate to energy efficiency, renewable energy or sustainable development. Prior to 2014 the definitions of energy security in Ukraine often reflected a typical hierarchization—where the economic aspects were put ahead of issues such as environmental acceptability or social stability—with the latter, more often than not, being omitted altogether.[7] Additionally, as opposed to the German context, where factors such as security of energy supply and environmental protection tend to be seen as complementary, in Ukraine they used to be perceived as mostly contradictory goals. Some studies even explicitly argued that aspects of energy security such as ecological impact, physical accessibility of resources, the economic value of energy resources and their efficient use, are in fact conflictual.[8] Not surprisingly, in this context, calls for adopting more inclusive approaches to energy security that would incorporate environmental or societal aspects used to be rare and confined mostly to the "green" actors. For example, some early analyses on the topic highlighted the link between energy security and the possibilities of sustainable development and—among the areas that require special focus—listed not only the reduction of energy dependence and improvement of energy efficiency, but also environmental and social stability.[9] Similarly, some local environmental actors would point to the development of the "inclusive energy market" as Ukraine's main priority in terms of energy security,[10, 11] or point to the necessity of finding a modern solution for the country's energy mix—regarding all its factors: economic, ecological and climate included.[12]

The outbreak of the war with Russia shifted the Ukrainian energy policy course closer to the EU agenda. Ukraine's multi-vector policy, which for many years allowed it to maneuver between the West and the East, created different sources of external pressure that contributed to two main stances on energy policy in Ukraine. One of them was linked to the EU policy and promoted wider use of renewables with the contraction of nuclear and fossil fuels. The other was more Russia-oriented and favored more gas and nuclear in the energy mix—with little concern for environmental issues such as CO_2 emissions. Therefore, turning towards Western direction meant that Ukraine started to put a stronger focus on issues such as market liberalization, energy efficiency, renewable energy and sustainable development. All those dimensions were more strongly emphasized in the new Ukrainian Energy Strategy 2035 developed after the outbreak of the military conflict with Russia. The document envisions ambitious goals of energy sector reforms, modernization of energy infrastructure and sustainable energy development that stretch years into the future.[13] As such, the typical hierarchies of the Ukrainian energy security approach based on heavy dependence on fossil fuels are gradually shifting. It is also a unique chance for the so far marginalized "environmental" and "green" societal actors to promote alternative understandings of energy security and policy solutions. The latter are still rare, but growing within the changing constellation of domestic actors and with the financial and logistical aid of transnational "green" networks that increased in the aftermath of the 2014 events.

Although the rapid policy change caused a significant power reshuffle within domestic players, both mainstream energy security definitions and energy policymaking signify that the Ukrainian energy context remains dominated by the imperative of sustenance. The domestic bargaining over the goals of energy policy that accompanied the development of the Ukrainian Energy Strategy 2030 and the subsequent Energy Strategy 2035 is a good reflection of this dominant logic that plays out between multiple stakeholders. The workings on both strategies illustrate well the competing influences of the uneasy energy policymaking process marked by oligarchic interests, a lack of coordination between different governmental bodies and a slowly decreasing communication gap between state officials and wider civil society organizations. Given the lack of the risk logic in Ukraine's nuclear energy sector, the dominant logic of subsistence is challenged only by the logic of war. The imperative of survival has not only become ever-present in Ukraine's pipeline politics, but the grammar of conflict started to permeate other energy security debates and policy developments. Hence, in a centralized energy system still dominated by big industry interests, attempts at diversifying the energy portfolio aim at increasing energy independence from Russia and focus on the use of domestic energy resources. The rest of the chapter unpacks this dynamic and illustrates how the specifics of the Ukrainian context contribute to the rise of some energy security logics, while hindering others and how the Ukrainian complex energy security agenda emerges from within those competing security imperatives.

Eastern influences and the Ukrainian Energy Strategy 2030

The Energy Strategy 2030 was supposed to replace the outdated energy strategy from 2006. The latter, after one to two years of preparation with the help of the Ukrainian Academy of Science, which wrote its first draft, was heavily criticized by domestic experts for its unrealistic forecasts of economic growth and energy demand.[14] The strategy from 2006 shifted the focus towards nuclear energy and the coal market, paying little attention to alternative energy sources. The public consultations, conducted by the Ukrainian government at the time, took place after the document had been already approved.[15] Between 2011 and 2013 the Ukrainian Ministry of Energy developed a new document, "Energy Strategy 2030," which was promulgated by the Ministry of Energy and Coal Industry in February 2014.

The development of this document illustrates an uneasy dynamic of the Ukrainian energy policymaking process that revolves around the dominant logic of subsistence and involves multiple actors with competing interests and rationales. In this case, different governmental agencies responsible for different aspects of the energy portfolio lacked inter-institutional coordination and were heavily influenced by external pressures. One could distinguish among three relevant agencies at the time: the Ministry of Energy, which developed the general framework for energy strategy and worked with the electricity, gas and coal markets; the National Agency of Ukraine for the Effective Use of Energy Resources,[16] which mainly tackled the issue of energy efficiency and renewables; and the National Electricity Regulatory Commission (NERC),[17] which regulated electricity and gas markets.[18] Despite the division of energy policy areas, each of the agencies appeared to follow in practice a separate energy strategy, and as one energy expert noted back in 2013:

> The Ministry of Energy supports traditional fossil fuel generation, while the other two agencies support renewables, but each of them understands what is to be done in a different manner—with the National Agency of Ukraine for the Effective Use of Energy Resources being heavily influenced by the government and supporting only a few costly segments of renewables—wind and solar—despite the fact that Ukraine has big potential also in the field of bioenergy.[19]

The local NGO sector believed that the slow development and implementation of the regulation on renewables at the time was greatly down to this lack of coordination between the governmental bodies and their competing interests. For instance, a conflict between the Ministry of Energy and the State Agency on Energy Efficiency over the percentage of renewables to be included in the energy strategy[20] during the years preceding its adoption in late 2013 caused certain damage, despite quite significant interest in renewables on the part of energy businesses. Similarly, the units directly responsible for the promotion of energy-efficiency solutions did not have an easy task. First, according to local experts, the Energy Efficiency Agency, which should actively propagate energy alternatives, had very low capacity to lobby its interests because of the dominance of other industrial lobbies (gas, coal, nuclear) aiming to maintain the status quo.[21] Second, the political parties that were in government at the time were mainly pro-coal and pro-nuclear and the opposition could block any moves of the parliamentary committee working on energy efficiency. Speaking as of October 2013, an analyst from the Institute for Economic Research and Policy Consulting pointed out:

> Energy efficiency plans are not coordinated with the Ministry of Energy, they have completely different views on the problem and as a result they cannot submit this joint document to the Energy Community Secretariat. And now they decided to submit this document independently, so it's a bureaucratic game.... They submitted it to the Secretariat as a draft.[22]

Although this lack of coordination is not unusual, the situation in Ukraine is additionally complicated by strong industry groups and lobbyists, which are highly influential in the sphere of energy policy. A number of local observers highlighted that point during the interviews. As a member of the EU Delegation to Ukraine noted, although inter-agency ministerial cooperation is difficult in most countries, it is particularly bad in Ukraine: "Very informally I would call it a bit of a clan thinking.... That is something that hinders Ukrainian progress."[23] Similarly, some local energy experts suggested that Ukrainian state agencies that serve the interests of concrete oligarchic groups constitute the main problem of state governance and lead to a deficit of cooperation between agencies. As one Kiev-based energy expert stated in autumn 2013: "During previous years these oligarchic groups provided their 'human resources' to those agencies. Many bureaucrats who are in the chairs of concrete departments, deputy ministers, minister chairs—they are interest-keepers of ... [these] oligarchic groups."[24] The Ukrainian oligarchic system further complicates the already uneasy and non-transparent decision-making process. Local commentators speculated that the presence of the energy industries' representatives in the ministries and governmental agencies is one of the main reasons why the latter often struggle to reach compromise and make final decisions.[25] Workings on Ukraine's Energy Strategy 2030 was a prominent example of such a dynamic, as the preparation of the document was heavily influenced by the main business lobbies and the entire policy process lacked a meaningful societal dialogue.

To start with, the Ukrainian government ordered a draft of energy strategy from the Ministry of Energy, which asked the private Foundation for Effective Governance for support in its preparation. As the foundation is owned by an oligarch, Rinat Akhmetov, who controlled almost the entire domestic coal sector, some analysts highlighted a clear conflict of interests when a big industrial group develops the main energy document of the country.[26] Consequently, as a local energy expert noted: "the draft of the 'so-called' energy strategy integrated some wishes of different business lobbyists and put the main emphasis on the coal scenario—followed by further nuclear energy development plans."[27] The Foundation for Effective Governance organized a public hearing of the strategy together with the Ukrainian government at the time, partly because of the conditionality of the received EU funds that favored such an initiative. However, a number of NGOs, energy experts and international organizations (such as IEA, World Bank or European Energy Agency) that prepared their comments, suggestions and criticisms of the document complained that these did not have any significant impact and the whole process lacked transparency.[28] The comparative analysis of the revised draft of the Energy Strategy 2030 (from March 2013) and the draft presented for public discussion (in July 2012) pointed only to minor corrections—mainly in the area of coal.[29] More strikingly still, not only did energy strategy say little about prospects for renewable energy, but similarly little attention was given to the pressing and more widely debated topic of energy efficiency. Societal actors complained that the Ukrainian government does not devote enough effort to either issue and does not consider multiple societal voices that call for change. In the words of an energy expert from the Ecological Centre of Ukraine, which has been working on promoting energy efficiency and renewables for over two decades:

> I think that everybody knows what to do on the level of experts, and state agencies, think tanks and NGOs—they know what to do, but those in parliament and the government, like ministries—they live in a parallel world, they don't connect with other people and cannot feel the feedback from them and the expert community.[30]

And further, while commenting on the public consultations on the law on the efficient use of energy resources:

> Everybody tried to improve it—people from NGOs, think tanks, independent experts, there were roundtables, conferences, meetings that tried to make that law better, but in the end the final version is very poor. I'm not sure if it will help a lot in this sector.... It disappoints me, and we are all tired of trying to speak to them—it is always like knocking on the closed doors.[31]

Whereas a lack of societal dialogue was typical for the Ukrainian energy context prior to the war with Russia, the emphasis on coal among other options could be explained by several factors. First, the strength of the coal lobby meant that although the new energy strategy focused on both the coal and nuclear sectors, the coal power stations belonging to a private company (DTEK) were prioritized. As a local economist evaluated, DTEK was more interested in the modernization of its own objects, while no private investors showed interest in the modernization of state-owned nuclear power plants.[32] Apart from the industry interests, focus on cheap coal and nuclear energy for the consumers, the political importance of the coal regions and their short-term interests, as well as the reluctance to introduce expensive technologies for the modernization of the energy sector could have played a role. The prioritization of coal resources in the draft Energy Strategy 2030 also had another important underlying rationale—Ukrainian energy sovereignty.

Even before the military conflict with Russia, local energy experts noted that it was a common perception in Ukraine that coal should be favored and developed as an alternative to expensive gas, which was imported from a single supplier and distributed in the highly non-transparent Ukrainian market.[33] Similarly to the Polish context, "energy sovereignty" was often confused with the notion of "energy security." As a member of the Kiev-based Heinrich Böll Foundation office pointed out at the time:

> There are a lot of alternatives, but the government does nothing and tries to maintain the status quo until 2030. It is a very simple strategy: we use local resources, everything that we have—mostly nuclear—but not really because uranium has to be taken to Russia first [to be enriched]—coal and natural gas.... The strategy wants to use local resources to provide energy security in Ukraine, and *energy security in Ukraine is local resources*.[34]

This imperative of sustenance grounded in the Ukrainian "island thinking" in regards to energy security seemed to also resonate in the wider social context. For instance, the former reports of the Civicus Index Ukraine illustrated that the Ukrainian population considers the role of civil society in the preservation of the environment insignificant, limited or moderated, and only 25 percent of respondents see it as essential.[35] In the opinion of local observers, Ukrainians are also not interested in environmental or climate issues related to energy production and consumption—despite the fact that local ecology in many large Ukrainian cities and industrial regions is threatened.[36] Consequently, contrary to citizens in many EU states, Ukrainians are generally less hostile towards extensive use of their state's fossil fuels—even if such practices result in environmental hazards. An activist from Movement 350 working locally on the promotion of energy efficiency and renewables pointed to a specific type of socialization that could explain this attitude:

> In Ukraine [there is this] thinking that the country is rich in natural resources and that we should better manage them. And largely people still believe in coal. We were taught at school that we have good coal and should use it.... I also see how my colleagues—also from Mohyla Academy—support the argument of shale gas—which will help Ukraine to become independent—even the environmentalists are divided.... I think it is a matter of your very basic beliefs. What do you believe in, what do you value, what comes first: profit or the environment or social justice?[37]

The above statement points to the contestation over different priorities of energy security typical for the subsistence logic as well as to the significant distal factors. The latter illustrates how the context-specific process of socialization coupled with the historically determined perceptions of Russia favor the idea of energy sovereignty and largely explain the widespread support for the use of domestic energy resources among the population. Consequently, the environmental aspects of energy production and consumption stay at the bottom of the hierarchy of energy security dimensions.

The development of the Ukrainian Energy Strategy 2030 discussed above illustrates well the context of Ukrainian energy policymaking prior to the conflict with Russia. The multiplicity of stakeholders and their competing interests made that dynamic even more challenging. As an energy expert from the Nomos Centre put it: "We have many debates, discussions, roundtables, but no results. Different views between different political factions, interest groups, businesses, lobbyists etc. I don't know what is possible or how long it will take for the members of the parliament."[38] In the end, the draft of the Energy Strategy 2030 came closer to the pro-Russian approach. Despite the drive towards energy sovereignty, more gas in the energy mix would mean higher dependence on Russia, and given that half of the electricity in Ukraine comes from the Soviet-designed NPPs that work on Russian nuclear fuel—the same logic applied here. However, the document was short-lived because of the outbreak of the war in 2014. Although the main industry interests, centralized decision-making and the imperative of sustenance still prevail in its aftermath, the conflict marked a major reshuffle in the domestic constellation of actors, gave more voice to societal actors and led to a significant change in the energy policy course.

Western influences and the Ukrainian Energy Strategy 2035

The war with Russia put an end to Ukraine's maneuvering between Western and Eastern policy influences that were often a source of different pushes and pulls in the conceptual vision of Ukraine's energy security. In November 2011 Russia attempted to pull Ukraine away from the Energy Community when Gazprom proposed cheaper gas for the Ukrainian side in exchange for its exit from it. According to local energy experts, Ukraine did not accept this proposal at the time, as it was commonly perceived that the pressure from Moscow is not a "fair play" and that Gazprom's proposition might not be realized, but rather constitutes a "promise to *consider* the idea for cheaper gas."[39] On the other side, Ukraine initially perceived the very membership in the Energy Community as a factor that could improve its bargaining position with Moscow. Local policy analysts admitted that some of Ukraine's expectations were unrealistic, as it hoped that the Energy Community would adopt an active stance and help it with some disputes with Russia, promote Ukrainian interests or support Ukraine in obtaining investment funds for modernization of its domestic energy system.[40, 41] As the Energy Community, being a rules-based system aimed primarily at market integration, did not meet those expectations, relations between the two parties became colder over the years.

Nevertheless, Ukraine's membership in the Energy Community served as an important trigger for establishing the national action plans for renewables and energy efficiency. Ukraine also started to gradually implement various EC directives and obligations. Prior to that, despite a number of local NGOs working in these issue areas, the general population did not perceive of them as important and it was considered to be purely an "imported" effect."[42] Local actors acknowledged that even the initial limited plans for the increase of the share of renewables and energy-efficiency measures in Ukraine—and related to that minor revision of the Energy Strategy 2030—would not be in place without some pressure from international stakeholders.[43] Apart from the Energy Community, international actors such as the EU, the US embassy and the World Bank also played a role—even if it was hard to evaluate the actual strength of their influence on key decisions at the time. Some related projects were also supported by the American government, British, Swedish, Austrian and German funding as well as corporate funding. Germany clearly stood out among the multiple foreign actors in terms of intensity of involvement and the variety of projects supported in the area of energy efficiency and expertise sharing in the field of clean coal technology and renewables.[44] GIZ, a technical aid program of the German government, included projects on the isolation of public buildings, assisted in organizing training on the municipal and urban levels for energy managers to increase energy efficiency, and supported some initiatives in public transport in the big Ukrainian cities. Prior to the war with Russia some projects were also realized on the Azov Sea and the Crimean Peninsula with the participation of Austrian and German companies and experts. Yet, the multiple competing interests so prevalent in the Ukrainian energy context also played a role here. Although it was perceived in Kiev that Germany was seeking an active involvement of Ukraine in the new conceptual vision of European energy security,[45] the German–Ukrainian cooperation faced some obstacles due to competing views on energy security among their respective governmental agencies and a lack of inter-institutional coordination. For instance, attempts at cooperation between the FNR (German renewable energy agency) and the Ukrainian side (mainly the Ministry of Agriculture) were not very successful. Local observers noted that although the former tried to transfer some German experience in the area of energy solutions to Ukrainian policymakers, changes in the policy framework on the part of Germany (refocus on pilot projects in biomass by the Ministry of the Environment) and lack of support on the Ukrainian side (no cooperation or a common vision among its governmental agencies working on renewables) complicated the process.[46]

If this type of cooperation appeared challenging for a number of years, the Ukrainian–Russian conflict that started at the beginning of 2014 shifted Ukraine's energy policy course clearly towards the Western agenda and facilitated new solutions in the area of renewables and energy-efficiency measures. As Moscow unilaterally terminated the 2010 Kharkiv Accords, which had provided a discounted gas price in exchange for its lease of the naval base in Sevastopol until 2042,[47] the resulted increase in gas prices has finally sparked a policy debate on energy-efficiency measures at the highest levels, as the urgency of the issue became evident to everyone.[48] Additionally, the occupation of the Donbas region severely disrupted coal supplies,[49] and even if the eastern territories were to be taken back, it would be difficult to exploit and transport coal because of damage to the local infrastructure. Consequently, the Cabinet of Ministers of Ukraine stated on its website that the dramatic events that took place in Ukraine at the beginning of 2014 had fundamentally changed the situation in the energy sector, rendering its energy strategy out of date.[50] It also called for the establishment of a new document that would set out the plan for ensuring energy safety and sustainable development of the energy sector under the new circumstances.

The new energy policy course puts much more emphasis on nuclear energy[51] and energy efficiency. In the changed situation the Energy Community was in a stronger position to lobby not only for the implementation of stronger energy-efficiency measures in Ukraine, but also the new policy on renewables. The new Energy Strategy 2035, under the theme "Safety, Energy Efficiency, and Competitiveness," was approved on August 18, 2017. The strategy focuses on the reduction of import dependence, development of energy-efficiency measures, domestic modernization of the energy sector and closer integration with the European energy market.[52] Its three phases focus on the energy sector reforms on the basis of EU legislation (e.g., third energy package), development of energy infrastructure (e.g., smart grids), and sustainable energy development respectively. The document also puts more emphasis on increasing the share of renewable energy with a goal of up to 25 percent of RES in the total primary energy supply by 2035.[53]

Work on the new strategy also illustrated a significant power shift within the domestic constellation of actors, where societal actors gained more leverage. First, the new document was developed on the initiative and with direct participation of the Razumkov Centre—a non-governmental public policy think tank. Second, according to the NGO actors themselves, they appeared to have much "more of a say" this time around, as many of their comments on the initial draft were taken into account.[54] This appeared to be a wider trend, as local green energy organizations pointed out that since the beginning of the conflict, the authorities started to pay attention to the solutions offered by them: "they are not accepting everything, they are accepting very limited part of our proposals, but there is a slow dynamic moving towards understanding [these issues]."[55] The gradually changing governmental stance towards the NGO sector and energy issues also found some new discussion platforms. For instance, the regular roundtables co-founded by the British Embassy and organized monthly by Kiev-based think tank Dixi Group at Verkhovna Rada gather a number of experts, parliamentarians, NGOs and media to discuss the critical energy challenges in Ukraine.[56] The establishment of the regular dialogue with all the stakeholders to discuss current policy issues appears to be an improvement upon the ad hoc public consultations on energy topics just a few years ago. For the first time a small group of parliamentarians supports the development of renewable energy and cooperates with local NGOs on developing some scenarios in this area.[57] The public consultations also became more common because of certain institutional reforms. For instance, some of the governmental regulatory bodies in the energy sector gained more independence—such as the National Energy and Utility Regulatory Commission (NEURC) (formerly NERC), re-created in 2016 in line with a new law[58] that ended its subordination to the office of the president, which in the past liquidated the body twice in order to dismiss the regulator's management.[59] Since its re-establishment, the NEURC has already held public consultations on a number of important secondary legislation drafts related to energy market reform.[60] Third, an introduction of a number of policy reforms enhances societal involvement in progressive energy solutions. The new governmental program undertook a number of steps towards a more sustainable energy policy as it focused on promoting energy efficiency, new legislative requirements for heat/hot water meters and energy-efficient buildings, and the establishment of the Energy Efficiency Fund, which provides loans to citizens.[61] Additionally, the decentralization reform implemented after the outbreak of the conflict with Russia (as prior to it the reform was discussed, but there was a lack of political will to introduce it) led to the diffusion of power and responsibilities to the newly formed territorial-administrative units. Since the emergent amalgamated communities have more resources available in their local budgets, the NGOs focus mostly on working with them to show them how the extra funds could be spent for green energy solutions in energy efficiency, new technologies or citizens' energy.[62] The decentralization of power coupled with more efficient energy consumers signify a significant loss of lobbying power on the part of the traditional energy businesses. However, although Ukrainian "green" actors for the first time have an opportunity to promote their agenda in the energy sector more efficiently, the introduction of the democratic means does not come easy in the Ukrainian distal context. Both technical and the socioeconomic/historical factors hinder the rise of the imperative of self-reliance. Whereas the workings on the consecutive energy strategies illustrate the shift of the Ukrainian energy policy towards the West, a domestic power reshuffle and change of certain energy policy priorities, they are still driven by the logic of subsistence, which revolves around big energy businesses and their economic interests. Simultaneously, although the war with Russia serves as a powerful trigger of social mobilization in the energy field, the fact that energy security lies at the core of the national security agenda heightens the influence of the war logic and its confrontational rationale permeates to everyday local energy politics. The next sections scrutinize this dynamic.

Democratic solutions in the Ukrainian context: obstacles to the emancipatory agenda

Whereas in neighboring Poland the emancipatory agenda was sparked by the ideas and debates "imported" from abroad by local actors, the same process appears to be happening in the Ukrainian context—albeit to a much lesser extent. The notion of energy democracy, although non-existent several years ago in the Ukrainian context, currently functions among a few NGOs that are trying to slowly introduce it to the public debate.[63] The NGO sector gradually engages in the pilot citizens' energy projects, informational campaigns and increasingly also in the social dialogue. The Ukrainian NGOs also highlight the potential benefits of the gradual decentralization of the domestic energy system. First, as a member of Greencubator put it:

> The core thing here is what do you do when somebody pulls a cord? In a country that is at war you should have more of these resilient communities and grid units, which can supply at least 30 percent of their own energy needs.[64]

Therefore, the development of micro-grids that could go in an autonomous mode is in line with enhancing both national and energy security in times of crisis. Second, as NGO actors emphasize, the democratization of the energy system would be preferred from the societal point of view, as it not only gets rid of connection troubles, but is as democratic as it gets—with people internally deciding all of the rules for their own small local grid.[65] The decentralization of energy production could also increase social participation in democratic processes and empower local communities financially, as the money formerly spent on purchasing gas could be used for creating new jobs and providing more resources to the local budget. Third, in more general terms some local NGOs believe that the inclusive energy system would improve the system's efficiency over time and mark significant societal progress. As one energy activist noted:

> The distributed generation model is very positive—it is like the Internet [...] and the energy harvesting is the basic right for any human.... The problem with the current energy model, the model from Eisenhower and Khrushchev time, is that energy consumer is considered to be a dumb terminal ... and when the utilities and the government keep treating consumers like dumb terminals that means the degradation that means a limitation of the progress.... I'm sure that when you add people to the system the efficiency of the system improves.[66]

Whereas a number of societal actors agree that democratization of the energy sector in the future would benefit Ukraine's energy security and public participation alike, both the technical and societal obstacles have to be addressed first. When it comes to the former, a continuous monopolization of the electricity market constitutes the main challenge.

Energy monopolies

Prior to the military conflict with Russia the Ukrainian renewables market was monopolized by two oligarchs—Rinat Akhmetov (wind power) and Andriy Kluiv (solar power). Whereas the annexation of the Crimean Peninsula, where a large part of the solar power plants was located, drove the latter out of business, Akhmetov's company DTEK, which is in control of most of the coal business, currently runs the biggest wind farm in Ukraine.[67] Despite the changes in the market shares, not much has changed for ordinary Ukrainians. As individuals who want to invest in renewables have to buy the necessary technology from the monopolists, it is the oligarchs who profit the most. Hence, as the local analysts admit, the potential widespread use of renewables by individuals would not lead to the market de-monopolization, but could end up upholding the existing monopolies.[68] Moreover, the grid ownership is monopolized, as OPAL energo owns the regional grid and the state enterprise Ukrenergo owns the higher voltage lines; it is also currently forbidden for citizens to own their own grid. Local societal actors highlight that other technical aspects, such as the lack of basic technology to support the shift to renewables, high prices for connection to the grid for each particular household, and huge energy losses on grids (11–12 percent), complicate the matter further.[69] Therefore, the NGO sector working in the field of local energy is waiting for the liberalization of the electricity market (third energy package and electricity market reform) to be implemented in full.

The projects in renewables are also still being developed by big energy companies—mostly foreign capital as well as the local oligarchs. The governmental agency that deals with renewables and energy efficiency, although very active, deals mostly with foreign and national investors to facilitate big projects, e.g., the 100 MWatt solar power plant near Chernobyl.[70] Developing renewables with private funds by big industry groups is seen by many societal actors working in the area of green energy as the worst case scenario—as it diminishes the wide range of potential benefits of renewable energy for average Ukrainians and for the democratization of the energy system in favor of continuously narrow business interests. According to the NGO sector, governmental bodies are not noticing the small players and not making any effort to promote the benefits of renewable energy to the population.[71, 72] An ongoing debate on green feed-in tariffs versus the auction system is a case in point here. The former is preferred and advocated by societal actors (e.g., Ecoaction, Reanimation Package of Reforms that emerged after Maidan), as it is believed that cutting the feed-in tariff and switching to the auction system would make small and medium producers of electricity uncompetitive on the market and eventually lead to further monopolization and "oligarchization" of the energy system in Ukraine.[73] As an activist from Movement 350 put it: "If it's small scale, it's energy democracy. If it's large-scale projects, then it is the same as now. It is better for the environment, but when it comes to people's power…."[74] The voice of societal actors on this issue has not been influential so far. Moreover, the media coverage of a couple of scandals connected to the big renewable energy projects had a negative impact on the image of renewables in Ukraine. As a local NGO worker put it: "We started it all from the wrong foot. […] in the minds of people renewable energy is another toy of the oligarchs. This is what the media was mostly writing about."[75] One of these scandals was connected to an oligarch, while the other to the small hydropower in Carpathia, where the company started to develop the project without the consent and engagement of the local communities, violating the agreements that were in place.[76] This led to a big public campaign against the development of renewables—in the view of the local NGOs the biggest public campaign against some sort of development in the last ten years in Ukraine.[77]

Apart from the monopolized market, the local NGO sector working on the development of small-scale energy projects points to a number of additional obstacles. These include lack of sufficient infrastructure and a better legislative framework that would set in law, e.g., energy cooperatives, and lack of capacity, proper energy management or expertise in the field of renewables and energy-efficiency measures at the local level.[78] The financial barriers also play a role and although many cities already have programs to co-fund materials for energy-efficiency projects, the general public lacks access to cheap loans, and the "warm loans" scheme proved to be insufficient to meet current demand. Societal actors hope that the State Energy Efficiency Fund established in 2017 will partially remedy that situation.

The sociohistorical obstacles

Technical obstacles aside, the emancipatory logic could only emerge in the local energy system if a sufficient number of individuals would be both *able* and *willing* to regain control over their own energy production and consumption—thus leading to an increase in self-reliance via bottom–up democratization processes. Apart from the technical barriers, some sociohistorical factors additionally hinder the rise of this imperative.

Some expert analyses published prior to the conflict with Russia argued that Ukraine's problems with energy security require the efforts of the whole society, as the directed actions and activities should be designed in relation to all branches of power and rely on the "competent management of personnel, mutual trust of authorities and citizens and their willingness to *social participation* and to taking the *responsibility*."[79] Moreover, they emphasized that to improve energy efficiency, the Ukrainian population should form the "national" attitude to consumption and payment for energy and other utilities.[80] However, changing the attitudes and regaining control over one's energy usage does not come easily in the Ukrainian sociohistorical context.

Societal actors consistently highlight that the Soviet legacy of the lack of trust and unwillingness to take responsibility are the main obstacles to cooperation and the development of local energy projects. As a member of Movement 350 pointed out: "When you are taking control, you are also taking responsibility. But here in the post-Soviets, we have this thing with the responsibility—'we don't really want to be responsible for anything.'"[81] Similarly, a member of Greencubator notes:

> We have a lack of trust everywhere to tell you the truth. It's one of the biggest issues. We have this internal communist or paternalist approach that the state should solve the problems of the communities and that it owes them something.[82]

This dynamic plays out in relation to local projects targeted at both energy-efficiency measures and renewables. When it comes to the former a number of issues arise while forming condominiums by the inhabitants of the buildings. As local activists point out, even when establishing a condominium would qualify the residents to participate in some newly introduced incentive programs, the interest was often not high as the residents did not want to cooperate and take responsibility for the common spaces.[83] Because the apartments were given to their tenants free of charge in the early 1990s, many people did not realize that since they became owners of the flats they also received both the rights of the owners as well as the responsibilities to maintain the estate that they received. Especially the older generation is used to the municipality taking care of the common areas. Trust is again a major factor here and local NGOs note that it is very hard to unite people in the emerging condominium system, as they constantly think that other residents will "cheat them." As a member of the Kiev-based NGO noted: "This is not going to change very fast. It's been 70 years during people survived only by not trusting each other."[84] Some youth networks that conducted specific projects on promoting energy-efficiency measures among the population note that residents often do not take active participation even within the established condominiums, but rather look for someone to take control and take care of all the affairs, e.g., one person in a building of 144 flats who manages it all.[85] Therefore, buildings at the local level often lack properly educated managers with a good understanding that a multi-floor building is a joint responsibility. As a representative of the Ukrainian Energy Efficiency Agency put it: "The biggest challenge which is happening in this country is the change in understanding who owns what and who is responsible for what."[86] Apart from the attitude change, some necessary regulations and technical improvements in municipal buildings are needed, as currently introducing energy-efficiency measures in many cases does not lead to significant savings and, as a representative from Movement 350 noted, it "does not really give people power over energy back."[87]

Ukraine's low social capital and lack of trust are also one of the main obstacles to establishing future energy cooperatives and other local programs related to renewables. Energy activists admit that also here people struggle to join to work together, as they are afraid of being taken advantage of, and the historical experience of involuntary cooperation makes the very promotion of "cooperation" tricky in rural areas, as it brings back the bad connotations with former "collectivization" and forced mergers of properties.[88, 89] Hence, local organizations plan to promote the democratization of energy not only in terms of energy cooperatives, but also in a broader sense of citizens' energy based on individual households, the cooperation between individuals and individuals with businesses.

This specific sociohistorical context makes the potential democratization of the domestic energy system extremely challenging. Problems with collective decision-making and reaching compromise, hard fights between investors in the condominiums, among the expert communities, or among rural populations which often avoid cooperation on local initiatives due to the mutual lack of trust mirror wider obstacles on the path to Ukrainian democracy. Additionally, historically determined unwillingness to take responsibility makes the rise of the imperative of self-reliance much less likely. Local NGOs note that some type of facilitation is needed for the projects and initiatives to take off from the ground and to overcome inherent trust issues, as: "People are not good yet at making decisions together, taking responsibility, they don't have the culture of discussing issues, conflict resolution, debating."[90] Therefore, the initial projects in energy tend to work better if there is clear leadership from the start. Simultaneously, if some studies noted that the emerging neighborhood associations might serve as the "grassroots schools of democracy" where citizens learn cooperation for the common good,[91] similar hope is at times expressed by green energy activists. As one pointed out: "One of my partners and friends in Poland says that energy is a backdoor to democracy. I think this is very true."[92] Yet, given the mounting challenges, local experts point to a perspective of several decades before a culture of prosumers could develop in Ukraine. Some of them argue that each country should find a system that suits the mentality of people and local conditions,[93] others that deciding which model of the energy system is better depends on the economics of scale.[94] Given the Ukrainian context, some experts point to a "hybrid" system as the best solution—decentralized for individual households and centralized for big energy projects.[95] Here, local NGO workers also highlight the urban–rural divide regarding energy capacities and suggest that diffused energy solutions would work better in the countryside.[96] Regardless of different opinions, the Ukrainian energy system remains highly centralized and monopolized, and the governmental focus on developing big projects is likely to continue. Simultaneously, in the years following the outbreak of the military conflict with Russia, a number of factors contribute to the increased social mobilization in energy-related topics and projects locally that go against that general trend.

Factors of change

The events at Maidan in 2013/14 and their aftermath served as a powerful trigger for changes in the Ukrainian energy sector, not only at the policy level, but also at the societal level. Kiev-based Heinrich Böll Foundation's informal internal survey among partner NGOs that measured the impact of civil society organizations in Ukraine on decision-making in the area of climate and green energy transition[97] showed a significant change in societal attitudes after Maidan (2014–2017)—especially locally.[98] The data indicated a higher level of civil society activity and participation, both in terms of quantity and quality, as people started to express more interest in local policies (municipal participatory budgets, programs, etc.) and to learn the necessary skills and mechanisms for influencing the decision-making process (open governance, electronic governance, petitions, etc.).[99] More civil society organizations appeared after Maidan, and as local activists point out:

> People became more reflexive about their lives and the power which they have. Because this really happened, the revolution or Maidan happened. And maybe they can say it was the oligarchs, and the US, and foreigners who made it happen, but it still happened. We got what we wanted.[100]

According to local observers, the events of 2013/14 changed the public perception that the political elite is untouchable, and made them realize that its activities should be transparent and accountable to citizens.[101]

This increased social mobilization, driven largely by the younger generation, fits into a wider trend that started with the Orange Revolution. The civic protests at the Maidan Square in 2004/05 were seen by some as signs of the awakening of Ukrainian civil society and some experts even hoped for the potential evolution of Maidan (sociopolitical) into socioeconomic and environmental civic engagement.[102] Activists from local organizations also consistently highlight that it is much easier to work with youth on topics connected to energy efficiency, green energy and climate change, as they are better informed and motivated to participate and, as opposed to the elderly, financially better off to make changes.[103] The generational change also has its sociohistorical dimension. If Soviet legacy and historical factors largely determine social disengagement from a number of important issues—current energy policy design included—local green energy activists point to the ongoing changes. As one of them noted when comparing Ukraine to Poland:

> In Poland, despite several decades of communist history, Poles were … [having] a sense of community and they never lost millions of population during the famine—we did.… So this is not the energy policy, this is not the renewable thing—this is *the social aspect*. And one great thing, which I see now, are the changes that are brought about by millions. Those who don't remember the Soviet Union—they are a different kind of people.[104]

Hence, somehow inversely to the Polish context—where some local voices express the hope that through civic empowerment in the energy sphere individuals will realize the power of their agency and transform the entire socioeconomic model—in Ukraine the anticipation is rather that it is political empowerment that could bring about changes in the energy and environmental sector. Local NGOs hope that the whole movement for change in energy affairs will start from the younger generation and they often rely on young people educated in the West in their own work.

These ongoing social changes make it easier to work locally on new energy-related initiatives with the involvement of society. Currently, NGOs frequently focus on working with the amalgamated communities that emerged only two to three years ago after the recent Maidan events. The latter combine territorial entities where people know each other and where the trust level is estimated by local actors to be higher than in urban areas.[105] As the communities have a new structure, not the one inherited from Soviet times, local activists find them more conducive to fresh ideas and a joint decision-making process. They also consider those that formed first as the most progressive: "They have a chance to change the country. That's why we work with them."[106] Currently, despite the ongoing transfer of power to the community level and existing conditions for the introduction of some progressive energy measures—in terms of money, land or biomass—local actors lack information on how to use their resources. Hence the NGO sector focuses on organizing workshops, information-sharing activities and identifying spots for the first energy cooperatives in Ukraine. Environmental organizations also engage in a number of grassroots activities in different Ukrainian cities, such as bus informational tours with small photovoltaics,[107] meetings at schools and with youth, educational forums, roundtables, training with foreign experts,[108] public consultations with citizens, public debates[109] or programs for children.[110] Some more advanced activities, such as Greencubator's "energy camps," also serve as networking platforms, as they involve informal activities and discussions on energy-related topics and cooperation with a number of public and private actors to promote green innovation programs.[111] All these activities focus on two main areas—local projects in renewable energy and energy-efficiency measures.

Energy efficiency not only finally became a policy priority for the Ukrainian government itself, but is also actively supported by a number of societal actors. After the outbreak of the war with Russia, the NGO sector together with the mass media ran a big informational campaign on energy efficiency. This time the topic proved to be very popular among the general population because of increased gas prices. Despite the lack of official opinion poll data on this topic, interviewees noted that as long as the prices for heat and electricity were kept low, the Ukrainian population showed little interest in saving energy, renewables or protesting any developments in the direction of the country's energy portfolio.[112] The drastic changes forced by the new geopolitical situation shook this status quo, although shifting public attitudes does not come easy. As a representative of the Energy Efficient Cities of Ukraine noted: "It took us enormous efforts to run the campaign explaining why we have to stop subsidizing energy at the national level" [and that it is not the international actors who push us to do so[113] (IMF, World Bank), but rather a need to stop the ineffective use of public money].[114] Although the Ukrainian government has been trying to bring the cost of gas closer to the economic level and the consumption of gas keeps decreasing in residential areas,[115] huge governmental subsidies for the utilities are still in place "just to make people less angry."[116] Whereas rising costs have caused many houses and multiple-apartment houses to consider switching from central heating (e.g., installation of small boilers), the "warm loans" credit system proved extremely popular[117] and local communities began to form condominiums in greater numbers to be eligible for different grants and projects on energy efficiency. The NGO sector attempts to aid this transition by developing the municipal capacity for running energy-efficiency programs in terms of monitoring, energy management, and the establishment of local policy plans.[118] Regular seminars on energy management in the municipalities are also conducted by the state Energy Efficiency Agency, whereas the association of the Energy Efficient Cities of Ukraine promotes the topic through its annual sustainable energy weeks, energy days and public campaigns.[119]

Similarly, although to a much lesser degree, the interest in small-scale renewable energy is increasing. Local environmental NGOs noted that prior to 2014, societal interest in renewables was extremely low and confined largely to some small groups and ecological organizations because of existing regulations and low electricity prices.[120] Even some affordable local projects (e.g., project on solar collectors and water heaters in rural areas)[121] were not met with a wide interest at the time.[122] Yet, a high renewable energy tariff has led to an increase in the energy capacity in this area. The feed-in tariffs law was extended to individual households in 2015, and in 2018 more than 3000 households were using it, despite no promotion and no public information campaigns from any government bodies.[123] Despite the lack of studies on the motivation behind the development of small-scale renewable energy in Ukraine, some state officials point to three key factors here: (1) economic motivation and ownership—"they want to own their station"; (2) affordability of green energy among those who are financially better off; (3) energy security—in regions with regular and lengthy shutdowns of the centralized system, where it especially pays off for local businesses to set up their own power station.[124]

Although it would seem that this increased social mobilization coupled with heightened awareness about the country's energy security is a particularly fertile ground for green actors to promote energy self-reliance through bottom–up energy democratization, their task is a more complex one. Namely, in the current geopolitical situation, higher social activity also has its dark side, and a number of interviewees expressed their concerns regarding the direction of the ongoing changes and the potential political radicalization since 2014.[125] As analysts from the Kiev-based think tank DixiGroup point out, the issue of high gas prices dominates the entire political agenda much more than just the energy topics.[126] The rise of political populism is attributed to the politicians who, instead of focusing on energy-efficiency measures, focus on how not to increase gas prices. As a representative of the Energy Efficient Cities of Ukraine put it:

> High gas prices motivate people to do something, but we haven't created sufficient mechanisms to support energy efficiency. And that's the problem because we are leaving a lot of people facing the challenge of high bills without really understanding what to do with that.... I think that high bills for the utilities are one of the highest risks for the national security at the moment, because they lead to a high rise of political populism: "We will come and reduce the gas price, we will make it as it was before"—which is either a lie or a threat, either incompetence or basically populism. What pains me, people are buying that.[127]

Activists working locally on the promotion of renewables and energy-efficiency measures highlight that the nationalistic rhetoric started to be successfully utilized even by grassroots organizations in Ukraine. As a member of Movement 350 described it:

> I have observed how these groups evolved after Maidan. More organizations make their way into stable NGOs and even campaign for small issues, such as protection of the local parks or lobbying against the illegal constructions. And even their members, often coming from the middle-class background, already try to use this pro-national rhetoric to bring more people out.... It obviously works, but for me playing with this national rhetoric is like playing with the devil, because of the nationalist appraisal all over the world.[128]

Whereas the rhetoric of energy independence underpinned by the confrontational and nationalistic stance is used to promote some domestic energy sectors, such as nuclear energy (despite nuclear fuel coming largely from Russia), the development of small-scale renewables and energy efficiency as a way of gaining independence is not yet well recognized by the general population.[129] Some societal actors highlight that in the country that is at war, establishment of the community-managed energy micro-grids is a matter of national security and increases the resilience and self-reliance of these communities.[130] However, given the current radicalization trend, the societal organizations working on the promotion of citizens' energy face a certain dilemma here. Namely, invoking the slogan of energy independence could further contribute to the rise of right-wing nationalism, as it became strongly tied to anti-Russian feelings. As a member of Movement 350 highlighted when mentioning their forthcoming nationwide information campaign on renewable energy:

> Now I'm also thinking what I would like more: to win this campaign and to use this nationalistic message or to stay true to our values.... Energy independence is good, I understand it my way and it would be hard to explain it to people who understand it just in terms of hatred towards Russia.[131]

Hence, their strategy will emphasize energy independence, but focus on its democratic aspects—the possibility of free energy for all that could lead to a stronger and more prosperous Ukraine.[132] In theoretical terms this is an example of how the rationale of self-reliance rooted in the democratic agenda will be positioned against the mainstream imperative of survival that currently reigns in Ukraine's politics and energy affairs alike.

Interviewees from other NGOs speculated that energy democracy has the potential to develop once people realize its economic benefits and possibilities for ownership.[133] Some have additionally pointed to the historical legacy that is likely to play a role in this process:

> Because of nearly 300 years' long foreign rule, authority of the state was seen as something opposing us, something alien, something not representative

> of our interests, and that's why people have been trying to distance themselves from the government and from the authorities at least until recent years. Now things are changing slowly and steadily, but it doesn't prevent people from uniting at their level. So they try to trust on the horizontal lines, and they are reluctant to be trusting people on the vertical ones.[134]

In practice this could mean that whereas the general population still distrusts and dislikes the government and the energy monopolies, it might welcome an opportunity to also distance itself from them in energy affairs—by cutting the grid off and sustaining their needs by their own capacities, as local NGOs stress, provided it is within reasonable costs for them. Some societal voices speculate that such a shift could take up to two to three decades and go, not in the direction of democratic, but anarchic—against all power structures.

NGO sector and its problems

Foreign actors have influenced the ongoing changes in the area of small-scale renewables and energy-efficiency measures not only on the policy level, but also in wider societal terms. The impact of Ukraine's political shift towards the West and its combined energy and climate goals in the domestic NGO sector is particularly noteworthy. Local NGOs admit that Western influence in the form of expertise and funds for the civil society organizations who cannot count on any government support or donations was visible in the way of framing the debate on green energy solutions.[135] Whereas international funding agencies have been the most active players in the area of renewables, the high number of foreign investors created the impression that there are many donors around and not enough movement on the government side. After 2014 the international technical assistance to Ukraine has further increased and enhanced the capacity of societal actors.[136] If prior to Maidan local NGOs focused on awareness-raising, as there were not so many opportunities to put pressure on the authorities, in recent years the focus shifted towards the training conducted by international donors[137] and more direct societal involvement in energy-related projects. However, despite gaining more influence in the ongoing energy policy changes, the Ukrainian NGO sector is not free of its problems—foreign funding included.

Societal actors agree that a lot of projects in the "green" energy sector were enabled by international donors and that the impact of foreign aid stretches further than that:

> It's the only way this can work. It's soft power. Maidan was enabled by the long-lasting period of such funding. Without it, it would not be possible to move to the next step of Maslow's hierarchy of needs or it would have taken many more years.[138]

Moreover, local NGOs highlight that the foreign assistance needed goes beyond financial support, as, e.g., many officials who are willing to implement changes at the local level often have to maneuver in an unfavorable political/administrative environment and need mental support from external partners and organizations to feel that "they are not alone."[139] However, overreliance on foreign funding causes many NGOs to work towards donor-driven rather than local agendas. It is especially the case with NGOs that are not issue-specific, but rather hunt for consecutive grants. As a co-founder of Greencubator put it:

> I don't believe in NGOs that care about election rights one day, gender rights the next day, and energy the third day. It is not going to work.... It's not a problem [that money comes from abroad]—it's a good thing. The not so good thing is on our side, those who are taking money are not necessarily the right institutions for implementing [such projects].[140]

Many Ukrainian NGOs function rather like private businesses than typical NGOs—as according to the local non-governmental sector it is often the case that private persons, who want to earn some money by receiving a grant from abroad, open their own NGOs.[141] Local actors point therefore to crowdfunding, corporate support and other types of financing to support NGO networks and to develop a certain level of self-resiliency. They also stress that the NGO sector needs a stronger vision of where the country should be heading regarding its energy agenda. As an analyst from the DixiGroup noted in autumn 2013:

> As a part of our project we tried to contact different NGOs and 80 percent of them are not really aware what the policy on renewables is or should be, so they work very generally: "we have to stop shale gas development," "we have to abandon nuclear power plants"; ... . They are also not constructive with the government—they criticize a lot, but they do not propose anything. [And] ... since our government is still living in some post-Soviet era, at least some of us should show them in which way we should go.[142]

It has been a general trend that Ukrainian NGOs work in a very closed circle and do not have much connection to the public. Previous studies showed that over a half of Ukrainians who are familiar with NGOs do not know what function they perform.[143] Engaging people in the issues related to green energy also remains problematic. Although the activity of the "green" NGOs has been improving in recent years, as the pressing energy challenges that increased rapidly since 2014 push it to work with the wider public, there is still a long way to go—especially since the efforts at the state level to educate or incentivize society are currently confined to energy-efficiency measures.

In summary, it could be said that the outbreak of the conflict with Russia set in motion important policy and societal changes that are driving and continuously reframing the Ukrainian energy security dynamic. Although a number of technical and socioeconomic obstacles to progressive energy solutions remain, an ongoing conflict accelerated key energy policy reforms and heightened societal mobilization. However, as every security lies at the core of the current national security agenda, the promotion of democratic energy solutions does not come easily to societal actors. The potential emergence of the emancipatory logic based on self-reliance is instantly challenged not only by the profound technical and socioeconomic factors, but also by the more confrontational imperative of survival that might feed populism and lead to political radicalization. The logic of war frequently comes to the fore of the public policy agenda and either permeates or outright dominates it. The next sections uncover the dynamic of the imperative of survival in a wider Ukrainian energy context.

Pipeline politics and the logic of war

Similarly to many other countries in the CEE region, the gas conflicts with Russia in 2006 and 2009 sparked a vivid debate and reconsideration of the energy policy course in Ukraine. If the grammar of conflict became entrenched in the mainstream debate ever since, the outbreak of the military conflict with Russia in 2014 made the issue of energy security inextricably intertwined with the national security agenda and strengthened the dominance of the survival imperative in Ukraine's energy affairs.

The rise of the logic of war

The the logic of war first emerged in Ukraine in the context of gas cut-off episodes from Russia in 2006 and 2009. The incidents themselves were referred to as "gas attacks" on Ukraine prepared in the "Gazprom headquarters."[144] Most strikingly, a number of Ukrainian energy experts from different political camps considered the signing of the January 2006 gas agreements with Russia as the biggest defeat of Ukrainian foreign policy in 2006, and called it the Pearl Harbor of Ukrainian energy diplomacy.[145] The Ukrainian–Russian gas conflict from January 2006 was also widely referred to as "gas war" in the numerous expert and media analyses in its aftermath.[146] This rhetoric applied not only to the Ukrainian–Russian gas dispute, but also to the Russian–Georgian one that took place at the end of January 2006—when Georgia accused Russia of energy blackmail and called on it to restore gas supplies to Georgia. The Ukrainian newspapers reported on the situation under headlines such as, "Gas War 2" or "Gas in the Soviet blitzkrieg."[147] Similar rhetoric was used in relation to the 2009 dispute, with Ukrainian media headlines like: "Gas War: new Cold War: nothing justifies Russian nostalgia for USSR,"[148] and politicians' analyses that saw the "gas war" between Russia and Ukraine as a continuation of the Georgian conflict through "economic aggression."[149] Crucially, as opposed to other countries in the region—where the grammar of conflict periodically rose and fell triggered by policy developments in the energy sphere—in Ukraine it became entrenched in the mainstream debate. Therefore, subsequent analyses kept referring to the gas cut-off episodes as the "so-called gas war,"[150] framed the potentially undesirable policy developments in relations with Russia in a similar manner (e.g., "New 'gas war' on the horizon"),[151] referred to the prospects of new tariffs or a decrease in the amount of gas supply from Russia as "gas attacks,"[152] and further expressed the rhetoric typical for the logic of war over the years, as reflected in newspaper headlines containing phrases such as "gas hostage state,"[153] "gas blitzkrieg,"[154] or "gas blackmail."[155]

Russian maneuvering in the energy sector was also depicted as part of a conscious strategy for domination. Starting from January 2006 with media stories such as "Empire and us,"[156] the crisis was seen as a further extension of the Ukrainian–Russian conflict that existed from the dawn of the independence of Ukraine.[157] The Russian side was perceived as having planned to create an international image of Ukraine as an unreliable partner in the transportation of natural gas to Europe, with one analysis referring to the head of Gazprom Alexey Miller and his spokesman Sergei Kupriyanov as "the most active propaganda heroes" who run the "reality show" with their turning-off of the tap at the Ukrainian border.[158] However, as the analysis stated, "Russian imperialists" failed to achieve their main strategic goal—the establishment of full control over the Ukrainian gas system.[159] The perception that the Russian side acted deliberately was visible also throughout the years, with the Ukrainian weekly *Zerkalo Nedeli* stating, for example, in 2011 that Russia started another propaganda campaign on a large scale and that it cannot be ruled out that it contains the script of the "third gas war."[160] Not surprisingly, the gas crises negatively impacted the perception of Russia as a reliable supplier.[161]

The logic of war was also manifested in a widespread belief that gas conflicts with Russia are a zero-sum game. Therefore, the Ukrainian daily *Dzen* pointed to the increase in Gazprom revenues as a result of the January 2006 crisis and asked the rhetorical question: "Who won?"[162] The same month *Dzen* asked a number of international experts for their opinion on "which side won in the Ukrainian–Russian gas dispute,"[163] while subsequent analyses suggested that the "gas wars" were indeed lost.[164] Similar rhetoric applied to the reporting on the energy sector developments in neighboring states. For example, in June 2010 the analysis titled "Dictatorship 'Gazprom' " noted that the decrease in gas supplies to Belarus by 15 percent could proceed further if the latter does not repay its debt—which in fact means that "the gas conflict entered a hot stage with no chances for Minsk of winning."[165] Most importantly, the zero-sum rhetoric entailed that in the gas conflicts with Russia it is not merely the gas supply at affordable prices that is at stake, but the very sovereignty of Ukraine itself. As President Yushchenko announced at the beginning of January 2006 in relation to the "gas war": "This is a real war for the independence of Ukraine."[166] On the expert level it was then claimed that since Ukraine already depends on Russia for hydrocarbons, Russian control over Ukrainian pipelines would transform Ukraine into "a sort of a colonial dominion."[167] Consequently, while the Kremlin was seen as aiming for dominance of the European energy market, Ukraine tried to "retain its sovereignty in the very literal sense."[168] As a result, the gas dispute was seen as promoting the "nation-building" efforts—especially in the western and central parts of Ukraine.[169] Simultaneously, any developments that were seen as "pro-Russian" were also considered unpatriotic at the time. Some media outlets were then criticized for keeping the Russian side in their coverage of the crisis and some Ukrainian politicians were accused of being willing to help Russia keep the Ukrainian people "on their knees"—with a harsh critique falling especially on a number of MPs who were aiming to grant an official status to the Russian language "at a time when the country was on the brink of the energy disaster."[170]

The logic of war and "energy sovereignty"

Apart from the "grammar of conflict" in the official rhetoric, the imperative of survival caused Ukrainian energy policy decision-making to be moved to the top political levels and the diversification plans refocused on domestic energy resources. Both moves aimed at ensuring "energy sovereignty" as opposed to "energy security" only. Therefore, the National Security and Defence Council of Ukraine was reformed in the aftermath of the 2006 gas crisis to include a separate unit for dealing with energy security, as its Secretary Vitaliy Haiduk stated in February 2007: "energy independence—this is the issue of state sovereignty. [And] we are paying great attention to [it]."[171] The Chief of the Ukrainian Security Service also warned later that year about the danger to Ukraine caused by Russian political integration and a lack of transparency in the area of energy supply.[172] Similarly, in the aftermath of the 2009 gas dispute, the Ministry of Fuels and Energy promised to implement the decision of the Council of National Security and Defence from February 2009 regarding urgent means for ensuring energy security.[173]

In practical terms, it was the diversification of energy portfolio that was seen as a means of reducing "the temptation to use energy supplies by Russia to attack the sovereignty of Ukraine."[174] Therefore, diverse projects throughout the years that focused on domestic energy production were justified on the grounds of greater independence from Russia. This trend was most prominent in relation to the gas market, with Ukrainian newspapers announcing " 'the formula' of gas independence,"[175] or with the chairman of the Committee for Energy Independence of Ukraine seeing the "chance for energy sovereignty" in the formation of a nationwide public movement that could pressure the government to decrease its reliance on gas monopoly and focus on diversification and domestic energy resources.[176] Similarly, a director of the National Investment Agency called November 26 "the day of energy independence of Ukraine" while referring to plans to build a domestic LNG terminal.[177] The same rhetoric applied to further nuclear energy development plans, as the media noted how the latter decreases Ukraine's dependence on a gas monopoly, while "freedom, [and] energy security is not measured in millions, ... [but] in the percentages of dependence or independence."[178] It was also argued that in the mentality of a growing number of Ukrainians, nuclear energy became linked to energy independence, reliability and the promising scientific and technological development of the country.[179]

The two gas disputes—especially the one in January 2006—also raised the issue of energy-saving measures. President Yushchenko called on the members of the government at the Cabinet meeting in January 2006: "In every ministry and department, I would like us to have a clear answer regarding the implementation of the new energy saving policy in the country."[180] As later years showed, this feeling of urgency to radically change the attitudes towards energy saving into more sustainable ones did not bring satisfactory results. Not surprisingly, the rationale of energy independence was also behind the ideas of further exploration of the domestic ores of uranium and coal in energy production as well as of the gradual development of wind and solar renewable energy.[181]

Generally speaking, though, although different energy supply diversification plans were seen as politically justifiable at the time, expert opinions regarding their economic rationale varied.[182] Different energy experts evaluated the economic and technical viability of plans for the development of an LNG terminal, extraction of shale gas, reversed gas flow from the West, or further development of NPPs differently.[183] Some pointed to the high politicization of certain diversification projects—such as Odessa-Brody, when the terminal was built and only then a real search for the supplier started,[184] whereas Ukraine did not have much problem with oil security in the first place.[185] Interestingly, although the development of the Odessa-Brody project signaled high politicization of the issue of energy security during Yushchenko's presidency, more diversification attempts took place with Viktor Yanukovich in office.[186] Yushchenko tried to realize the policy of energy independence, which as an energy expert from the Nomos Centre pointed out, "was included in the state's schedule in the Yushchenko times, but without any concrete results, correct vision, correct ideas."[187] Moreover, as local policy analysts pointed out, the political life during Yushchenko's presidency was dominated by his conflict with Julia Tymoshenko, and it was only during the presidency of Yanukovych that a number of projects under the slogan of "energy independence" as well as the monitoring of economic reforms within the ministerial administration were implemented.[188] Therefore, paradoxically, despite winning the elections based on the pro-Russian electorate, the unfavorable conditions at the time (high prices for the contracted gas from Russia and disillusionment with its energy policy) forced Yanukovich to look for alternative sources of energy supply (shale gas, reversed gas flow, LNG).[189]

War with Russia: the strengthening of the survival imperative

If Ukraine's diversification attempts following the two gas crises proved not very successful in the long run, the outbreak of the military conflict with Russia in 2014 brought the issue of energy security back to the fore of the national security and policy agenda. The resulting increase in gas prices finally sparked a serious policy debate on energy-efficiency measures and led to increased mobilization at the local level. Even the eastern regions directly affected by the conflict became highly mobilized in the energy sector. As a representative from the Energy Efficiency Agency noted:

> Even in the regions of Kramatorsk local municipalities ... developed an energy concept. The regional authorities were very active to show the rest of Eastern Ukraine—"if we can do it, how come you don't." ... The main reason for doing that was again an increase in gas prices.[190]

The loss of the eastern regions with their coal mines, the damage of the local infrastructure, and the annexation of the Crimea where the big solar power plants were located, put additional strain on national energy security. The imperative of survival came back to Ukraine's energy affairs with a double force, as the geopolitical factors were as pressing as ever.

The shift from the logic of subsistence back to the logic of war was best illustrated by the Ukrainian changing responses to the Nordstream 1 and Nordstream 2 projects. As opposed to neighboring Poland, the development of the initial North European Pipeline in 2011–2012 (Nordstream 1) did not invoke the imperative of survival in the Ukrainian context. On the one hand, given that Ukraine had spare capacities and could not see the justification for the bypassing project, there was disappointment on the side of the Ukrainian government—with media pointing to the loss in revenues. On the other hand, some experts highlighted that the Nordstream pipeline would not have much impact on the Ukrainian gas transit because of its limited capacity. A former energy security commissioner of the president of Ukraine, Bohdan Sokolovski, even stated that such a policy trend might be for the better as Ukraine should not rely so heavily on being a transit state—as the profits do not outweigh the political costs here.[191] Therefore, although Nordstream 1 was perceived as a certain manifestation of Russia's power in relation to Ukraine (but also the Czech Republic and Slovakia), and—according to the former adviser to the president of Ukraine, John Diyak, its construction had even accelerated the energy conflict in 2009, where Russia used "horror stories" to scare Europeans and to imply that Ukraine is not a reliable partner[192]—its relative impact on the Ukrainian energy security debate was low.

The war over eastern territories brought geopolitical considerations back into energy politics. As the network of pipelines crossing Ukraine gave it a certain advantage in its war with Russia—especially as the Gazprom–Naftogaz transit agreement is set to expire on January 1, 2020,[193] the development of Nordstream 2 caused a much stronger reaction. With press headlines such as "A gas noose on the neck of Europe,"[194] or "The battle of transit... ,"[195] the new pipeline project not only raised an alert in Kiev, but Ukrainian politicians actively campaigned in Brussels against its establishment.[196] Ukrainian President Petro Poroshenko announced his plans to create a consortium of EU companies in Brussels that would help to stop this "political project against Ukraine," which he considered an economic and energy blockade of no economically justifiable basis established to harm his country.[197] The rhetoric went even further than that, as the Ukrainian side started to question the integrity and motives of the EU players in the face of a "political bribe for loyalty to Russia."[198] With headlines such as "Values or Nord Stream 2?"[199] Ukrainian commentators wondered whether the terms of EU solidarity and common values are just empty words for German businesses and politicians alike, who insist on the project's economic nature whereas the US administration and EU countries agree that it is a geopolitical measure.[200] As some argued, if Russia used energy as a weapon on a number of occasions against Ukraine, the German stance not only gave the impression that the West is not united, but that it can be easily bought and corrupted.[201] As a director of the Ukrainian New Europe Center stated: "'Schroederization' represents the higher, overt degree of cynicism and corruption.... These steps raise more questions, casting doubt on the reputation of the whole of the EU."[202] In a similar, albeit lighter tone, Rada Deputy Chairperson Oksana Syroyid stated in an interview with Ukraine's Channel 112: "Russia will win victories, and we do not know when it will stop, because today, the Nordstream 2 project is a weapon that Russia has already delivered to Berlin; and the only question is when she will use this weapon."[203] Given this political stance, the Ukrainian side attempted to portray its fight as motivated not only by its own domestic concerns, but by the common European good. Petro Poroshenko called Nordstream 2 the Trojan horse for European security, which threatens not only the energy security of the European Union, but also its geopolitical security.[204] He added that increasing the EU's dependence on Russia leads to the monopolization of the European market and poses a geopolitical threat, hence Ukraine makes every effort at its disposal to stop this project and to protect the interests of Ukraine, Poland, the Baltic and Scandinavian states, the whole EU and the whole world.[205]

The imperative of survival remains high in Ukraine's energy affairs and is likely to strengthen further, as the prospects for ending the military conflict and normalizing economic relations with Russia remain out of reach. The logic of war is vividly present in both the political rhetoric and the policy moves that put the issue of energy supply at the top of the national security agenda and frequently overshadow the dominant subsistence logic (e.g., low economic viability of diversification plans). Moreover, the war logic became deeply embedded in the Ukrainian context on all levels, as it leads to the further conflation of the notion of "energy security" with "energy sovereignty" and "energy independence" and has far-reaching consequences for national and local energy affairs alike. In this light, the joint EU–Russian energy projects conducted without the involvement of Ukraine are likely to be seen as a betrayal of a vulnerable state at war. Energy security lies at the very core of the current Ukrainian national security, and geopolitical considerations will be ever present in its energy policy for years to come.

The nuclear energy debate

The puzzling lack of prevention imperative

Although the military conflict with Russia understandably caused the energy policy to shift more strongly towards alternatives such as nuclear energy (which is now providing close to 60 percent of electricity in the country),[206] and safety concerns related to the exploitation of nuclear energy are not a priority, the Ukrainian energy context has been marked by a surprising lack of the risk logic, both now and in a wider historical perspective. On the one hand, the 1986 nuclear accident in Chernobyl gave rise to the green movement in Ukraine (establishment of Zelenyi Svit "Green World," the Ukrainian Environmental Association) that transformed into the Party of Greens, which entered the Ukrainian Parliament as a part of the Democratic Bloc during the 1990 elections, when environmental issues were high on the agenda.[207] On the other hand, the history of this catastrophe had no impact on the subsequent developments in the domestic nuclear energy sector over the years.

It is then a common expert opinion in Ukraine that the accident in Chernobyl was an example of the incompetence and mismanagement at all levels of the totalitarian state—from the political to the scientific one—which implies that the tragedy was simply inevitable.[208] As far as public opinion is concerned, similar to other countries, the Chernobyl disaster raised awareness about the safety of nuclear energy in general and Ukrainian nuclear power plants in particular—and as some analyses stated, the emotional perceptions largely prevailed over the rational ones.[209] However, the initial impact of the catastrophe has been diminishing in the Ukrainian context ever since. One of the opinion surveys that asked the question "what are people most afraid of?" over the years showed a steady decline in the declared fear of the consequences of Chernobyl—from 47 percent in 1992 to only 16 percent in 2010.[210, 211] Moreover, the same data showed that the consequences of the Chernobyl catastrophe were ranked low among the Ukrainian population among other fears—albeit still at eleventh place.[212] They were preceded mostly by various economic concerns (an increase in prices, unemployment, not being paid salary), and issues such as an increase in crime, infection harmful for life, hunger, cold, or disintegration of Ukraine as a state.[213] Some local actors also pointed to both psychological factors and a lack of public debate on nuclear energy when explaining the relative non-importance of the Chernobyl legacy. As a member of Movement 350 stated in 2013:

> Why is Chernobyl not an issue? I don't know. I think it is something psychological. I think people just tend to forget or are trying to forget about Chernobyl. And right now, that the nuclear blocks of the nuclear power stations are being discussed, people are not protesting, people are not blocking the sites of the construction—it is strange. Of course many people don't know about the plans, because they are not being discussed everywhere—these are decisions that are made in the closed circle.[214]

Similarly, other energy experts point out that nuclear energy is discussed mostly by professionals, and not only is there a lack of wider public debate, but it is hard to get the media's attention on the issue even on the anniversary of the Chernobyl disaster.[215] Although the "green" energy activists attempted to utilize the "Chernobyl rhetoric" to criticize the plans for the construction of new nuclear power plants on a number of occasions, their efforts have not brought any tangible results so far. According to the NGO sector, such persistent social attitudes towards nuclear energy in Ukraine have been heavily influenced by the effective promotion of this type of energy as cheap, clean and secure—and therefore appealing to the general population concerned mostly with prices for utilities.[216] As a representative from the Kiev-based Institute for Economic Research and Policy Consulting noted in autumn 2013: "The government from time to time sends a message to the public: 'OK, we have cheap nuclear, we will proceed further'—and nobody cares about the fact that it is outdated."[217] Whereas the outbreak of the conflict with Russia served as an additional trigger for the justification of the further development of the NPPs, this policy move was not difficult to implement in a context where the debate on the potential phase-out of nuclear facilities never took place and where the population seemed to agree on the status quo.

In the aftermath of Fukushima

The accident at the Japanese Fukushima nuclear power plant did not alter the Ukrainian mainstream energy policy approach. First, there was no political debate in Ukraine after Fukushima, as the accident was discussed primarily at the level of NGOs and the Ukrainian expert community. Second, the Ukrainian government itself—similar to the aftermath of the Chernobyl disaster—assured the Ukrainian population that additional safety tests at all of the Ukrainian nuclear power plants would be conducted and the Cabinet of Ministers approved a program for increasing the level of safety of power units of nuclear power plants later that year.[218] Third, Ukrainian media reported on the developments in Japan in a non-emotional manner, as the focus was clearly kept on the casualties and people missing as a consequence of an earthquake and tsunami rather than on the accident in the nuclear power plant.[219] The tendency was to point to a chain of events and their unlikely accumulation that led to the nuclear leak rather than to the uncontrollability of nuclear energy per se.[220] With the newspaper headlines in the immediate aftermath of the Japanese catastrophe such as "'Fukushima -1' is not Chernobyl," the Ukrainian media reported on the technical details of an earthquake and tsunami that were additionally "complicated" by the damage made to the Fukushima nuclear power plant.[221] Simultaneously, the Ukrainian media quoted Japanese authorities that evaluated the probability of nuclear contamination as small and international expert opinions, which emphasized that the Japanese nuclear accident was very different from the catastrophes in Chernobyl or Three Mile Island, as it did not pose a serious threat to the health of people or natural environment.[222] The nuclear accident was therefore depicted as a historical precedent of very limited impact—with no reported cases of post-radiation disease.[223] In light of this general rhetoric, analyses that resembled the German media reaction to Fukushima—as they pointed to "a contemporary *Homo Economicus* occupied with the fulfillment of its endless needs through economic activity and technological advancement—a root cause of both Ukrainian and Japanese tragedies"—were in a clear minority.[224] Therefore, the imperative of prevention failed to rise in the Ukrainian energy context. Although some political statements ensured the population of the safety of the NPPs' safety, the general rhetoric of calculation and precaution was lacking as it did not fall on fertile ground. The post-Fukushima approach to nuclear energy in Ukraine was not about the manageability of risk, but rather "business as usual."

Similarly, the catastrophe in Japan did not significantly influence Ukrainian attitudes towards nuclear energy. On the one hand, as the opinion polls mentioned earlier showed over the years, other pressing problems of the current social agenda overshadowed its relative importance.[225] On the other hand, some local observers pointed to general social disengagement:

> After Fukushima there was news about the losses in Japan, but not really a huge debate on whether we should continue with nuclear power. My only explanation is that people feel powerless, it's a very deep internalized feeling that you cannot change anything, so you better not worry.[226]

Some voices also pointed out that even if Ukrainians are afraid of nuclear energy—that fear is not necessarily strong enough to motivate them to take part in anti-nuclear initiatives. First, many people do not believe that their opposition could have any tangible effects. Second, a lot of protests that took place in Ukraine so far were "paid for" by different actors—and many people do not want to be associated with such protests.[227]

Crucially, the rise of the risk logic has also been hindered by the growing idea of energy independence among the Ukrainian political circle, which even prior to the conflict with Russia considered nuclear energy as a key means to that end.[228] As one energy expert stated in 2012:

> We have a moral right to think about our energy future, energy independence and security. We already have nuclear reactors. They will pose minimal risk, once we devote serious money to further development and improvement of nuclear technology and training.[229]

This rhetoric strengthened even more after the outbreak of the military conflict, despite the fact that Ukraine still imports nuclear fuel from its eastern neighbor. Local observers of the ongoing energy security debates point out that because of increased gas prices and loss of the coal regions, nuclear energy is often presented as "the only option left."[230] The general public disengagement from the issue coupled with the ongoing military conflict with Russia and a new policy approach makes it hard for the NGO sector to actively oppose the development of the nuclear power plants (or old coal-burning plants) and to promote alternative solutions (e.g., decentralized renewable energy). If "green" NGOs, which have been consistently concerned with the outdated nuclear units and a critical dependence on Russia for nuclear fuel, have advocated a gradual nuclear phase-out for years,[231] but have lost the battle with big industry lobbyists, their current efforts in this area appear even less likely to be successful. With

15 active reactors, Ukraine ranks seventh among the world's nuclear energy producers, and the Ukrainian government plans to both extend the operation of the existing NPPs from the 1980s[232] and construct new units at Khmelnytskyi power plant.[233] It also seeks to diversify its nuclear fuel supplies in order to limit its dependence on Russia. The first successful steps in this direction have already been taken.[234]

Overall, the Ukrainian debate on nuclear energy fits into wider energy policy considerations and is marked by the surprising lack of the risk logic. The absence of the imperative of prevention is down to the specifics of the domestic context. First, the typical constellation of actors with big industry lobbyists, centralized decision-making and "rational" media are not conducive for the rhetoric of precaution to emerge on the public policy agenda. Second, the distal context with the historically determined perceptions of Russia that puts the focus on domestic energy resources, as well as the specific socialization processes that result in societal disengagement (feeling of powerlessness), play a role. Third, such a setting is easily dominated by the subsistence logic that is increasingly underpinned by the idea of energy independence and sought in the domestic energy projects—such as nuclear energy.

Conclusion

The analysis of the Ukrainian case reveals uneasy maneuvering between different priorities of energy security in the country at war. The contextual dynamic marked by the multiplicity of actors, interests and agendas became even more complicated as a result of the Russian–Ukrainian military conflict. Energy security lies at the core of Ukraine's security considerations, and the powerful policy shift towards the West shook up the domestic status quo. Although centralized decision-making, dominant interests of big energy businesses and societal disengagement still prevail, the events of 2014 set in motion new energy security approaches and solutions and increased societal mobilization, both at the national and local levels.

With the rise of gas prices and a loss of strategic coal regions, Ukraine increasingly turns towards nuclear energy and big renewable energy projects. The imperative of sustenance gives a strong drive to energy policies that focus on the fulfillment of societal needs in times of crisis. Simultaneously, the conflict with Russia strengthens the already present logic of war in Ukraine's energy affairs. The imperative of survival leads to extraordinary measures and conflictual rhetoric that aim at energy independence from the Russian supplier at all costs. Moreover, the idea of energy independence started to permeate to grassroots initiatives in energy, as the economic impact of high gas prices give rise to political populism and make appealing to nationalistic and anti-Russian sentiments an efficient strategy. Therefore, although the ongoing decentralization of power and increased funding make it easier for the local NGO sector to promote alternative energy solutions, advocating self-reliance based on democratic energy does not come easy in a context with a deeply internalized survival rationale. While the big projects in renewables are developing, the prospects for wider democratization of the domestic energy sector are a remote future because of technical aspects as well as the Soviet legacy of lack of trust and unwillingness to cooperate and take control by the general population. In the context where the imperatives of sustenance and survival set the energy policy course within a shifting constellation of political and social actors, nuclear energy constitutes yet another sector that fits this broader dynamic. If the Chernobyl legacy played no role in the Ukrainian approach to nuclear energy prior to the war with Russia, in its aftermath the economic calculations of cheap electricity from nuclear were additionally strengthened by the notion of energy independence and used to justify further development of the NPPs. The societal disengagement and business-like approach to the nuclear sector meant that even in the post-Fukushima context, the imperative of prevention did not emerge in the Ukrainian approach to nuclear energy. Given the ongoing political developments, the latter is likely to become further dominated by the logic of war that currently rules both Ukraine's high-level politics and energy affairs.

Notes

1 Movement 350, Interview; EU Commission Delegation in Kiev, Interview; Institute for Economic Research and Policy Consulting, Interview; Institute for Energy Studies, Interview; International Finance Corporation, Interview.
2 Dixi Group II, Interview; Energy Efficient Cities of Ukraine, Interview.
3 Dixi Group, Interview; Nomos Centre Kiev, Interview.
4 Consolidation that would make these networks work more efficiently as a part of the Ukrainian energy system rather than as part of the former USSR transit system.
5 Prokin, *Harantuvannya Energetychnoi Bezpeki*, 102–3.
6 Institute for Energy Studies, Interview.
7 Prokin, *Harantuvannya Energetychnoi Bezpeki*, 13–15.
8 Ibid., 14.
9 Shevtsov, *Energetyka Ukrainy Na Shlyakhu Do Evropeyskoi Integratsyi*, 71.
10 Followed by shifting financial resources from subsidizing utilities to subsidizing energy efficiency, diversification of gas supply routes and development of renewables.
11 Greencubator, Interview.
12 Heinrich-Böll-Stiftung Kiev, Interview.
13 Ministry of Energy, "Energetichna Strategija Ukraïni Na Period Do 2035."
14 National Ecological Centre of Ukraine, Interview; Institute for Economic Research and Policy Consulting, Interview; Dixi Group, Interview.
15 Ibid.; Dubrovyk, "Povazhayte Alternativu."
16 Currently the State Agency on Energy Efficiency and Energy Saving of Ukraine.
17 After its dissolution in 2014, the National Energy and Utility Regulatory Commission (NEURC) was re-created by presidential decree; Decree of the President of Ukraine No 694/2014 of August 27, 2014. http://zakon3.rada.gov.ua/laws/show/694/2014.
18 But also deals with a number of related regulatory procedures, such as setting the green tariffs for renewables.
19 Institute for Economic Research and Policy Consulting, Interview.
20 With the Ministry insisting on around 5–6 percent and the Energy Efficiency Agency on at least 11–12 percent.

21 National Ecological Centre of Ukraine, Interview; Heinrich-Böll-Stiftung Kiev, Interview.
22 Institute for Economic Research and Policy Consulting, Interview.
23 EU Commission Delegation in Kiev, Interview.
24 Nomos Centre Kiev, Interview.
25 Institute for Energy Studies, Interview.
26 Nomos Centre Kiev, Interview.
27 Ibid.
28 Dixi Group, Interview; National Ecological Centre of Ukraine, Interview; National Ecological Centre of Ukraine, *Energy [R]evolution*, 1.
29 National Ecological Centre of Ukraine, *Energy [R]evolution*, 1.
30 National Ecological Centre of Ukraine, Interview.
31 Ibid.
32 Institute for Economic Research and Policy Consulting, Interview.
33 International Finance Corporation, Interview; Nomos Centre Kiev, Interview.
34 Heinrich-Böll-Stiftung Kiev, Interview. Emphasis added.
35 Leukhina, "Stages of Development of Ecological Non-Governmental Organizations in Ukraine after Chernobyl Accident."
36 Institute for Economic Research and Policy Consulting, Interview; Kiev Post, Interview.
37 Movement 350, Interview.
38 Nomos Centre Kiev, Interview.
39 Ibid. Emphasis added.
40 Institute for Energy Studies, Interview.
41 Ukrainian Institute for Public Policy, Interview.
42 Institute for Economic Research and Policy Consulting, Interview.
43 National Ecological Centre of Ukraine, Interview.
44 Skuba, "Energoefektyvnist Myslennia"; Nomos Centre Kiev, Interview.
45 Nomos Centre Kiev, Interview.
46 Ibid.
47 Antonenko et al., "Reforming Ukraine's Energy Sector."
48 Ecoaction, Interview; Opora Rivne, Interview; Sweet Osvit, Interview; Greencubator II, Interview.
49 Antonenko et al., "Reforming Ukraine's Energy Sector."
50 Ibid.
51 Now providing approximately 55 percent of electricity in the country.
52 "Energy Strategy for 2035."
53 Ibid.
54 Ekoklub Rivne, Interview.
55 Greencubator II, Interview.
56 With the average number of participants oscillating around 120.
57 Ecoaction, Interview.
58 Law no. 1540 "On the National Commission for the State Regulation of Energy and Utilities" of 22.09.2016 entering into force on 16.11.2016.
59 "The National Energy Regulatory Authority of Ukraine," 6.
60 Antonenko et al., "Reforming Ukraine's Energy Sector."
61 Ibid.
62 Heinrich-Böll-Stiftung Kiev II, Interview; Greencubator II, Interview; Ekoklub Rivne, Interview.
63 Dixi Group II, Interview; Ecoaction, Interview; Heinrich-Böll-Stiftung Kiev II, Interview.
64 Greencubator II, Interview.
65 Heinrich-Böll-Stiftung Kiev II, Interview.
66 Greencubator, Interview.

67 https://dtek.com/en/about/, DTEK company website.
68 National Ecological Centre of Ukraine, Interview; Institute for Economic Research and Policy Consulting, Interview.
69 Dixi Group, Interview; Institute for Economic Research and Policy Consulting, Interview; Nomos Centre Kiev, Interview; Heinrich-Böll-Stiftung Kiev, Interview; Ecoaction, Interview.
70 "Chernobyl Begins New Life as Solar Power Park."
71 Ecoaction, Interview.
72 Greencubator, Interview.
73 Heinrich-Böll-Stiftung Kiev II, Interview.
74 Movement 350 II, Interview, Kiev.
75 Ecoaction, Interview.
76 Matveev, "Carpathian Resistance."
77 Ecoaction, Interview.
78 Ekoltava, Interview; Ekoklub Rivne, Interview.
79 Shevtsov, *Energetyka Ukrainy Na Shlyakhu Do Evropeyskoi Integratsyi*, 71–111. Emphasis added.
80 Ibid.
81 Movement 350, Interview.
82 Greencubator II, Interview.
83 Opora Rivne, Interview.
84 Ecoaction, Interview.
85 Opora Rivne, Interview.
86 Ibid.
87 Movement 350, Interview.
88 Heinrich-Böll-Stiftung Kiev II, Interview.
89 Greencubator II, Interview.
90 Movement 350 II, Interview.
91 Lutsevych, "How to Finish a Revolution," 8.
92 Greencubator II, Interview.
93 Heinrich-Böll-Stiftung Kiev, Interview.
94 Ukrainian Institute for Public Policy, Interview.
95 Dixi Group, Interview, Kiev.
96 Movement 350, Interview.
97 The survey covered approximately one-third of the Ukrainian territory and 20 organizations working in collaboration with HBF.
98 Heinrich-Böll-Stiftung Kiev II, Interview.
99 Ibid.
100 Movement 350 II, Interview.
101 Ibid.
102 Kniazhanskyi, "'Ozelenennia' ekonomiki."
103 Sweet Osvit, Interview; Opora Rivne, Interview; Ecoaction, Interview; Ekoltava, Interview.
104 Greencubator, Interview. Emphasis added.
105 Ekoklub Rivne, Interview.
106 Ibid.
107 Ekoklub Rivne, Interview; Ekoltava, Interview.
108 Opora Rivne, Interview; Sweet Osvit, Interview.
109 Heinrich-Böll-Stiftung Kiev II, Interview.
110 Greencubator II, Interview; Opora Rivne, Interview.
111 http://greencubator.info/, Greencubator organization website.
112 National Ecological Centre of Ukraine, Interview; Movement 350, Interview; Institute for Economic Research and Policy Consulting, Interview; International Finance Corporation, Interview.

113 IMF, World Bank, etc.
114 Energy Efficient Cities of Ukraine, Interview.
115 "Natural Gas Consumption in Ukraine by User Category."
116 Dixi Group II, Interview, Kiev.
117 "Ukrainian Government Extends 'Warm Loans' Program for 2017."
118 Ecoaction, Interview; Sweet Osvit, Interview.
119 Energy Efficient Cities of Ukraine, Interview; http://enefcities.org.ua/en/.
120 Heinrich-Böll-Stiftung Kiev, Interview.
121 "Building Local Capacity for Domestic Solar Heating."
122 Movement 350, Interview.
123 "Number of Households with Solar Panels on Roofs in Ukraine Increases 2.5-Fold."
124 Energy Efficient Cities of Ukraine, Interview.
125 Movement 350 II, Interview; Heinrich-Böll-Stiftung Kiev II, Interview; Energy Efficient Cities of Ukraine, Interview.
126 Dixi Group II, Interview.
127 Energy Efficient Cities of Ukraine, Interview.
128 Movement 350 II, Interview.
129 Ibid.
130 Greencubator II, Interview.
131 Movement 350 II, Interview.
132 Ibid.
133 Ekoklub Rivne, Interview.
134 Dixi Group II, Interview.
135 Movement 350, Interview; Heinrich-Böll-Stiftung Kiev II, Interview.
136 Wolczuk and Zeruolis, "Rebuilding Ukraine"; Deychakiwsky, "Analysis: U.S. Assistance to Ukraine."
137 With the most active ones being the EU, Germany and USAID.
138 Ekoklub Rivne, Interview.
139 Ibid.
140 Greencubator, Interview. Emphasis added.
141 International Finance Corporation, Interview.
142 Dixi Group, Interview.
143 International Foundation for Electoral Systems, "Key Findings."
144 Savytskyi, "Gazovo Imperski Paraleli"; Diyak, *Gazova Promysovist I Energetychna Bezpeka Ukrainy*, 53–4.
145 Chornei, "Ocherednaia Gazovaia Ataka"; Kniazhanskyi, "Navishcho Ukrayini Energetichna Strategiia."
146 E.g., Murtazaiev, "Monetizatsiia Liubovi"; Kniazhanskyi, "Prognoz Negatyvnyi"; Diyak, *Gazova Promysovist I Energetychna Bezpeka Ukrainy*, 131–2.
147 Danylov, "Gazovyi Blitskryg Po-Sovetsky"; Solodkyi, " 'Gazovi Viyni'—2."
148 Kadare, "Gazova Viyna."
149 Yahno, "Viacheslav Kyrylenko."
150 Gaidai, "Zorianyi Chas Mistsevoi Energopolityky."
151 Rozer, "Na Gorizonti—Nova 'gazova Viyna'."
152 Chornei, "Ocherednaia Gazovaia Ataka"; Kniazhanskyi, "Gazova Ataka"; Gonchar and Alinov, "Gazovyi Natisk c Vostoka."
153 Kniazhanskyi, "Kraina Gazovyh Zarushnykiv."
154 Gonchar and Alinov, "Gazovyi Natisk c Vostoka."
155 Kniazhanskyi, "Ukraina Pidigruie 'gazovomu' shantazhu?"
156 Kulchytskyi, "Imperiia I My."
157 Diyak, *Gazova Promysovist I Energetychna Bezpeka Ukrainy*.
158 Ibid., 50–4.
159 Ibid.
160 Gonchar and Alinov, "Gazovyi Natisk c Vostoka."

161 National Ecological Centre of Ukraine, Interview; Institute for Economic Research and Policy Consulting, Interview.
162 Kniazhanskyi, "Prognoz Negatyvnyi."
163 Zhluktenko, "Zdvig Po Gazu."
164 Kniazhanskyi, "Zakony Tysku"; Petkova, "Volodymyr Semynozhenko."
165 Raihel, "Dyktat 'Gazpromu'."
166 Voswinkel, "Moskaus Rohrkrepierer."
167 Diyak, *Gazova Promysovist I Energetychna Bezpeka Ukrainy*, 59.
168 Ibid., 131–2.
169 Voswinkel, "Moskaus Rohrkrepierer."
170 Diyak, *Gazova Promysovist I Energetychna Bezpeka Ukrainy*, 59.
171 "Vitalii Gaiduk: Naigolovnishe—Tse Vlasna Energobezpeka."
172 Olearchyk, "Golova SBU Zasterigaie pro Nebezpeku."
173 "Mintopenerg Obeschaet Vypolnit Reshenie SNBO I Obespechit Energobezopasnost Ukrainy."
174 Diyak, *Gazova Promysovist i Energetychna Bezpeka Ukrainy*, 63.
175 Gonchar, " 'Formula' gazovoi Nezalezhnosti."
176 Kniazhanskyi, "Shans Na Energetychnyi Suverenitet."
177 Bilousova, "Den Energetychnoi Nezalezhnosti Ukrainy."
178 Ibid.
179 Kylnytskyi, "Yuryi Nedashkovskyi."
180 Kniazhanskyi, "Truba."
181 Nadeyn, "Alternativnaya Energetika"; Gaidai, "Zorianyi Chas Mistsevoi Energopolityky"; Ryzhkov, "Alternatyva Gazu Lezhyt Pid Nogamy."
182 International Finance Corporation, Interview.
183 Heinrich-Böll-Stiftung Kiev, Interview; Institute for Energy Studies, Interview; Ukrainian Institute for Public Policy, Interview; Institute for Economic Research and Policy Consulting, Interview; International Finance Corporation, Interview; Nomos Centre Kiev, Interview.
184 Institute for Economic Research and Policy Consulting, Interview.
185 Ukrainian Institute for Public Policy, Interview.
186 International Finance Corporation, Interview; National Ecological Centre of Ukraine, Interview; Institute for Energy Studies, Interview.
187 Nomos Centre Kiev, Interview.
188 International Finance Corporation, Interview; Movement 350, Interview.
189 National Ecological Centre of Ukraine, Interview; Institute for Energy Studies, Interview; Nomos Centre Kiev, Interview.
190 Energy Efficiency Agency, Interview.
191 Dubrovyk, "Pro Golovnu intrygu 'Pivnichnogo Potoku'."
192 Ibid.
193 Cohen, "Russia's Nord Stream II Pipeline Is Ukraine's Worst Nightmare."
194 Siruk, "A Gas Noose on the Neck of Europe."
195 Harchenko, "Bitva Za Tranzit, ili 'Severnyj Potok-2' kak Jabloko Razdora."
196 "NordStream 2 to Pump, but Ukraine Gas Transit Will Remain."
197 MacDonald, "Poroshenko Tells Germany Nord Stream 2 Gas Pipeline Is a 'Political Bribe' "; Rusheva, "Ukraine Creating EU-Based Consortium to Stop Nord Stream-2."
198 Ibid.
199 Kapsamun, "Values or Nord Stream 2?"
200 Siruk, "A Gas Noose on the Neck of Europe."
201 Kapsamun, "Values or Nord Stream 2?"
202 Ibid.
203 Sputnik, " 'Russian Weapon Already in Berlin': Ukrainian MP Has Meltdown Over Nord Stream 2."

204 "Poroshenko Nazval Severnyj Potok-2 Trojanskim Konem Dlja Evropejskoj Bezopasnosti."
205 "Poroshenko on Nord Stream 2."
206 "Poroshenko: Ukraine to Increase Nuclear Share to 60%."
207 Yekelchyk *Ukraine: Birth of a Modern Nation*, 181–7; www.globalgreens.org/fr/node/4651?language=en
208 Shvec, "Yenerhetycheskaia Bezopasnost Ukrayny."
209 Kuzmenko, "Risk Society," 194.
210 Data from the Institute of Sociology HAH of Ukraine.
211 Konoplytska, "Strah Pered Naslidkamy Avarii Na Chaes Ta Inshi Strahy Naselennya Ukrainy," 66.
212 Ibid., 67.
213 Ibid., 67.
214 Movement 350, Interview.
215 Ecoaction, Interview.
216 Dixi Group, Interview.
217 Institute for Economic Research and Policy Consulting, Interview.
218 Cabinet of Ministers of Ukraine Resolution, December 7, 2011, nr. 1270, Kiev, On approval of the integrated (consolidated) program for increasing the level of safety of power units of nuclear power plants, http://zakon.rada.gov.ua/laws/show/1270-2011-%D0%BF.
219 Kan, "Yaponiia Shliah Do Vidnovlennia."
220 Maskalevych, "Fukusima Uroki Ekonomiki."
221 Siruk, " 'Fukusima-1' ne Chornobyl."
222 Ibid.
223 Shvec, "Yenerhetycheskaia Bezopasnost Ukrayny."
224 Tunytsia and Tunytsia, "Chernobylskii Sindrom Otrazhaet Antyekologicheskuiu Suschnost Rynochnoi Ekonomiki."
225 National Ecological Centre of Ukraine, Interview; Konoplytska, "Strah Pered Naslidkamy Avarii Na Chaes Ta Inshi Strahy Naselennya Ukrainy," 66.
226 Movement 350, Interview.
227 International Finance Corporation, Interview.
228 Starchevskyi, " 'Zalezhnist' i 'dyversyfikatsiia'."
229 Shvec, "Yenerhetycheskaia Bezopasnost Ukrayny."
230 Ecoaction, Interview.
231 Heinrich-Böll-Stiftung Kiev, Interview; Greencubator, Interview; Heinrich-Böll-Stiftung Kiev II, Interview.
232 Including the South-Ukraine NPP, untis 1 and 2 of the Rivne NPP, and units 1 and 2 of the Zaporizhzhya NPP.
233 Antonenko et al., "Reforming Ukraine's Energy Sector."
234 "Ukrainian Nuclear Reactor Now Using All Non-Russian Fuel for the First Time."

References

Antonenko, Anton, Roman Nitsovych, Olena Pavlenko, and Kristian Takac. "Reforming Ukraine's Energy Sector: Critical Unfinished Business." *Carnegie Europe*, February 6, 2018. https://carnegieeurope.eu/2018/02/06/reforming-ukraine-s-energy-sector-critical-unfinished-business-pub-75449.

Bilousova, Nataliia. "Den Energetychnoi Nezalezhnosti Ukrainy." *Den*, November 27, 2012. http://day.Kiev.ua/uk/article/den-ukrayini/den-energetichnoyi-nezalezhnosti-ukrayini.

"Building Local Capacity for Domestic Solar Heating, Hot Water and Insulation for Rural and Remote Areas in the EEC Region." *www.wecf.eu*, March 25, 2011. www.wecf.eu/english/about-wecf/issues-projects/projects/localcapacity-eecregion.php.

"Chernobyl Begins New Life as Solar Power Park." *www.phys.org*, October 5, 2018. https://phys.org/news/2018-10-chernobyl-life-solar-power.html.
Chornei, Yurii. "Ocherednaia Gazovaia Ataka." *Zerkalo Nedeli*, January 19, 2007. http://gazeta.zn.ua/ECONOMICS/ocherednaya_gazovaya_ataka_s_1_yanvarya_2007_goda_grazhdane_budut_platit_za_potreblennyy_gaz_po_novy.html.
Cohen, Ariel. "Russia's Nord Stream II Pipeline Is Ukraine's Worst Nightmare." *Forbes*, June 18, 2018. www.forbes.com/sites/arielcohen/2018/06/18/russias-nord-stream-ii-pipeline-is-ukraines-worst-nightmare/.
Danylov, Sergei. "Gazovyi Blitskryg Po-Sovetsky." *Zerkalo Nedeli*, January 27, 2006. http://gazeta.zn.ua/POLITICS/gazovyy_blitskrig_po-sovetski.html.
Deychakiwsky, Orest. "Analysis: U.S. Assistance to Ukraine." *U.S. Ukraine Foundation*, February 26, 2018. www.usukraine.org/analysis-u-s-assistance-ukraine/.
Dixi Group. Interview, Kiev, October 19, 2013.
Dixi Group II. Interview, Kiev, April 24, 2018.
Diyak, Ivan Vasylovych. *Gazova Promysovist I Energetychna Bezpeka Ukrainy*. Kiev: Svit Uspikhu, 2009.
Dubrovyk, Alla. "Povazhayte Alternativu." *Den*, April 20, 2010. http://day.Kiev.ua/uk/article/ekonomika/povazhayte-alternativu.
Dubrovyk, Alla. "Pro Golovnu intrygu 'Pivnichnogo Potoku.'" *Den*, November 9, 2011. http://day.Kiev.ua/uk/article/ekonomika/pro-golovnu-intrigu-pivnichnogo-potoku.
Ecoaction. Interview, Kiev, April 30, 2018.
Ekoklub Rivne. Interview, Rivne, April 27, 2018.
Ekoltava. Interview, Poltava, May 7, 2018.
Energy Efficiency Agency. Interview, Kiev, May 3, 2018.
Energy Efficient Cities of Ukraine. Interview, Kiev, April 26, 2018.
"Energy Strategy for 2035." *International Energy Agency*, March 2018. www.iea.org/policiesandmeasures/pams/ukraine/name-167037-en.php.
EU Commission Delegation in Kiev. Interview, Kiev, November 26, 2013.
Gaidai, Andrii. "Zorianyi Chas Mistsevoi Energopolityky." *Den*, March 18, 2009. http://day.Kiev.ua/uk/article/ekonomika/zoryaniy-chas-miscevoyi-energopolitiki.
Gonchar, Mychail. "'Formula' gazovoi Nezalezhnosti." *Den*, July 17, 2008. http://day.Kiev.ua/uk/article/ekonomika/formula-gazovoyi-nezalezhnosti.
Gonchar, Mychail, and Maksim Alinov. "Gazovyi Natisk c Vostoka." *Zerkalo Nedeli*, July 1, 2011. http://gazeta.zn.ua/ECONOMICS/gazovyy_natisk_c_vostoka.html.
Greencubator. Interview, Kiev, October 30, 2013.
Greencubator II. Interview, Kiev, May 1, 2018.
Harchenko, Aleksandr. "Bitva Za Tranzit, ili 'Severnyj Potok-2' kak Jabloko Razdora." *Zerkalo Nedeli*, April 17, 2018. https://zn.ua/energy_market/bitva-za-tranzit-ili-severnyy-potok-2-kak-yabloko-razdora-281123_.html.
Heinrich-Böll-Stiftung Kiev. Interview, November 5, 2013.
Heinrich-Böll-Stiftung Kiev II. Interview, April 25, 2018.
Institute for Economic Research and Policy Consulting. Interview, Kiev, October 10, 2013.
Institute for Energy Studies. Interview, Warsaw, October 17, 2013.
International Finance Corporation. Interview, Kiev, November 19, 2013.
International Foundation for Electoral Systems, "Key Findings: Public Opinion in Ukraine, 2011." www.ifes.org/~/media/Files/Publications/Survey/2011/Public_Opinion_in_Ukraine_2011_Report.pdf.
Kadare, Ismail. "Gazova Viyna—Nova Holodna Viyna." *Den*, February 5, 2009. http://day.Kiev.ua/uk/article/den-planeti/gazova-viyna-nova-holodna-viyna.

Kan, Naoto. "Yaponiia Shliah Do Vidnovlennia," *Den*, April 27, 2011, http://day.Kiev.ua/uk/article/den-planeti/yaponiya-shlyah-do-vidnovlennya.

Kapsamun, Ivan. "Values or Nord Stream 2?" *Den*, March 29, 2018. https://day.Kiev.ua/en/article/day-after-day/zz-1-values-or-nord-stream-2-expert-russia-exports-gas-and-corruption-parallel.

Kniazhanskyi, Vitalii. "Gazova Ataka." *Den*, March 5, 2008. http://day.Kiev.ua/uk/article/panorama-dnya/gazova-ataka.

Kniazhanskyi, Vitalii. "Kraina Gazovyh Zarushnykiv." *Den*, September 12, 2007. http://day.Kiev.ua/uk/article/ekonomika/krayina-gazovih-zaruchnikiv.

Kniazhanskyi, Vitalii. "Navishcho Ukrayini Energetichna Strategiia." *Den*, February 27, 2009. http://day.Kiev.ua/uk/article/nota-bene/navishcho-ukrayini-energetichna-strategiya.

Kniazhanskyi, Vitalii. " 'Ozelenennia' ekonomiki." *Den*, December 21, 2010. http://day.Kiev.ua/uk/article/ekonomika/ozelenennya-ekonomiki.

Kniazhanskyi, Vitalii. "Prognoz Negatyvnyi." *Den*, January 18, 2006. http://day.Kiev.ua/uk/article/panorama-dnya/prognoz-negativniy.

Kniazhanskyi, Vitalii. "Shans Na Energetychnyi Suverenitet." *Den*, August 31, 2011. http://day.Kiev.ua/uk/article/panorama-dnya/shans-na-energetichniy-suverenitet.

Kniazhanskyi, Vitalii. "Truba: Istoriya Ta Isteriya." *Den*, January 13, 2006. http://day.Kiev.ua/uk/article/panorama-dnya/truba-istoriya-ta-isteriya.

Kniazhanskyi, Vitalii. "Ukraina Pidigruie 'gazovomu' shantazhu?" *Den*, April 11, 2012. http://day.Kiev.ua/uk/article/ekonomika/ukrayina-pidigruie-gazovomu-shantazhu.

Kniazhanskyi, Vitalii. "Zakony Tysku." *Den*, January 13, 2009. http://day.Kiev.ua/uk/article/ekonomika/zakoni-tisku.

Konoplytska, T. "Strah Pered Naslidkamy Avarii Na Chaes Ta Inshi Strahy Naselennya Ukrainy: Dynamika Zmin." In *Sotsialni Naslidky Chornobylya: Chas Vidrodzhennya*, 65–72. HAH Ukrainy, 2011.

Kulchytskyi, Stanislav. "Imperiia I My." *Den*, January 24, 2006. http://day.Kiev.ua/uk/article/cuspilstvo/imperiya-i-mi.

Kuzmenko, T. "Risk Society: Chornobyl Determinant." In *Chornobyl I Sotsium*, Vol. 12. Foliant, 2006.

Kiev Post. Interview, Kiev, October 19, 2013.

Kylnytskyi, Oleg. "Yuryi Nedashkovskyi: 'V Ukraine Net Realnoy Alternatyvy Atomnoy Energetike.' " *Zerkalo Nedeli*, February 24, 2006. http://gazeta.zn.ua/ECONOMICS/yuriy_nedashkovskiy_v_ukraine_net_realnoy_alternativy_atomnoy_energetike.html.

Leukhina, Anastasia. "Stages of Development of Ecological Non-Governmental Organizations in Ukraine after Chernobyl Accident: Tendencies and Problems." In *Crossroads Digest*. 5, 2010. www.ehu.lt/files/periodicals/Digest_5_2010%20small.pdf.

Lutsevych, Orysia. "How to Finish a Revolution: Civil Society and Democracy in Ukraine, Georgia and Moldova." *Russia and Eurasia*. London: Royal Institute of International Affairs, 2013.

MacDonald, Euan. "Poroshenko Tells Germany Nord Stream 2 Gas Pipeline Is a 'Political Bribe.' " *KievPost*, October 4, 2018. www.Kievpost.com/ukraine-politics/poroshenko-tells-germany-nord-stream-2-gas-pipeline-political-bribe.html.

Maskalevych, Igor. "Fukusima Uroki Ekonomiki." *Zerkalo Nedeli*, April 22, 2011. http://gazeta.zn.ua/TECHNOLOGIES/fukusima_uroki_ekonomiki.html.

Matveev, Mikhail. "Carpathian Resistance: Has the 'Green Blessing' Turned to a 'Green Curse'?" *350.org*, August 20, 2014. https://350.org/carpathian-resistance/.

Ministry of Energy. "Energetichna Strategija Ukraïni Na Period Do 2035 roku 'Bezpeka, Energoefektivnist', 'Konkurentospromozhnist.'" July 9, 2017. http://mpe.kmu.gov.ua/minugol/control/publish/article?art_id=245234085.

"Mintopenerg Obeschaet Vypolnit Reshenie SNBO I Obespechit Energobezopasnost Ukrainy." *Zerkalo Nedeli*, February 13, 2009. http://gazeta.zn.ua/POLITICS/mintopenergo_obeschaet_vypolnit_reshenie_snbo_i_obespechit_energobezopasnost_ukrainy.html.

Movement 350. Interview, Kiev, November 22, 2013.

Movement 350 II. Interview, Kiev, May 12, 2018.

Murtazaiev, Akram. "Monetizatsiia Liubovi." *Den*, January 17, 2006. http://day.Kiev.ua/uk/article/svitovi-diskusiyi/monetizaciya-lyubovi.

Nadeyn, Ivan. "Alternativnaya Energetika: V Ukrainu Okolnymi Putyami Cherez Evropu." *Zerkalo Nedeli*, July 9, 2010. http://gazeta.zn.ua/ECONOMICS/alternativnaya_energetika_v_ukrainu_okolnymi_putyami_cherez_evropu.html.

National Ecological Centre of Ukraine. *Energy [R]evolution: Analytical Note*. Kiev: National Ecological Centre of Ukraine, 2013.

National Ecological Centre of Ukraine. Interview, Kiev, October 26, 2013.

"Natural Gas Consumption in Ukraine by User Category." *www.naftogaz-europe.com*, February 16, 2017. https://naftogaz-europe.com/article/en/naturalgasconsumptioninUkrainebyusercategory.

Nomos Centre Kiev. Interview, Kiev, October 21, 2013.

"NordStream 2 to Pump, but Ukraine Gas Transit Will Remain." *Deutsche Welle*, March 7, 2018. www.dw.com/en/nordstream-2-to-pump-but-ukraine-gas-transit-will-remain/a-44511681.

"Number of Households with Solar Panels on Roofs in Ukraine Increases 2.5-Fold." *Ukraine Open for Business* [blog], October 29, 2018. https://open4business.com.ua/number-of-households-with-solar-panels-on-roofs-in-ukraine-increases-2-5-fold/.

Olearchyk, Roman. "Golova SBU Zasterigaie pro Nebezpeku." *Den*, June 12, 2007. http://day.Kiev.ua/uk/article/den-planeti/golova-sbu-zasterigaie-pro-nebezpeku.

Opora Rivne. Interview, Rivne, April 27, 2018.

Petkova, Marina. "Volodymyr Semynozhenko: Nova Konstytutsiia—Test Dlia Starogo Uriadu." *Den*, February 8, 2006. http://day.Kiev.ua/uk/article/podrobici/volodimir-seminozhenko-nova-konstituciya-test-dlya-starogo-uryadu.

"Poroshenko Nazval Severnyj Potok-2 Trojanskim Konem Dlja Evropejskoj Bezopasnosti." *Zerkalo Nedeli*, October 8, 2018. https://zn.ua/UKRAINE/poroshenko-nazval-severnyy-potok-2-troyanskim-konem-dlya-evropeyskoy-bezopasnosti-291333_.html.

"Poroshenko on Nord Stream 2: 'Geopolitical Project Aimed to Weaken Ukraine' | UNIAN." Accessed January 5, 2019. https://economics.unian.info/10181456-poroshenko-on-nord-stream-2-geopolitical-project-aimed-to-weaken-ukraine.html.

"Poroshenko: Ukraine to Increase Nuclear Share to 60%." *www.world-nuclear-news.org*, February 17, 2017. www.world-nuclear-news.org/NP-Poroshenko-Ukraine-to-increase-nuclear-share-to-60-17021701.html.

Prokin, Andrian Volodymyrovych. *Harantuvannya Energetychnoi Bezpeki: Mynule, Sohodenn*. Lviv, 2011.

Raihel, Yurii. "Dyktat 'Gazpromu.'" *Den*, June 23, 2010. http://day.Kiev.ua/uk/article/den-planeti/diktat-gazpromu.

Rozer, Tomas. "Na Gorizonti—Nova 'gazova Viyna.'" *Den*, August 23, 2006. http://day.Kiev.ua/uk/article/den-planeti/na-gorizonti-nova-gazova-viyna.

Rusheva, Violetta. "Ukraine Creating EU-Based Consortium to Stop Nord Stream-2." *New Europe*, June 18, 2018. www.neweurope.eu/article/ukraine-creating-eu-based-lobbyist-consortium-stop-nord-stream-2/.

Ryzhkov, Vadym. "Alternatyva Gazu Lezhyt Pid Nogamy." *Den*, March 18, 2009. http://day.Kiev.ua/uk/article/ekonomika/alternativa-gazu-lezhit-pid-nogami.

Savytskyi, Oleksii. "Gazovo Imperski Paraleli." *Den*, March 31, 2009. http://day.Kiev.ua/uk/article/podrobici/gazovo-imperski-paraleli.

Shevtsov, A.I. *Energetyka Ukrainy Na Shlyakhu Do Evropeyskoi Integratsyi*. Dnipropetrovsk: Natsionalny Instytut Stratehichnykh Doslidzhen, 2004.

Shvec, Valerii. "Yenerhetycheskaia Bezopasnost Ukrayny—v Chem Ona." *Zerkalo Nedeli*, April 27, 2012. http://gazeta.zn.ua/ECONOMICS/energeticheskaya_bezopasnost_ukrainy__v_chem_ona.html.

Siruk, Mykola. "A Gas Noose on the Neck of Europe." *Den*, May 24, 2018. https://day.Kiev.ua/en/article/day-after-day/gas-noose-neck-europe.

Siruk, Mykola. "'Fukusima-1' ne Chornobyl." *Den*, March 15, 2011. http://day.Kiev.ua/uk/article/panorama-dnya/fukusima-1-ne-chornobil.

Skuba, Viktoriia. "Energoefektyvnist Myslennia." *Den*, February 9, 2011. http://day.Kiev.ua/uk/article/ekonomika/energoefektivnist-mislennya.

Solodkyi, Sergii. "'Gazovi Viyni'—2." *Den*, January 24, 2006. http://day.Kiev.ua/uk/article/den-planeti/gazovi-viyni-2.

Sputnik. "'Russian Weapon Already in Berlin': Ukrainian MP Has Meltdown Over Nord Stream 2." *Sputnik News*, June 17, 2018. https://sputniknews.com/business/201806171065486413-kiev-complains-of-nord-stream-threat/.

Starchevskyi, Yurii. "'Zalezhnist' i 'dyversyfikatsiia': Chy Mozhe Pershe Buti Krashchim Za Druge." *Den*, November 11, 2008. http://day.Kiev.ua/uk/article/ekonomika/zalezhnist-i-diversifikaciya-chi-mozhe-pershe-buti-krashchim-za-druge.

Sweet Osvit. Interview, Kiev, May 3, 2018.

"The National Energy Regulatory Authority of Ukraine. Governance and Independence." *Energy Community*, March 2018.

Tunytsia, Yurii, and Taras Tunytsia. "Chernobylskii Sindrom Otrazhaet Antyekologicheskuiu Suschnost Rynochnoi Ekonomiki." *Zerkalo Nedeli*, April 1, 2011. http://gazeta.zn.ua/ENVIRONMENT/chernobylskiy_sindrom_otrazhaet_antiekologicheskuyu_suschnost_rynochnoy_ekonomiki.html.

"Ukrainian Government Extends 'Warm Loans' Program for 2017." *Interfax-Ukraine*, August 2, 2017. https://en.interfax.com.ua/news/economic/401980.html.

Ukrainian Institute for Public Policy. Interview, Kiev, October 25, 2013.

"Ukrainian Nuclear Reactor Now Using All Non-Russian Fuel for the First Time." *Japan Times Online*, July 20, 2018. www.japantimes.co.jp/news/2018/07/20/business/ukrainian-nuclear-reactor-now-using-non-russian-fuel-first-time/.

"Vitalii Gaiduk: Naigolovnishe—Tse Vlasna Energobezpeka." *Den*, February 2, 2007. http://day.Kiev.ua/uk/article/panorama-dnya/vitaliy-gayduk-naygolovnishe-ce-vlasna-energobezpeka.

Voswinkel, Johannes. "Moskaus Rohrkrepierer." *Zeit Online*, January 5, 2006. www.zeit.de/2006/02/Ergas.

Wolczuk, Kataryna, and Darius Zeruolis. "Rebuilding Ukraine: An Assessment of EU Assistance." *Chatham House*, August 2018. www.chathamhouse.org/sites/default/files/publications/research/2018-08-16-rebuilding-ukraine-eu-assistance-wolczuk-zeruolis.pdf.

Yahno, Olena. "Viacheslav Kyrylenko: Teperishnii Gazovyi Konflikt—Tse Prodovzhennia Konfliktu v Gruzii. Inshymy Metodamy." *Den*, January 17, 2009. http://day.Kiev.

ua/uk/article/den-ukrayini/vyacheslav-kirilenko-teperishniy-gazoviy-konflikt-ce-prodovzhennya-konfliktu-v.

Yekelchyk, Serhy. *Ukraine: Birth of a Modern Nation*, Oxford: Oxford University Press, 2007.

Zhluktenko, Varvara. "Zdvig Po Gazu." *Den*, January 13, 2006. http://day.Kiev.ua/uk/article/panorama-dnya/zdvig-po-gazu.

5 The energy security logics in Europe revisited

Introduction

The analysis of this book illustrated that deciphering the nuanced contemporary energy policy in Europe through contextualized analysis of energy security logics provides a fresh perspective on the topic. Unpacking the wider historical, socioeconomic and political contexts from which energy security discourses and policies emerge, driven by different imperatives, contributes to a better understanding of the current sources of friction, the policy challenges ahead as well as the possible ways forward. This final chapter summarizes the theoretical and empirical findings of the book. First, it revisits the initial typology of the energy security logics from the first chapter and extends it by the logic of emancipation identified in the three countries studied. The workings of this logic in the energy sector are then conceptualized against the background literature on emancipation. The discussion highlights its analytical importance for critical security studies debates on security and its logics, the concept of emancipation, immanent critique and relation between emancipation versus democratic politics and desecuritization. Second, the chapter juxtaposes all energy security logics uncovered in the German, Polish and Ukrainian energy contexts in a two-fold manner. First, the logics are compared on an analytical level in order to highlight the distinctive features of the emancipation logic vis-à-vis the rest of the typology and to illustrate how all four logics relate to each other. Second, the logics' occurrence patterns across the cases are outlined to demonstrate how different logics are linked not only in the theoretical, but also empirical terms—with all the resulting normative and policy implications for the domestic energy contexts. The book concludes by providing wider implications of this study for critical security studies and the energy policy agenda.

Energy security and its logics: the state of the field revisited

Corry noticed that although "securitization theory has been widely criticized on methodological and normative grounds, the Copenhagen School account of the specific logic of 'security' has hitherto not been challenged by a rival description of a dominant logic of security."[1] The analysis of energy security illustrates that looking for an alternative dominant security logic is misguided, as the energy contexts display multiple security logics that come to the fore of the public debate and policy agenda at different times—with their scope and diversity often exceeding what even the more inclusive classifications or typologies would suggest.[2] Therefore, not only the logic of risk, war and subsistence interchangeably shape energy security dynamics in Europe, but the conducted research shows that the emerging logic of emancipation increasingly plays a role in various energy contexts. This logic manifests through the bottom–up democratization of the energy system and the rhetoric of social liberation, as it appears to be "growing out" of the local areas of contestation driven by the imperative of self-reliance.

In general terms, the analysis showed that all pre-identified logics of war, subsistence and risk play out to different degrees in the German, Polish and Ukrainian energy contexts. However, whereas the war and risk logics might periodically rise and fall triggered by important developments in the energy sector (e.g., nuclear accidents or gas cut-off episodes) and lead to sudden discursive and policy shifts, the local areas of contestation formed around the subsistence logic pull towards divergent trajectories as far as the meaning and priorities of energy security are concerned. Although growth, sustenance and environment might indeed constitute three dimensions of energy security that are reflected in all its logics,[3] the actual contestation over these aspects does not happen within the war or risk logic respectively, as the rise of the "grammar of conflict" or the rhetoric of "calculation and precaution" in the face of risks periodically overshadow incremental processes of contextual meaning formation. In the case of the logic of war, "survival" replaces the "sustenance" imperative and aspects such as "growth" or "environment" are moved to the background. In the case of the risk logic, all dimensions remain very present—yet they are not prioritized one over the other. Hierarchizing competing dimensions of energy security takes place around the logic of subsistence, which dominates in most energy policy contexts as it is driven by the economic calculations of the sustenance imperative. The logic of subsistence also implies the multiplication of voices, interests and agendas that come to the fore once the dominant sustenance rationale is contested. The analysis of this logic's operation across the German, Polish and Ukrainian contexts illustrated that the contestation over the competing meanings/priorities/practices of energy security tends to push in two different directions. On the one hand, prioritization of the "sustenance" rationale as reflected in the rhetoric of fulfilling societal needs and fueling economic growth that relies on energy consumption—even at the expense of the environmental agenda—points to a strong economic orientation that is typical for the subsistence logic. On the other hand, once this hierarchy reverses and the environmental aspect starts to set the frame of the energy security debate, other dimensions not only drop down the hierarchy, but are transformed in the process (see Figure 5.1).

Therefore, sustenance is replaced by the idea of sustainable development, while attention to growth is minimized—with some voices even calling for the decouplement of economic growth from energy consumption. Once that

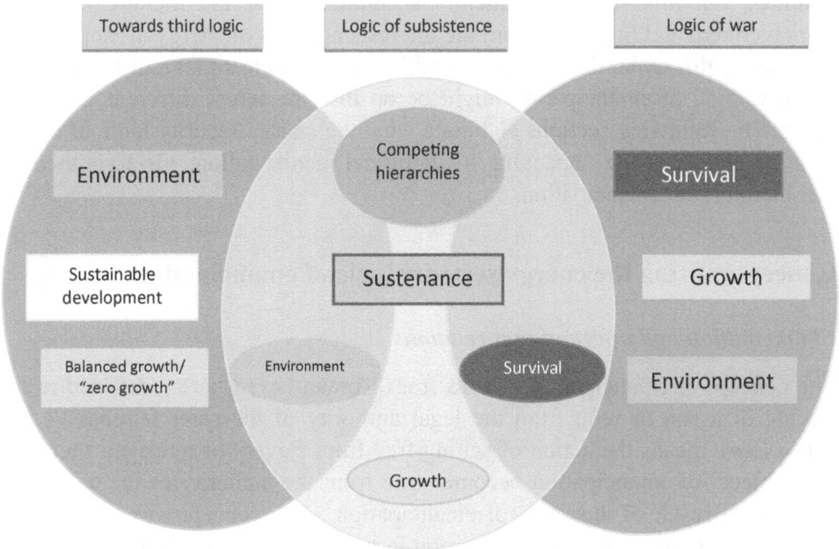

Figure 5.1 Competing energy security dimensions across the logics.

happens, the frame of the energy security debate shifts towards a more humanistic and sustainable approach to energy security within environmental limits.

The analysis showed that in the German case this re-hierarchization of energy security priorities goes hand-in-hand with the emergence of the imperative of self-reliance among the local communities that increasingly opt for bottom–up inclusive and democratic energy solutions with the use of renewable energy. The beginnings of this dynamic can also be spotted in neighboring Poland, where environmentalists try to contest the mainstream sustenance imperative while the first bottom–up initiatives of taking control over energy back are emerging. In this respect Ukraine constitutes a special case because of its difficult political situation and the strong war logic that permeates into other policy areas. Although the local "green" activists and NGOs hope for the promotion of democratic measures in the local energy sector, a number of technical and socio-economic obstacles as well as the rise of nationalism and political populism hamper their efforts. Therefore, depending on the context, the rise of the imperative of self-reliance might be dependent upon: (1) growing societal ecological awareness; (2) effective incentive programs (e.g., to introduce energy-saving measures or renewables on a wider scale) and other technical and legislative solutions; and (3) contextual susceptibility to participatory solutions that is often bound to "distal context"—e.g., history of social engagement and participation in the democratic process, stable domestic political situation that is conducive towards democratic solutions, etc. Crucially, the analysis illustrated that the rise of the imperative of self-reliance not only shifts the agency and responsibility for energy production and consumption to the level of individuals and local communities, but this shift is frequently accompanied by the rhetoric of social empowerment and liberation from the interests/agendas of energy monopolies. If we analyze this dynamic in greater detail, it becomes clear that a distinct energy security logic of emancipation might be on the rise across different European states. The following sections elaborate what the energy security logic of emancipation entails, while unpacking its empirical manifestations vis-à-vis theoretical literature on emancipation.

Conceptualizing the energy security logic of emancipation

Emancipation and international relations

The concept of emancipation derives from Roman law, where it referred to the freeing of a son or wife from the legal authority of the pater familias.[4] Latin *emancipare* means the action of setting free from slavery or tutelage,[5] therefore the "object" of emancipation becomes free from the authority or the control of others as a result of the "act" of emancipation.[6] The concept was used in this manner in relation to religious toleration in the seventeenth century, the emancipation of slaves in the eighteenth century and the emancipation of women and workers in the nineteenth century.[7] These conceptualizations inspired by the struggles against particular oppressions—monarchical despotism, religious intolerance, ignorance and inequality—with time gave place to emancipation as identified with political programs for a better world (based on liberty, progress, controlling nature, pursuing equality, and the perfectibility of humanity).[8]

Notably, some international relations scholarship was inspired by the Frankfurt School of Critical Theory's elaboration of the concept of emancipation. Max Horkheimer initially argued that the emancipatory potential for a better life was already a part of the existing forces of production, but remained unrealized because it was mobilized for the benefit of capital rather than humanity.[9] He equated emancipation with the domination of nature and the need to be freed from its vicissitudes, but later altered his understanding of the concept towards a "reconciliation" with nature.[10] Wyn Jones derived from Horkheimer's earlier work an assumption that emancipation does not refer "to an idealized end-state that has yet to be reached, but to unfulfilled *potentialities* extant within the current order."[11] As such, he conceptualized emancipation as a gradual process of removal of oppressive structural constraints (emancipatory change) rather than the realization of an ideal endpoint (emancipation).[12] Emancipation implied then utilization of the existing forces of production for bringing nature under rational human control in an ongoing and open-ended process.[13] Wyn Jones has also argued that if critical security studies are to be concerned with human emancipation, they need to pay equal attention to the issue of liberation of individual human beings not only from military threats, but also non-military ones such as environmental threats, poverty and state-based oppression. This link between security and emancipation was developed further by Booth, who stated that whereas security means the absence of threats:

> as a discourse of politics, emancipation seeks the securing of people from those oppressions that stop them carrying out what they would freely choose to do, compatible with the freedom of others. It provides a three-fold framework for politics: a philosophical anchorage for knowledge, a theory of progress for society, and a practice of resistance against oppression. Emancipation is the philosophy, theory, and politics of inventing humanity.[14]

Security and emancipation are according to Booth two sides of the same coin, as: "Emancipation, not power or order, produces true security. Emancipation, theoretically, is security."[15] While trying to elaborate further on the security–emancipation nexus, Booth stated that a more effective way of explaining the relationship is to conceive "security *as the means* and emancipation *as the end*."[16] Most recently he added that security and emancipation form in fact a kind of a virtuous circle: as the pursuit of security (understood as reducing the threats that impose life-determining conditions of insecurity on individuals and groups) promotes emancipation (freeing people from oppression and so giving them some opportunity to explore being more fully human), while pursuit of emancipation (reducing structural oppression) promotes security (opening up space in which people can feel safer).[17] The belief that it is individual humans, not states, that should be the ultimate referent object of security is a key assumption behind Booth's reasoning as he declares that it would be his aim:

> to contribute to conceptualizing world security away from its nationalist and statist orthodoxies—which promote the idea of security *against* others—to an approach that conceives security as an instrumental value concerned to promote security *reciprocally*, as part of the invention of a more inclusive humanity.[18]

Booth's concept of "emancipatory realism"—although rooted in the Frankfurt School's notion of emancipation—also subscribes to the Kantian idealism as it propagates "gradual reforms" as "the only means of approaching the supreme political good."[19] As such, emancipation itself became a practice of resistance and "a framework for attempting to actualize both nearer-term and longer-term emancipatory goals through strategic and tactical political action based on immanent critique."[20, 21] The latter aims to make visible the internal contradictions of dominant security arrangements in given contexts and to foster alternative visions of security that are often promoted by marginalized actors.[22]

Both the idea of inclusive solutions and immanent critique have been taken up by other scholars working with emancipatory approaches to security. Since the promotion of the emancipatory agenda could take not only material, but also discursive, form, McDonald propagated the vision of emancipation as freeing up space for dialogue and inclusion of marginalized voices to "speak security."[23] In his work on environmental change, he sought to identify the possibilities for the emergence of an emancipatory security discourse, which would constitute "a framework of meaning about security that is concerned with overturning structures of oppression or exclusion, is radically cosmopolitan [and] is predicated on the rights and needs of the most vulnerable."[24] By shifting attention to the ways in which certain voices are empowered or marginalized in "speaking" security and how broadly the spaces for meaningful political contestation are drawn in different contexts, McDonald aimed to enable the "subjugated" voices.[25] The latter could articulate alternative definitions of "core values" and means to protect them, but were not strong enough to influence dominant security practices within the given community. As such, the immanent critique could be used as an emancipatory tool in the process of "emancipation" accelerated by the agency of the "emancipator."

The emancipatory logic of energy security on the rise in Europe closely reflects the above approaches and conceptualizations at various points. However, its workings in the specific energy sector often have different practical and analytical implications. The next section unpacks this argument at greater length in its attempt to conceptualize the emancipatory logic of energy security.

The emancipatory logic of energy security

Identifying the emancipatory logic of energy security in different European energy contexts might seem quite puzzling, as given its usual "hard security" standing it would seem that energy security does not lend itself as easily as some other "soft security" issues (e.g., environment) to the alternative understandings and interpretations of security. Nevertheless, the comparative analysis of the German, Polish and Ukrainian energy contexts shows that apart from the war, subsistence and risk logics, the logic of emancipation gradually emerges from the local sites of contestation and increasingly plays a role in them. Different contextual factors largely determine whether the imperative of self-reliance will bring about the emancipation logic in its full spectrum in a given national setting. However, this logic has a number of distinct characteristics, as the analysis in the three case study chapters showed that situated actors ("green energy" activists, NGOs, civic movements and local authorities): (1) talk about individuals and local communities as the ultimate referents of energy security—as opposed to states and big energy companies; (2) call for "freeing people from the centralized energy systems," "dismantling of oppressive energy monopolies," "taking things into their own hands," "further democratization of society through energy democracy" and "change of the social-economic/political model into a more inclusive one, where people 'have a say' "; (3) use the rhetoric of liberation, empowerment and social inclusion in relation to energy security solutions or even put social inclusion at the top of energy security's dimensions when asked about their own definition of energy security; (4) engage in local projects and practices that embody the above rhetoric (e.g., establishing first citizens' energy cooperatives, bottom–up energy projects at the level of local communities and municipalities, or production of renewable energy and implementation of energy efficiency measures by individual households); (5) in line with the statement that: "Emancipation is a process rather than an endpoint, a direction rather than a destination,"[26] talk about long-term plans that often stretch decades from now.[27] The emergence of the emancipatory logic in the energy sector provides new insights into conventional energy studies that tend to focus on national-level energy policy analysis, as well as adds a new quality to critical security studies, which tend to deal with emancipatory issues within the "soft security" or "societal sector." Although the logic of emancipation in the energy sphere reflects Booth's take on emancipation, its dynamics simultaneously challenge at many points critical security studies' assumptions regarding the nature of emancipation as well as its relation to the securitization/desecuritization mechanisms.

To start with, if we link the above indicators back to the theoretical debates in the discipline, it appears that calling for the diffusion of energy systems and basing the new model on individuals as the ultimate referent objects of energy security is in line with Booth's understanding of emancipation. It is therefore no longer the state or the major sub-state actors, such as large energy companies, that are of primary concern, but the focus is shifted to the level of individual users and local communities. The latter stop being mere consumers of energy, dependent on domestic providers and external suppliers, but in the process of producing and consuming their own energy and establishing different bottom–up energy projects become more self-reliant in attaining their own energy security. This increase in self-reliance can be achieved either on the individual level (e.g., energy prosumers—simultaneous producers and consumers of energy) or on the local level (e.g., energy-autonomous cities). The diffusion of energy systems—from centralized ones towards participatory energy systems with the use of renewables—is often accompanied by the rhetoric of liberation and social empowerment. Therefore, numerous local actors talk about the "dismantling of energy monopolies" and "freeing themselves from their power" and "taking things into their own hands" when it comes to local energy projects and initiatives. Social empowerment here does not result from a legal process, but is a natural consequence of individual and local energy practices. Regaining control from larger actors, who are often perceived as "oppressing forces" or even "occupying powers," resonates well with Wyn Jones' reading of Horkheimer on emancipation, who saw it as the liberation of individual human beings from suffering not only from military threat, but also from threats such as environmental threats, poverty and state-based oppression.[28] In the energy context, even when termed as "energy revolution" (e.g., the German case), energy transition is in fact a gradual process of liberation. This liberation is also of a dual nature—as becoming independent from energy monopolies not only shifts the power and agency back to the people, but the energy practices in which they engage—e.g., production of renewable energy or implementation of energy-efficiency measures—might simultaneously diminish environmental threats that the local communities face in the long run.[29] Therefore, emancipatory practices in the energy sphere have both a material and an idealistic aspect to them, as gaining ownership of the means of energy production leads to increased control over one's energy security in a way that might be consistent with the long-term environmental and wider social agenda. In this sense, "emancipation" understood as giving away of ownership (*ex*: away; *mancipum*: ownership),[30] involves utilizing material means not for the benefit of capital, but for the individual actors and communities who take charge of their own energy affairs. The emancipatory logic of energy security relies therefore on the process of diffusion of the energy system, which, once set in motion, has potentially far-reaching consequences for the environmental, political and social areas. As, given favorable contextual conditions, a wide range of individuals can become involved in the transformation of the energy system, the entire socioeconomic model changes and social participation leads to further democratization of society. The analysis of the German case, and to a lesser extent also the Polish and Ukrainian one, showed that different societal voices on the ground talk about "energy democracy" that can be brought about by the gradual diffusion of energy systems and a change of the socioeconomic model into a more inclusive one, where people "have a say." Additionally, a number of actors who propagate the participatory energy model prioritize "social inclusion" among energy security's dimensions when asked about the definition of energy security and the relative importance of its various aspects, whereas energy security, social participation and democratization are linked together in key publications that introduce the idea to wider national audiences.[31] The drive towards self-reliance underpinned by the inclusive and democratic rhetoric is also increasingly manifested in practice, as more and more local projects and citizens' energy initiatives emerge. In this sense, the energy sphere indeed shows, following Aradau, that "emancipation is the concept that should be able to enact a radical 'democratization' of security. [As] emancipation radically tackles the concept of democratic politics and the issue of institutional authority in claiming a voice for the … 'security have-nots'."[32] Similarly, Nunes notices that by embracing critique within emancipatory approaches, we can move:

> beyond the idea that "security" is merely a representation of reality or a modality for dealing with issues. Rather, critique sets out to impact upon political actors' perceptions and actions, so as to pave the way for a reconstruction of security along the more open, inclusive and democratic lines.[33]

The emerging rhetoric of liberation and social inclusion that accompanies energy transition in Germany, and that can be spotted to different degrees in the other two contexts, stands in sharp contrast to the divisive and confrontational rationale underlying the logic of war that plays out in the pipeline politics and global distribution of fossil fuels. On the contrary, the language of the increasingly diffused energy systems with active prosumers and growing local energy initiatives is marked by the positive notion of energy security—one that is not divisive and exclusive, but that can be embraced by all of humanity. In other words, as opposed to the realist-informed security logic that quite adequately grasps the dynamics of competition over energy resources—which because of the diminishing amount of fossil fuels became a zero-sum game—energy revolution based on the democratization of energy indicates that one person's win does not equal another person's loss. In theoretical terms, this particular case of the positive notion of energy security mirrors Booth's argument about the promotion of reciprocal security—as a part of the invention of more inclusive humanity. As Booth noticed:

> Outside the seminar room ... the language trends describing what is happening have been moving away from the neat and orderly world of mainstream theory. The dominant traditional language of the subject remains sharp-edged, and is mostly a language of division and exclusion.[34]

Different contemporary national energy contexts illustrate that this does not have to be the case, as positive notions of energy security that propagate inclusive solutions are already in place. However, because of frequent unfavorable contextual factors as well as the existence of other dominant security logics in the energy sphere, the logic of emancipation often implies that "freeing energy for people" is a long-term project. Therefore, in line with the statement that "emancipation is a process rather than an endpoint, a direction rather than a destination,"[35] "green" actors in different contexts talk about long-term plans—that often stretch decades from now. However, if Booth described "security" as means and "emancipation" as ends,[36] the sphere of energy indicates a reversed dynamic—as it is through social empowerment and emancipatory practices that individual prosumers achieve energy security. Energy security has a tangible element to it—energy output, therefore, is the very dismantlement of monopolies, removal of intermediaries and production of energy that make individuals more "secure" in terms of their own energy supply. A number of actors on the ground additionally express the hope that increased local energy practices with societal involvement will change the way in which society thinks about energy security in particular and wider design of the socioeconomic system in general.[37] Therefore, decentralization of traditional energy systems can imply much more than a technical redesign of energy sector solutions—as the diffusion of the energy system has the potential to empower local communities and lead to democratization of the energy sphere.[38] This is especially the case in the CEE region, where centralized political power is additionally strengthened by the Soviet legacy of keeping a strict division between the management of resources and societal relations—which impacts both the energy and environmental sectors.[39] The democratization of energy shifts the responsibility for energy production and consumption to citizens, who become subject and sovereign rather than an object of energy policy,[40] and has the power to transform common beliefs regarding the possibilities of widely defined sociopolitical change that can be brought about by individuals and local communities. In many cases, this process is based on the small-scale renewables that additionally enable local users to invest and benefit from their development.

Therefore, the emerging emancipatory logic that arises driven by the imperative of self-reliance and that manifests both in the rhetoric and local energy security practices is geared not only towards transforming the future design of the energy systems. The analysis of this book showed that, depending on the context, its goals expressed by the local actors might be more ambitious and aim at the holistic transformation of the domestic political and socioeconomic settings. The latter might imply further democratization of society that will spill over from the democratic solutions in the domestic energy sector (Poland) or simply the promotion of the wider democratic ideals in the times of crisis (Ukraine).

Overall, this emerging logic has a strong normative agenda that clearly distinguishes it from the energy security logics of war, risk or subsistence that are in operation in Europe. The long-term planning and a firm belief in the possibility of societal transformation that will result in better, more just and equal—as well as environmentally, politically and economically sound—energy solutions represents a shift towards an entirely different energy security paradigm. In a way, given its normative implications, this logic resembles what Booth and Wheeler described as *a transcender logic*—one of the three a priori logical positions defined in relation to their analysis of security dilemma. Booth and Wheeler's "logics of insecurity" included: *the fatalist logic*—indicating that insecurity can never be escaped in international politics; *the mitigator logic*—assuming that insecurity can be ameliorated for a time, but not eliminated; and *the transcender logic*—underpinned by the idea that human society on a global scale can become what it wants to be, and is not determined.[41] In their own words:

> The transcender logic argues that systemic insecurity, including that deriving from the security dilemma, can be escaped if human society reforms or re-invests the structures and processes within which it lives, globally. The transcender logic assumes that this is not the best of all possible worlds.... Consequently, human society could do much better according to transcender logic, for human societies have the capacity to reject the oppressive insecurities that have dominated the global political condition by making appropriate political, economic and social changes.[42]

The emancipatory logic in the energy sector resonates with the above statement. Moreover, the highly practice-oriented energy sector illustrates that the process of this logic's rise has already begun—although it was neither marked by the revolutionary changes nor did it require the figure of "emancipator" to be triggered.

Energy democracy: emancipation without emancipator?

If this book followed an interpretivist research design and a contextual approach to security analysis to uncover the multiplicity of logics in the energy sector, the local manifestations of the emancipatory logic were one of its major findings. However, giving voice to the multiplicity of actors and embracing a wide range of empirical sources uncovered a distinct imperative that drives the rhetoric and praxis of emancipation that is already in place among other energy security logics operating across the three countries studied. In other words, the contextualized approach revealed the emancipatory agenda across energy contexts without having a specific a priori intention to do so.

That stands in sharp contrast to a number of scholars who intentionally employ immanent critique as a part of their research approach aimed at identifying possibilities for emancipatory change. McDonald, for example, in his analysis of emancipation and the environment, uses immanent critique to free up space for dialogue and inclusion of marginalized voices that "speak security" in order "to identify immanent possibilities for the emergence of an emancipatory security discourse" in the environmental sphere.[43] Such discourse, according to McDonald:

> constitutes a framework of meaning about security that is concerned with overturning structures of oppression or exclusion, is radically cosmopolitan; is predicated on the rights and needs of the most vulnerable; and wherein the means envisaged to achieve or preserve "security" will not deprive others of it.[44]

The analysis of energy security dynamics in Germany, Poland and Ukraine shows that a similarly inclusive and cosmopolitan discourse and practice aimed at energy liberation of individuals is already present in all three contexts to a different degree. Therefore, a broader contextual approach was able to depict it and draw attention to it. However, the research undertaken did not carry the strong normative agenda that marks the work of McDonald on the environment—as similar attention was paid to other security logics that are at play in different contexts—and the very interaction between them.

The analysis confirmed, though, that "far from constituting an unrealizable, utopian vision, emancipation is in fact articulated and practiced in the every day of world politics."[45] Moreover, emancipatory changes in the energy realm resemble what could be termed as "emancipation without emancipator." Namely, they are brought about by the intersubjective processes, where—given favorable local conditions—individuals drive emancipatory agenda on a wide scale. Despite the fact that various "green" actors often provide some guidance and expertise to bottom–up energy initiatives, the whole process defies the "emancipator versus emancipated" dynamics. In this sense energy emancipation falls into Biesta's category of "new emancipation," as it implies "[that it] is not something that is done to people but instead is something that is done by people."[46]

Whereas "old emancipation" talked about lifting people from the workings of power and put the emancipator as a "master-explicator in a position above everyday world," the "new emancipation" no longer relies on a relationship of dependency as it starts from the assumption of equality—everybody is able to make a move.[47] As Biesta puts it:

> That is not to suggest that society is equal. But what it aims to do is to take away from the logic of emancipation the idea that there is a fundamental, almost ontological inequality that only can be overcome through the interventions of the emancipator.[48]

Emancipatory logic in the energy sphere seems to follow this "new emancipation" trajectory. Although a number of green political actors and activists across the three analyzed cases call for social empowerment in the energy sphere, their role is rather of a facilitating nature as emancipatory changes rely largely on grassroots movement and bottom–up citizens' and municipal initiatives operating within given contextual conditions.

Energy security logic of emancipation and the Copenhagen School

The rise and operation of the emancipatory logic in the energy sphere also shed some light on the recent debate on the relation between securitization versus desecuritization and emancipation. According to Aradau, the concepts of desecuritization and emancipation are closely related as they both aim at establishing alternatives to certain social practices.[49] Drawing on the work of Jacques Ranciere and Etienne Balibar, Aradau argued that whereas securitization instituted the politics of enmity and exceptionalism and is enacted through the non-democratic constitution of authority, desecuritization should learn the democratic politics of emancipation.[50] As such, it should present the challenge to securitization by being inscribed institutionally and by creating a relation that is not rooted in the exclusionary and non-democratic logic of security.[51] In this sense, desecuritization could be seen as "a political choice of restoring democracy" and the question of securitization versus desecuritization as the ultimate choice of the kind of politics that we want—one of the exceptional measures or one of the democratic politics of slow procedures which can be contested.[52] However, linking "emancipation" with "democratic politics" meant for Aradau that "emancipation" should not be simultaneously conflated with "security," as the latter often implies exclusionary practices associated with militarization and "securitization." Therefore:

> When equated with security, emancipation becomes problematic as it can no longer envisage social transformations outside of the logic of security.... The struggle for security is restyled as a struggle for emancipation, without any qualms about the relationship between emancipation and security.[53]

According to Aradau the implications of "emancipation" are yet to be fully realized regarding equality and democratic participation—with all the complexities of protest, resistance, violence and counter-violence of the politics of emancipation.[54]

The most obvious criticisms of the above argument challenge a number of assumptions regarding the nature of security that Aradau takes for granted. Assuming that security and emancipation operate under incompatible logics, exclusive and inclusive respectively, implies that the politics of security is always a zero-sum game achieved at somebody's expense—a deterministic view that overlooks numerous ways in which security is understood and practiced.[55] Naturally, this argument mirrors a wider debate regarding the nature of security, yet here the consequences of equating security with exclusionary logic are made even more explicit when it comes to conceiving of the possibilities for progressive change. As McDonald noted, the analytical consequence of this position implies that security has a meaning and logic that is fixed and problematic, whereas the derivative from the above normative consequence is that the normative progress can only be realized through resisting and ultimately escaping security.[56] As Nunes put it: "By assuming the form of a damning verdict on the supposed logic of the security–securitization nexus, the contestation of security becomes synonymous with the refusal of security."[57] Learning democratic politics of emancipation by desecuritization and decoupling "emancipation" from "security," as discussed earlier by Aradau, also serves that purpose. However, the analysis of energy security indicates that the emancipatory logic in the energy realm does not equal the desecuritization of the issue, but is rather synonymous with the transformation of the very meaning and practice of energy security.

The common assumption that we know what the logic of security is, leads to the conclusion that Aradau's argument contributes to our understanding of "how, in practice, can security be *unmade*?"[58] However, the energy sphere shows that it is through social emancipation that energy security is *made*—albeit in line with a distinct security imperative. Energy security presents a special case as it is because of prior social emancipation in the energy field that individuals can engage in practices (e.g., energy-saving measures or production of renewable energy), which increase their energy security. The fact that we are still talking about "energy security" here and not just participatory solutions in the energy field is confirmed by the individuals themselves, who often put "social inclusion" and "social participation in the energy system" as the prerogatives of their definition or their understanding of "energy security" itself.[59] If we are to take the assumption that "actors do speak security" seriously, such local conceptualizations have to be taken into account. In this case, the expressed rhetoric and practices that aim at increasing local self-reliance in energy affairs point to another energy security logic at play. Within this logic there is no need for security trade-offs—as one individual's security does not happen at the expense of the other. Consequently, the traditional assumption that security logic is one of "discrimination [and] of creating hierarchies of subjects who need to be secured"[60] is strongly contradicted. Emancipatory energy practices show that once we go down to the level of individual prosumers—there are no more hierarchies to be made among actors, who are capable of "securing themselves." In this respect security among equals becomes possible. Thus, if Balzacq et al. argued that "desecuritization seeks to transform the register of meanings which previously organized the interactions among people,"[61] the same can be said about emancipation in the sphere of energy. However, whereas Balzacq et al. claimed that the transformative way of desecuritization derives from its ability to institute "a new intersubjective relation embedded in democratic politics, not security, values (e.g., equality, fairness, transparency, etc.),"[62] the sphere of energy shows that there is no contradiction between security and democratic politics, as the latter might bring about the former. Therefore, against the statement that "critical and feminist security studies function more as a 'counter-securitization' and not desecuritization, as this move leaves intact the logic of security that shapes social relations,"[63] emancipatory practices in the energy sphere indicate that social practices might be reshaped along different security logic altogether. One could then agree with McDonald that:

> If we acknowledge that the meaning of security has changed and can change further; that it is understood in different ways in different political communities; and that the practices to flow from particular security discourses are related to the structure and logic of the discourses themselves, then the rejection of security is less obvious as a strategy for enabling progressive change.[64]

Moreover, the emancipatory logic in the energy realm teases out the perceived theoretical tension between the idea that security has a mobilizing power politically and the view that security should be defined and practiced in positive, progressive terms.[65] In the three analyzed cases—especially in the German, but also Polish, context—energy security based on the diffusion of the energy system indeed has a mobilizing political power, yet simultaneously the proclaimed "energy revolution" is brought about by peaceful, evolutionary changes. Whereas there is no inherent violence underlying the emancipatory agenda in the energy sector, there is a hope among local environmental and green energy circles that societal empowerment in the energy sphere will have far-reaching consequences for other socioeconomic and political sectors.[66]

Therefore, the energy security logic of emancipation challenges the poststructuralist essentialist version of security as it exemplifies another valid security logic at operation. Its unique character is down to the complexity of the energy security phenomenon itself, and as such, the logic often diverges from or contradicts assumptions regarding the nature of emancipation and its relation to security voiced in critical security studies. First, since "security" is expressed here in positive terms and is of a reflexive nature, its relation to emancipation is a more complex one. If Booth saw security as "the absence of threats" and emancipation as "freeing of people from physical constraints,"[67] in the energy sphere it is social empowerment that removes the technical barriers and that through individual energy practice leads to transformation of the very meaning of security. Second, a strongly practice-oriented energy field embraces the emancipatory logic that is already in place—where normative agendas emerge from the congruence of contextual factors rather than being imposed by a circle of "emancipators" or enabled by the empowerment of certain discourses by various scholars and analysts.[68] Third, democratization in the energy sphere serves as the actual security mechanism—and as such cannot be equated with "desecuritization" since energy security is *made* rather than *unmade* in this process.

All the above points illustrate the differences in the conceptualization of emancipation in the literature on the subject as opposed to one which emerges from the practice of energy security and often escapes such conceptualizations. Consequently, they also highlight the analytical purchase of the contextual approach to security analysis, as only the latter could account for such differences.

The purchase of contextual analysis

This book's focus on the widely defined contexts allowed it to depict a number of energy security logics that drive contemporary energy security policies and debates in Europe. Such an analytical approach required a certain "sociological" orientation that would not only embrace diverse security mechanisms and local factors, but also allow for the foregrounding of various actors and their respective agency—individuals included. As McSweeney put it in his *Security, Identity and Interests*:

> A nation can only be mobilized for national security in peacetime if the majority of the people identify the state and its enemies as the highest expression of their own personal security and fear. But what drives the security project, and defines its content and appropriate instruments, is the internal logic of the state. In the name of the people, and of a philosophical conception of human nature rooted in a human ideal of liberty, solidarity and order, security was appropriated by the state and operationalized by its theorists and specialist agencies.[69]

It was then the acceptance of the realist logic of security as timeless and universal that led to the centrality of state and its leaders in defining threats and responses to them—which in turn often resulted in the association of security means and tools with military action.[70] Moreover, as McSweeney noted, later attempts at the contextualization of security analysis—such as the Copenhagen School framework—often retained the analytical focus on the state's political elites for methodological rather than substantive reasons, as "to pursue individual security as a subject in its own right would take one deeply into the realms of politics, psychology and sociology."[71] Therefore, challenging this status quo would require an openness to other security logics, diverse local voices and a sociologically grounded methodological approach that could account for such broader security dynamics. Prominently, Balzacq attempted to reformulate the securitization framework towards a more sociologically oriented one that would see all its conceptual elements as intersubjective.[72] Invariably, equating security with threat-based modality could not take the analysis beyond the Copenhagen School's initial problems with context and a single logic approach. Therefore, while conducting energy security analysis, this book chose to approach the very security contexts in a broad manner and to operationalize them against three elements: distal factors, "embeddedness" of security articulations and a constellation of actors. In general terms this allowed the analysis to give voice to numerous actors, recognize diverse security mechanisms and grasp the multiplicity of security logics. More specifically, the research depicted the energy security logic of emancipation across the countries studied and was able to recognize its "transformative" character by scrutinizing the operation of this logic within the broader contexts.

Namely, the analysis showed that within a favorable distal context (historical and socioeconomic background), the constellation of domestic actors gives more leverage to the societal actors vis-à-vis big market players, who in turn driven by the imperative of self-reliance engage in local energy security practices that lead to the democratization of the energy sphere. The very democratization process serves here as a de facto security mechanism that can have a spillover effect on other sectors and in turn lead to further democratization of the political and socioeconomic setting ("distal context"). Simultaneously, the distal context further enhances the embeddedness of security articulations (calls for energy democracy) and strengthens the given constellation of actors (that empowers individuals and local communities) (see Figure 5.2). Since via democratization of the energy sphere societal actors not only regain control over their energy affairs, but over time might also realize the power of their own political agency, the emancipatory logic has a potential to transform the entire socioeconomic setting.

It could then be said that the energy security logic of emancipation could be transformative on two levels. First, it transforms how individuals understand and "go about" their own energy security needs, as the internalization of the rationale of self-reliance drives them towards local practices of energy production. As green energy propagators on the ground recognize that understanding of energy security transforms as a result of such practices, they are more focused on facilitating conditions that will remove technical and economic barriers to the development of citizens' energy projects. Therefore, if, as McSweeney noted, security was appropriated by the state and the logic of the state was internalized by its theorists and specialist agencies,[73] a sociologically grounded approach points to individuals who might "internalize" an entirely different logic. However, just as the realist logic of the state derived from historical experience and practice of international politics often marked by confrontation and conflict, the internalization of the emancipation logic might come about through the experience of positive, inclusive and reflexive energy practice. Second, once that

Figure 5.2 The energy security logic of emancipation within an operationalized context.

happens, individuals themselves can lead to the further cross-sectoral transformation and democratization of the system.

The strength of this transformative potential varies as more centralized political and energy systems appear more challenging—yet, the possibilities for metamorphosis are also higher in such contexts. Therefore, in Germany, where social empowerment within the energy sphere is taken more for granted (favorable distal context and a constellation of actors that gives strong standing to the societal and "green" actors), the emancipatory logic is strong and the imperative of self-reliance underpins the rhetoric of liberation and drives local energy practices on a wider scale. On the other hand, although Poland and Ukraine are less conducive to the rise of the energy security logic of emancipation, its transformative potential is also higher there. As the interviewees pointed out, the democratization of the energy sector could serve as a "backdoor to democracy" in both cases—with its beneficial impact for the entire socioeconomic model (Poland) and for the strengthening of the fragile democracy in the state at war (Ukraine).

The energy security logics revisited

The German, Polish and Ukrainian cases showed complex dynamics of contextual logics of energy security. Table 5.1 summarizes all four energy security logics that were identified across the analyzed cases. The first three logics (the logic of war, the logic of subsistence and the risk logic) were conceptualized in Chapter 1 based on the two typologies reviewed,[74] whereas the fourth logic—the logic of emancipation—was detected to different degrees in all contexts under investigation. The identified energy security logics are driven by different imperatives and manifest differently as far as the rhetoric invoked, an aspect of control, policy actions, nature and value of security within each logic are concerned.

Table 5.1 Energy security logics—rethinking the typology

	Rationale/ imperative	*Rhetoric*	*Control*	*Action*	*Manifestation*	*Nature of security*	*Value of security*
Logic of war	Survival	Grammar of conflict	Centralized	Policy moves above "normal politics"	"Zero-sum" energy game	Absence of war/ winning the war	Exclusive negative
Logic of subsistence	Sustenance	Utility of trade-offs	Unequally shared among stakeholders	Hierarchizing energy security dimensions	Establishment of energy security priorities	Fulfillment of needs	Exclusive positive
Risk logic	Prevention	Calculation and precaution	Lack of control/ attempting control	Strategies for alleviating risk	Precautionary measures in place	Manageability of risk	Inclusive negative
Logic of emancipation	Self-reliance	Empowerment and liberation	Diffused	Reflexive practice of energy production	"Energy democracy"	Self-made safety	Inclusive positive

The juxtaposition of the logics clearly illustrates that the energy security logic of emancipation differs from the other a priori conceptualized propositions across all of the reference points. Therefore, whereas the logic of war was driven by the "survival" imperative, which was replaced by "sustenance" in the logic of subsistence, and "prevention" in the risk logic, the primary drive behind the logic of emancipation is that of "self-reliance." This shift happens through regaining control over one's own energy affairs by the local actors. Hence, if the logic of war was mainly concerned with control over globally diminishing energy resources and the subsistence logic implied that multiple actors aim to control diverse aspects of widely defined energy security, the control within the logic of emancipation becomes diffused. It could be said that within the logic of emancipation control collapses, but only at the level of the state and energy monopolies, as it is gradually dispersed and regained at the level of local actors, who become responsible for their own energy security. Their practices of energy production and consumption that happen in a circular manner imply that energy security is ultimately becoming a "self-made safety." It is also of a reflexive nature, as since local actors can improve their energy security through their own practices, the distinction between threatening actors and referent objects of security becomes blurred—similarly to the risk logic. However, in the risk logic "energy" becomes a "security" issue because of our own actions in a negative sense of the process, due to man-made hazards, such as the construction of nuclear energy power plants or terrorist attacks on energy infrastructure. Such hazards imply that every individual actor within a given context is vulnerable to them, which points to the inclusive character of contemporary global risks. On the other hand, in the logic of emancipation "energy" becomes a "security" issue because of our own actions—in a positive sense of the process. Here, favorable contextual factors coupled with the agency of local actors lead to energy security that is conceptualized and manifested in the inclusive, positive and not threat- or risk-dependent way. The entire process is driven by the imperative of self-reliance and accompanied by the rhetoric of empowerment and social liberation. The ultimate empirical manifestation of the logic of emancipation is the gradual democratization of the energy sphere.

The analysis of the German, Polish and Ukrainian energy contexts also highlighted different dynamics through which logics of energy security come about. The logics of subsistence and emancipation appeared to operate and emerge via incremental processes within domestic sites of contestation and as such are often "intertwined" at various points. The subsistence logic, driven by the imperative of sustenance, revolved around the economic factors and dominated most energy contexts. Its workings also marked the multiplication of different dimensions, understandings and interests of energy security that are continuously renegotiated in domestic policy settings. The analysis revealed that a shift in its typical hierarchies and prioritization of the environmental aspect of energy security set a favorable ground for the emancipatory logic to rise. On the contrary, the logics of war and risk appeared to "rise and fall," often triggered by important developments in the regional or global energy sector. The rise of either the imperative of survival or prevention was always enabled by a number of favorable background conditions (distal context). Once on the rise the logics manifested differently and could invoke certain rhetoric ("grammar of conflict" or calculation and precaution) or also lead to further policy measures. Moreover, the risk logic was more likely to play out in its full spectrum if it reflected the totality of risks in the energy sector—more in line with Ciută's total security logic and Becksian risk society dynamics. The empirical analysis also suggests that despite a number of elements of the respective security logics at play, their impact varies—and often does not lead to permanent or tangible outcomes.

Energy security logic of emancipation versus other logics

The emancipatory logic of energy security appears then to be one of the security logics operating in the energy realm and, as such, it shapes and embraces contextual understandings and practice of energy security and might come to the fore of public policy agenda and mainstream debate at various times. It is not to claim, however, that this is either the new dominant logic or the only energy security logic worth paying attention to. Corry questioned the critical security studies project on the grounds that it aims at changing the dominant culture of security instead of identifying a new existing security logic.[75] The analysis of the energy sphere illustrates that security as emancipation is present there, although it is one among several competing security logics. Critical security studies criticized the Copenhagen School for reifying the wrong notion of security that does not address the needs of most of the world's population and argued that security should be seen in terms of emancipation.[76] If anything, the analysis of the three cases shows that security dynamics are highly contextual and complex as diverse security logics compete within the same context. Consequently, just as security does not simply equal the Schmittian logic of exclusion and exception, it cannot be equated only with emancipation. The analysis of the energy sphere illustrates a number of points. First, "the basic account of security hinging on an emergency threat–defense modality concerned with 'survival' and existential threats"[77] is challenged in the energy sphere and, indeed, there is nothing inevitable about the Schmittian logic of security capturing the essence of security in a universal and timeless sense.[78] Second, and consequently, if some have argued that it is difficult to employ security in an emancipatory way in the context of societal questions, as "the security formation in this field is a conservative one with strong roots in a 'vulgarised' Hobbesian version of the human condition,"[79] the energy realm shows that it is not always the case, as emancipatory energy practices both derive from socioeconomic contexts and have further transformative effects on them. For these reasons, more attention should be paid to the specific local dynamics when determining what security logics guide them.

In broader terms, the above findings strongly confirmed the need for the contextualization of security analysis. As Trombetta pointed out:

> A de-contextualized, self-referential approach to security underestimates two aspects: first, different contexts can have different logics and practices

of security; … Second, the logic of security itself can change, as new principles, actors, capabilities and threats gain relevance and different security discourses emerge.[80]

Indeed, the analysis of the energy security field, in line with Trombetta's argument, showed the multiplication of actors and interacting security logics, which manifested to a different degree in different contexts. However, the adoption of a contextualized approach had even more profound implications than Trombetta would imply. Namely, the analysis illustrated that the very energy security logics are *contextual*. This means that first, the same triggers will not invoke the same logics across different contexts, and what is seen as a security issue in one domestic setting may not be perceived as such in another—even in relation to the same development, threat or risk. Second, not only new threats and discourses transform security logics, but the same security logic might mutate, play out differently and have diverse normative and policy implications depending on the context. The energy security logic of emancipation illustrated that point—as although it was present to the highest degree in the German context, its transformative character was exhibited in the national settings of the post-Soviet space. The next section scrutinizes in greater detail the occurrence patterns of all four logics of energy security across the cases.

The energy security logics in empirical contexts: a cross-case comparison

Based on the strength of the security imperatives that give rise to the manifestation of different energy security logics in rhetoric and practice, Table 5.2 juxtaposes all four logics uncovered in the analysis of the German, Polish and Ukrainian energy contexts. The occurrence patterns of the logics' manifestation shed light on the existing interdependencies that have both analytical and policy implications.

To start with, as the logic of war implies division and confrontation and manifests itself through the "grammar of conflict" and "survival" policy mode that usually involves some sort of an "external adversary," not surprisingly, in the European context, this logic was often triggered by the crises related to gas

Table 5.2 Occurrence of energy security logics across the analyzed cases

	Logic of war	*Logic of subsistence*	*Risk logic*	*Emancipatory logic*
Germany	Low	High	High	High
Poland	High	High	Medium	Medium
Ukraine	High	High	Low	Low

supplies from Russia. The analysis of the three cases illustrated that once triggered, the war logic has a tendency to periodically dominate and overshadow other security logics—most commonly the logic of subsistence. When that happens, sustenance is replaced by the survival imperative as economic considerations are secondary and zero-sum thinking dominates the immediate policy agenda. The Polish context was a case in point here, where in the aftermath of the Ukrainian gas crisis in 2006, its domestic energy policy was criticized for the "ideologized" character—with the economic agenda and the opinion of energy experts falling in importance and with politicians deciding on alternative energy supply routes in a way that resembled "country war defense preparations."[81] Not surprisingly, this logic was also high in Ukraine, and the survival imperative has further strengthened since the outbreak of the military conflict with Russia in 2014. As energy security lies at the core of the Ukrainian struggle for national independence from Russia, this logic easily permeates to different policy sectors and levels (from the state to the local) and is likely to play a key role in the Ukrainian energy sector for years to come. Because of contextual factors, the logic of war was of marginal significance in Germany—where despite strong "grammar of conflict" expressed across media outlets in the aftermath of the gas cut-off episodes, neither significant attempts at diversification of supply occurred nor did the perception of Russia as a reliable supplier change. The detailed analysis of the German case showed that the specifics of the distal context (historical and socioeconomic factors) and a traditional constellation of actors (that gives leverage to big energy businesses) are not conducive to the rise of the survival imperative in the context of the country's pipeline politics. The German response to the gas crises was therefore a matter of perceptions and "business as usual" conducted by energy companies. From the analytical point of view, it could be said that—as the earlier discussion already indicated—although the war logic competes with other logics, it does not "intertwine" with them as closely as, for example, subsistence and emancipatory logics do in the energy sphere, but rather rises and falls periodically.

Not surprisingly, the subsistence logic—driven by the sustenance imperative and oscillating mainly around economic dimensions of energy security—was highly visible in all contexts studied. As the changing domestic energy policy agendas are marked by the multiplicity of voices and interests, the latter was most visible once the rationale of sustenance was contested. This process was illustrated by the analysis of the changing hierarchizations of different energy security aspects that tended to push in two opposite directions—either emphasizing economic growth fueled by energy consumption or highlighting a broader humanistic approach to energy security and the environmental agenda. The latter challenges the traditional drive and rationale of the energy policy and has been put forward by a number of societal actors in all countries studied—"green" parties, environmental activists, NGOs and citizens' movements. These two competing trends were visible in the mainstream debates, official documents and as expressed by actors on the ground during the interviews. Particularly the analysis of the German and Polish contexts suggested that once a typical hierarchy of energy security priorities reverses, giving more weight to "sustainable" goals as opposed to the basic economic orientation, the entire frame of the energy security debate changes. Moreover, such a shift further strengthens the rise of the imperative of self-reliance in the energy sector.

The analysis of the emerging logic of emancipation illustrated that its contextual manifestations vary. The imperative of self-reliance proved to be very strong in the German case and manifested both in the rhetoric of social empowerment/liberation from energy monopolies and in the energy practice of local energy initiatives. The analysis showed that a wide number of favorable factors in the German distal context played a role here, including socioeconomic, historical and political. The logic of emancipation also appears to be slowly rising in neighboring Poland, although the rationale of self-reliance is not yet well internalized because of unfavorable distal factors. The latter include current government regulations, low ecologic awareness, economic factors, and much lower societal mobilization as compared with the German case. Nevertheless, the logic of emancipation already manifests in the rhetoric of some "green" NGOs and activists as well as in the first bottom–up energy initiatives. The analysis of the Polish context also revealed that a number of local voices hope that the gradual democratization of the energy system has a power to further transform the entire socioeconomic model through shifting the agency to individual actors in the post-Soviet states with a traditionally centralized political authority. Although such hopes were voiced much more prominently in Poland than in Ukraine, the Ukrainian energy context—with its increased societal mobilization after the outbreak of the war with Russia—could become more prone to the emancipatory agenda in the future. Hence, if the idea of "energy democracy" is not yet discussed in Ukraine (apart from a handful of NGOs), the progressive energy solutions are growing fast at the local level with the help of activists, municipalities and the recently introduced decentralization of power reform. Although the gradual attitude changes among the younger generation could aid in that process, the ongoing war poses a certain threat of increased political radicalization that could also hamper the democratic agenda in the energy sector.

Some counterintuitive findings also proved the purchase of the contextual approach to energy security analysis. For instance, despite the legacy of the Chernobyl disaster, the risk logic appeared to be nearly non-existent in relation to the Ukrainian nuclear energy policy and debate. The detailed analysis of the Ukrainian case illustrated that the combination of distal factors—historically determined perceptions of Russia and the recent outbreak of war that shift the focus towards domestic energy resources as well as specific socialization process that results in societal disengagement (feeling of powerlessness)—combined with the typical constellation of actors (big industry lobbyists and centralized decision-making) largely explain this phenomenon. On the other hand, the Polish context—with its commonly perceived conservatism in the area of energy solutions—manifested quite visible emancipatory logic—both in the rhetoric used and in the emerging practice of the local bottom–up initiatives. Such findings highlight the analytical advantages of utilizing a contextual approach and illustrate how the latter makes it worthwhile to analyze even the "obvious" cases.

Table 5.2 also points to certain patterns in the security logics' occurrence—suggesting that some logics are closely related not only in the theoretical, but also empirical terms. First, high energy security logic of war and high logic of emancipation do not seem to operate in the same contexts within the same timeframe. Second, the level of intensity of the risk and emancipatory logics seems to correlate within the same domestic settings closely. In general terms, whereas the risk logic did not manifest strongly in Poland (media rhetoric in the aftermath of the Fukushima accident) and was largely absent in Ukraine, in Germany the rise of the prevention imperative in the post-Fukushima context—reflecting the totality of risks in the global energy system—both invoked the rhetoric of calculation and precaution and led to drastic policy change. The accelerated nuclear phase-out could then be clearly seen through the prism of the manageability of risks. The way in which the risk logic played out also gave an additional push to the German transition to renewable energy and to the gradual diffusion of the centralized energy system.

The close correlation between the degrees of the risk and emancipatory logics' occurrence across contexts might suggest that the logic of emancipation appears to be "growing out" of contexts where the rationale of prevention plays an important role. The fact that both logics embrace a variety of actors—individuals included—seems to be crucial here, as it is the individual local actors who are directly affected and who are motivated to ultimately bring about the systemic change from within. In a way such progression from the risk to emancipatory logic resembles Ulrich Beck's argument about the possibilities of "ecological enlightenment."[82]

Beck argued that "the exposure of scientific uncertainty is the liberation of politics, law and the public sphere from their patronization by technocracy," as in the risk societies "new" social movements, which do not obey the traditional state or class boundaries, will challenge the prevailing techno-economic order and emancipate humanity from its grip.[83] Beck believed that unavoidable catastrophes that occur in contemporary societies would—with the help of the "sensationalist greed of the mass media"—expose the hazardous nature of the contemporary techno-economic order and lead social movements to challenge it.[84] He called such a far-reaching transformation "ecological enlightenment"—an emancipatory project aimed at the democratization of society that should be fought out at both the micro and macro levels.[85] Such radical democratization could be achieved by: first, realization on the part of society that the current governmental structures are losing their power as diverse monopolies are breaking up and the societal transformation changes the role, scope, and institutional expression of politics;[86] and second, democratization of the techno-economic development that would empower societal actors so that they no longer depend on the judgment of experts.[87]

The emancipatory logic that manifests in the three cases studied does not go as far as Beck's argument, yet it closely follows the aims of the above trajectory—especially in the German context. First, it is the social movements or local citizens' initiatives that (often accompanied by vivid media debate) bring about the change—starting mostly from the micro level. Second, local practices that contribute to the diffusion of energy systems aim, more or less explicitly, at the democratization of society in the energy sphere and at empowering the so far marginalized groups. Third, the whole process leads to the dismantling of energy monopolies, but to some extent also political monopoly over energy policy course—which in turn becomes more diversified and embraces a wider set of actors. Moreover, promotion of energy-efficiency measures and renewables often involves the efforts of local "green" actors to educate society about the consequences of the shift. As a number of interviewees stated, these efforts have in mind to change the way in which we produce, but also think about, energy security. In the process, and in line with Beck's argument, society gradually becomes less reliant on the judgment of experts as it regains control over its energy production and consumption.

Having said that, although in Germany the shift to renewables and rise of the emancipatory logic could be related to going away from the "risks of nuclear energy," it is not necessarily the case in Poland or Ukraine, where the emancipatory logic has different domestic implications. On the one hand, the analysis showed that there exist strong links between green energy and environmental activists from Germany, Poland and Ukraine—with the former sharing their experiences of "Energiewende" on a regular basis. Through workshops, conferences open to the public or translation of the German publications, progressive ideas reach a wider audience in the CEE region and influence the developing debate on alternative approaches to energy security that is taking place among the Polish and (to a lesser degree) Ukrainian green energy circles.[88] The existence of the transnational networks of "green" actors is in line with what Beck would say about the "new" movements that are not confined to state borders. These transnational networks surely influence domestic constellations of actors. However, it is the combination of such constellations and the distal factors that ultimately determine the degree to which the emancipatory logic can manifest in a given context and what form it can take. Despite its cosmopolitan character it is fully fledged in Germany, but present mostly in the rhetoric and slowly emerging bottom–up citizens' energy initiatives in Poland and Ukraine. However, although a cross-case comparison suggests a pattern of its gradual demise—from high in Germany, through to medium in Poland to a low one in Ukraine—the logic mutates and manifests differently in different empirical contexts and its eventual normative goals are defined and created locally. Therefore, they can neither be imposed by the international or national actors, nor is it sensible to formulate a distinct normative agenda outside of empirical energy contexts. From the analytical point of view, the analysis of the three contexts indicates that the higher the risk logic in the domestic setting in relation to the "total" risks of nuclear energy, the stronger the correlation between the risk and emancipatory logics' empirical occurrence.

Conclusion

Implications for critical security studies and energy policy analysis

The analysis of this book has important implications for both theoretical debates in the security studies literature and contemporary research on energy policy in Europe. From the theoretical perspective the research conducted showed that security is indeed a contextual phenomenon and that one-fits-all frameworks and approaches cannot grasp its empirical scope and complexity. In the example of energy security, the analysis illustrated that there are different security logics operating in energy contexts in Europe. Those logics are driven by different imperatives, employ different rhetoric and policy means, permeate all levels of actors, and manifest and interact differently depending on the specifics of the domestic setting in which they operate. As such, the book demonstrated that similar to the wider security studies, in the energy sector the realist logic of war is only one of the security logics at play. Moreover, there is nothing certain about this logic's dominant position or endurance, as it is continuously challenged by the logics of subsistence, risk and, increasingly, the logic of emancipation, which is on the rise in different energy contexts. Given the uniqueness of the energy security field, the logic of emancipation exhibits here some uncommon characteristics which led to its alternative conceptualization against the existing literature on emancipation. Subsequently, the argument elaborated how the "transformative" energy security logic of emancipation deviates from the critical security studies approach, immanent critique as well as from the emancipation/desecuritization argument.

The depiction of all four energy security logics in the analysis of the German, Polish and Ukrainian cases challenges both the theoretical frameworks based on a single logic approach (e.g., Copenhagen School) and some existing typologies of the security logics/grammars (e.g., Ciută and Corry). While it makes the advantages of the contextual approach to security analysis the more explicit, it also accounts for the key shifts in our contemporary understandings of the energy security phenomenon. As we move away from the state-centric logic of war, through the complex contestation processes within the logic of subsistence, and the totality of global risks towards the logic of emancipation, not only does the possibility of technical redesign and diffusion of the centralized energy systems emerge, but we see the very transformation of the meaning of energy security. The analysis of the German, Polish and Ukrainian energy contexts showed how, among the competing imperatives of survival, sustenance and prevention, that of self-reliance gradually emerges. Consequently, the rhetoric no longer resembles conflictual power struggles, the utility of trade-offs or calculation and precaution in the face of the possibilities of harm, but transforms into calls for empowerment and liberation. Such a shift implies the transfer of agency towards individual users and retaking control over their own energy security that starts to be conceived of in positive and inclusive terms. As we move down from the "anarchy" of international players competing over depleting fossil fuels, through the changing hierarchies within the logic of subsistence to the lateral power of the bottom–up civic energy movements, we simultaneously shift from "we versus others" towards "security among equals." This shift—although one among many possibilities and logics—has important normative and policy implications. On the one hand, it can transform the meaning and practice of energy security within a new progressive paradigm. On the other hand, it adds yet another layer to the already complex energy sector dynamics—this time at the very local level, where the gradual democratization processes can over time remodel the entire political and socioeconomic settings. At the very least, the emergence of the energy security logic of emancipation shows that the reality often escapes the determinism and pessimism of the mainstream theoretical approaches to security and that, indeed, "far from constituting an unrealizable, utopian vision, emancipation is … articulated and practiced in the every day of world politics."[89]

Most crucially, this book provided an alternative take on the analysis of contemporary energy policy across European states. If the conventional energy studies remain focused on the state-level technocratic energy policy, an in-depth study of the variety of actors and interests that operate within specific historical, political and socioeconomic backgrounds from which energy policies emerge offered a wider approach that gets to the root causes of many rationales, debates and policy decisions. Such a study is especially timely in the turbulent times ahead, when the consequences of progressing climate change, diminishing fossil fuels, and the geopolitical situation in CEE complicated by the military conflict with Russia will become even more dire. The narratives of the three case study chapters elaborated on the variety of contextual factors that influence the often controversial energy policy decisions, which are a source of friction and hamper European and regional cooperation. It became clearer, among other things, why German pipeline politics is driven by the sustenance imperative as opposed to its eastern neighbors, what the multiple reasons behind slow development of sustainable energy policy in Poland are, and how the domestic power reshuffle in Ukraine following the outbreak of war with Russia sets its domestic energy policy on a potential new progressive path that will be challenged by political struggles and potential radicalization. Whereas scrutinizing broader dynamics that impact energy security reasoning at the national policy level provided for a better understanding that could ease regional dialogue and make the task of finding common solutions easier, giving voice to the societal actors has pointed to the practices that work on the ground level. As such, the policy insights gained could aid in building concrete agendas and local strategies for the development of citizens' energy initiatives in line with the EU climate protection goals across the CEE region.

By analyzing diverse security logics that drive energy sector developments in the areas of gas, nuclear energy and renewables, this book sought to better comprehend the complexity of the national energy contexts in Europe. The broader contextual approach proved to be particularly helpful in scrutinizing how the political, historical and socioeconomic factors favor certain actors, interests and policy solutions, while hindering others. Further empirical research in this direction could analyze energy security logics' dynamics across other national contexts, as well as conduct more in-depth study into the emerging phenomenon of bottom–up citizens' energy initiatives more broadly. This type of research not only sheds more light on the key developments in diverse national energy policies, but also brings us closer to understanding how transformations within the energy sector are likely to further transform broader socioeconomic models in which we live and which will have to inevitably face the profound political, environmental and economic challenges of the twenty-first century ahead.

Notes

1 Corry, "Securitisation and 'Riskification'," 240.
2 E.g., Corry, "Securitisation and 'Riskification'"; Ciută, "Conceptual Notes on Energy Security."
3 Ciută, "Conceptual Notes on Energy Security."
4 Biesta, "Toward a New 'Logic' of Emancipation," 169.
5 Ibid.
6 Ibid.
7 Biesta, "Toward a New 'Logic' of Emancipation," 169.
8 Booth, *Theory of World Security*, 111.
9 Adorno and Horkheimer, *Dialectic of Enlightenment*, 54.
10 Ibid.
11 Wyn Jones, *Security, Strategy, and Critical Theory*, 230.
12 Ibid., 77.
13 Ibid.
14 Booth, *Theory of World Security*, 112.
15 Ibid.
16 Ibid., 115.
17 Booth, in Peoples, "Security after Emancipation?," 1116.
18 Booth, *Theory of World Security*, 111.
19 Booth, in Peoples, "Security after Emancipation?," 1129.
20 A means of detecting the societal contradictions which offer the most determinate possibilities for emancipatory social change.
21 Peoples, "Security after Emancipation?," 1129.
22 Nunes, "Reclaiming the Political," 352.
23 McDonald, *Security, the Environment and Emancipation*, 41; McDonald, "Emancipation and Critical Terrorism Studies."
24 McDonald, *Security, the Environment and Emancipation*, 41.
25 Ibid.
26 Fierke, *Critical Approaches to International Security*, 189.
27 See sections on the logic of emancipation in all three empirical chapters (Chapters 2, 3 and 4).
28 Wyn Jones, *Security, Strategy, and Critical Theory*, 23.
29 At least in regard to wider climate protection goals, as different projects in renewable energy might have some negative impact on the local environment.
30 Biesta, "Toward a New 'Logic' of Emancipation," 169.
31 E.g., Szwed and Maciejewska, *Demokracja Energetyczna*.
32 Aradau, "Security and the Democratic Scene," 397.
33 Nunes, "Reclaiming the Political," 351.

34 Booth, "Security and Emancipation," 314.
35 Fierke, *Critical Approaches to International Security*, 189.
36 Booth, *Theory of World Security*, 115.
37 Szwed, Interview; SGGW, Interview; demosEUROPA, Interview; Greencubator, Interview.
38 Szulecki, Ancygier, and Szwed, "Energy Democratization?"
39 Robbins, *Political Ecology*; Jehlicka and Smith, "Out of the Woods and into the Lab."
40 Szulecki, Ancygier, and Szwed, "Energy Democratization?"
41 Booth and Wheeler, *The Security Dilemma*, 10.
42 Ibid., 16–17.
43 McDonald, *Security, the Environment and Emancipation*, 52.
44 Ibid., 52.
45 Ibid., 55.
46 Biesta, "Toward a New 'Logic' of Emancipation," 175.
47 Ibid.
48 Ibid.
49 Aradau, "Security and the Democratic Scene," 397.
50 Ibid., 390.
51 Ibid., 400.
52 Ibid., 393.
53 Ibid., 398.
54 Aradau, "Security and the Democratic Scene."
55 Nunes, "Emancipation and the Reality of Security"; McDonald, "Contesting Border Security."
56 McDonald, "Contesting Border Security," 154.
57 Nunes, "Emancipation and the Reality of Security," 143.
58 Balzacq, Depauw, and Leonard, "The Political Limits of Desecuritization," 107–8. Emphasis added.
59 E.g., Szwed, Interview; Greencubator, Interview.
60 Aradau, "Security and the Democratic Scene," 401.
61 Balzacq, Depauw, and Leonard, "The Political Limits of Desecuritization," 107–8.
62 Ibid.
63 Aradau, "Security and the Democratic Scene."
64 McDonald, "Contesting Border Security," 160.
65 McDonald, *Security, the Environment and Emancipation*, 50.
66 *Green Paper: A European Strategy for Sustainable, Competitive and Secure Energy*; Szwed, Interview; demosEUROPA, Interview; SGGW, Interview; Chancellery of the Sejm, Interview.
67 Booth, "Security and Emancipation," 319.
68 McDonald, *Security, the Environment and Emancipation*.
69 McSweeney, *Security, Identity and Interests*, 21. Emphasis added.
70 McDonald, "Securitization and the Construction of Security," 579.
71 Buzan, *People, States and Fear*, 324; McSweeney, *Security, Identity and Interests*, 57.
72 Balzacq, *Securitization Theory*.
73 McSweeney, *Security, Identity and Interests*, 21.
74 Corry, "Securitisation and 'Riskification'"; Ciută, "Conceptual Notes on Energy Security."
75 Corry, "Securitisation and 'Riskification,'" 240.
76 Booth, *Theory of World Security*.
77 Corry, "Securitisation and 'Riskification,'" 240.
78 McDonald, *Security, the Environment and Emancipation*, 36.
79 Huysmans, "Defining Social Constructivism in Security Studies," 60.
80 Trombetta, "Rethinking the Securitization of Environment," 142.

81 Bieleń, "Deficyt Realizmu W Polskiej Polityce Zagranicznej"; Grzeszak and Ostrowski, "Taniec Na Rurach,"
82 Beck, "From Industrial Society to the Risk Society."
83 Ibid., 109.
84 Ibid., 116.
85 Ibid., 118.
86 Beck, *Risk Society*, 232; Wyn Jones, *Security, Strategy, and Critical Theory*, 82.
87 Beck, *Risk Society*, 228–31.
88 And this influence is often strengthened by Western financial and technical support for local NGOs.
89 McDonald, *Security, the Environment and Emancipation*, 55.

References

Adorno, Theodore, and Max Horkheimer. *Dialectic of Enlightenment*. London: Verso Editions, 1979.

Aradau, Claudia. "Security and the Democratic Scene: Desecuritization and Emancipation." *Journal of International Relations and Development* 7, no. 4 (2004): 388–413.

Balzacq, Thierry. *Securitization Theory: How Security Problems Emerge and Dissolve*. London: Routledge, 2010.

Balzacq, Thierry, Sara Depauw, and Sarah Leonard. "The Political Limits of Desecuritization: Security, Arms Trade, and the EU's Economic Targets." In *Contesting Security: Strategies and Logics*, 104–21. London: Routledge, 2015.

Beck, Ulrich. "From Industrial Society to the Risk Society: Questions of Survival, Social Structure and Ecological Enlightenment." *Theory, Culture and Society* 9, no. 1 (1992): 97–123.

Beck, Ulrich. *Risk Society: Towards a New Modernity*. London: Sage, 1992.

Bieleń, Stanisław. "Deficyt Realizmu W Polskiej Polityce Zagranicznej." *Stosunki Międzynarodowe*, no. 3/4 (t. 38) (2008): 9–29.

Biesta, G.J.J. "Toward a New 'Logic' of Emancipation: Foucault and Ranciere." *Philosophy of Education Society*, 2008.

Booth, Ken. "Security and Emancipation." *Review of International Studies* 17, no. 4 (1991): 313–26.

Booth, Ken. *Theory of World Security*. Cambridge: Cambridge University Press, 2007.

Booth, Ken, and Nicholas Wheeler. *The Security Dilemma: Fear, Cooperation, and Trust in World Politics*. Basingstoke: Palgrave Macmillan, 2011.

Buzan, Barry. *People, States and Fear: The National Security Problem in International Relations*. Hemel Hempstead: Harvester Wheatsheaf, 1991.

Chancellery of the Sejm. Interview, Warsaw, June 7, 2013.

Ciută, Felix. "Conceptual Notes on Energy Security: Total or Banal Security?" *Security Dialogue* 41, no. 2 (2010): 123–44.

Corry, Olaf. "Securitisation and 'Riskification': Second-Order Security and the Politics of Climate Change." *Millennium-Journal of International Studies* 40, no. 2 (2012): 235–58.

demosEUROPA. Interview, Warsaw, May 24, 2013.

Fierke, Karen. *Critical Approaches to International Security*. Cambridge: Polity, 2007.

Green Paper: A European Strategy for Sustainable, Competitive and Secure Energy. Brussels: European Commission, 2006.

Greencubator. Interview, Kiev, October 30, 2013.

Grzeszak, Adam, and Marek Ostrowski. "Taniec Na Rurach." *Polityka*, 2006.

Huysmans, Jef. "Defining Social Constructivism in Security Studies: The Normative Dilemma of Writing Security." *Alternatives: Global, Local, Political* 27, no. 1 (2002): 41–62.

Jehlicka, Petr, and Joe Smith. "Out of the Woods and into the Lab: Exploring the Strange Marriage of American Woodcraft and Soviet Ecology in Czech Environmentalism." *Environment and History* 13, no. 2 (2007): 187–210.

McDonald, Matt. "Contesting Border Security: Emancipation and Asylum in the Australian Context." In *Contesting Security: Strategies and Logics*, 154–68. London: Routledge, 2015.

McDonald, Matt. "Emancipation and Critical Terrorism Studies." *European Political Science* 6, no. 3 (2007): 252–9.

McDonald, Matt. "Securitization and the Construction of Security." *European Journal of International Relations* 14, no. 4 (2008): 563–87.

McDonald, Matt. *Security, the Environment and Emancipation: Contestation over Environmental Change*. London: Routledge, 2011.

McSweeney, Bill. *Security, Identity and Interests: A Sociology of International Relations*. Cambridge: Cambridge University Press, 1999.

Nunes, João. "Emancipation and the Reality of Security: A Reconstructive Agenda." In *Contesting Security: Strategies and Logics*, 141–53. London: Routledge, 2015.

Nunes, João. "Reclaiming the Political: Emancipation and Critique in Security Studies." *Security Dialogue* 43, no. 4 (2012): 345–61.

Peoples, Columba. "Security after Emancipation? Critical Theory, Violence and Resistance." *Review of International Studies* 37, no. 3 (2011): 1113–35.

Robbins, P. *Political Ecology: A Critical Introduction*. Oxford: Wiley-Blackwell, 2004.

SGGW (Warsaw University of Life Sciences). Interview, Warsaw, June 12, 2013.

Szulecki, Kacper, Andrzej Ancygier, and Dariusz Szwed. "Energy Democratization? Societal Aspects of De-Carbonization in the German and Polish Energy Sectors." *Environmental Studies and Policy Research Institute: Wroclaw*, March 9, 2015.

Szwed, Dariusz, and Beata Maciejewska. *Demokracja Energetyczna*. Warsaw: Zielony Instytut, 2014.

Szwed, Dariusz. Interview, May 27, 2013.

Trombetta, Maria Julia. "Rethinking the Securitization of Environment: Old Beliefs, New Insights." In *Understanding Securitisation Theory: How Security Problems Emerge and Dissolve*, 135–49. London: Routledge, 2010.

Wyn Jones, Richard. *Security, Strategy, and Critical Theory*. London: Lynne Rienner Publishers, 1999.

Index

For Product Safety Concerns and Information please contact our EU representative GPSR@taylorandfrancis.com Taylor & Francis Verlag GmbH, Kaufingerstraße 24, 80331 München, Germany